The Ottoman Twilight in the Arab Lands

Ottoman and Turkish Studies

Series Editor: Hakan T. Karateke (University of Chicago)

ACADEMIC
STUDIES
PRESS

The Ottoman Twilight in the Arab Lands

Turkish Memoirs and Testimonies of the Great War

SELIM DERINGIL

BOSTON
2019

Library of Congress Cataloging-in-Publication Data

Names: Deringil, Selim, 1951- editor.

Title: The Ottoman twilight in the Arab lands : Turkish memoirs and testimonies of the Great War / Selim Deringil.

Description: Brighton, MA, USA : Academic Studies Press, 2018. | Series: Ottoman and Turkish studies | Includes bibliographical references.

Identifiers: LCCN 2018057561 (print) | LCCN 2019006179 (ebook) | ISBN 9781618119599 (ebook) | ISBN 9781618119575 (hardcover) | ISBN 9781618119582 (pbk.)

Subjects: LCSH: World War, 1914-1918--Personal narratives, Turkish. | World War, 1914-1918--Turkey. | World War, 1914-1918--Middle East.

Classification: LCC D640.A2 (ebook) | LCC D640.A2 O86 2018 (print) | DDC 940.30917/4927--dc23

LC record available at https://lccn.loc.gov/2018057561

ISBN 978-1-618119-57-5 (hardback)
ISBN 978-1-618119-59-9 (electronic)
ISBN 978-1-618119-58-2 (paperback)

Book design by Lapiz Digital Services

On the cover: Yemeni Sheikhs visit the front as guests of Cemal Pasha. Library of Congress. American Colony of Jerusalem. Photo album "World War I: Palestine and Sinai."

Published by Academic Studies Press in 2019

1577 Beacon Street
Brookline, MA 02446, USA
press@academicstudiespress.com
www.academicstudiespress.com

For Carla

Contents

Acknowledgments

First and foremost, I would like to thank my friend and colleague Dr. Ayhan Aktar, who gave me the idea of writing a book consisting of extended annotated translations of memoirs of late Ottoman individuals in the Arab lands in the final years of the Ottoman Empire. As we were approaching the centenary year of the final Ottoman withdrawal from these lands, it seemed to be an appropriate project. I would also like to thank Dr. Tariq Tell for his tremendously knowledgeable suggestions during our many conversations and for reading and commenting on the Introduction. Sinan Kuneralp was, as always, extremely generous in providing suggestions for source materials and, indeed, the source materials themselves. Dr. Talha Çiçek, whose pioneering work on the governorship of Cemal Pasha in Syria was an essential reference, was also kind enough to read previous versions of my text and make valuable suggestions. My long-suffering friend Dr. Edhem Eldem was also very helpful in responding to my queries about decorations and other matters. My thanks also to Dr. Salim Tamari, whose work on war diaries served in many ways as a template for the present work. Thanks are also due to İclal and Tunca Örses for allowing me to use photographs from their valuable collection. Mr. Ergun Kocabıyık of the Boğaziçi University Press was extremely kind in providing much-needed technical support with some of the visual materials used in the book. My thanks also to Dr. Issam Nassar for kindly sharing the photograph of the surrender of Jerusalem with itemized personae. Thanks are also due to Dr. John Winterburn for allowing me to use some of the photographs from the GARP project. I would also like to thank Dr. Kaukab Chebaro and Samar Mikati Kaissi of the AUB Archives for their kind support during my research. Dr. Cengiz Kırlı and Dr. Nadir Özbek also provided important insights during our numerous conversations. I would also like to thank my copyeditor Louis Parks for his dedication and professionalism. Thanks are also due to the anonymous reviewers who provided very useful feedback. Above all, I would like to thank my wife and colleague, Dr. Carla Eddé, for her patience and support and for listening to what were no doubt, at times, less than consistent tirades about my work in progress.

Needless to say, all mistakes, overstatements, omissions, and oversights are entirely my own.

Selim Deringil, Ras Beirut, March 15, 2018.

Introduction

Aspects of the Ottoman Twilight

In Turkey's collective memory today, the Ottomans lost the First World War; the Turks won it.

Mustafa Aksakal, "The Ottoman Empire"[1]

Remembering is a very private act. Yet there are certain watersheds in history when private remembrance and collective memory overlap. In my generation everybody remembers exactly where they were and what they were doing when they heard the news of the assassination of John Fitzgerald Kennedy. For later generations it will be 9/11. For Eric Hobsbawm, it was when he and his sister were returning home from school in Berlin and they saw newspapers with banner headlines declaring that Adolf Hitler had become the Chancellor of Germany, "I can see it still as in a dream," Hobsbawm said.[2] For most Arabs in the late Ottoman Empire the watershed moment was the hanging of Arab patriots by Cemal Pasha in 1915 and 1916. The collective "shudder that shook the country," as memorably put by George Antonius, was transmitted across generations and has become the definitive moment in Arab-Turkish relations that shaped the collective memory of Arabs who saw the "days of the Turks" as a period of unmitigated catastrophe and destitution.[3] As admirably expressed by Salim Tamari:

---

1 Mustafa Aksakal, "The Ottoman Empire," in *The Cambridge History of the First World War*, ed. Jay Winter (Cambridge: Cambridge University Press, 2014), vol. 1, 464.
2 Eric Hobsbawm, *Interesting Times: A Twentieth-Century Life* (London: Allen and Unwin, 2002), 74.
3 George Antonius, *The Arab Awakening: The Story of the National Arab Movement* (London and New York: Kegan Paul, 2000), 190.

The Great War brought about a radical break with the Ottoman past in the whole Arab East, not only in the established constitutional regime but also in the system of governance, local administration, and identity politics. In popular memory of peasants and city folk alike, 1915 was the Year of the Locust ('am al Jarad). Even four generations later, the locust invasion continues to evoke the combined memory of natural disasters and the manmade devastation of war. These events erased four centuries of rich and complex Ottoman patrimony in which popular narratives of war and nationalist ideology colluded. An anti-Ottoman rewriting of history took place simultaneously, and in the same abrupt manner, both on the Turkish side (in the guise of the modernizing state and making it geographically manageable) and on the Arab side (in the sustained annals of nationalist historiography). The erasure replaced four centuries of relative peace and dynamic activity, the Ottoman era, with what was known in Arabic discourse as "the days of the Turks": four miserable years of tyranny symbolized by the military dictatorship of Ahmad Cemal Pasha in Syria, seferberlik (forced conscription and exile), and the collective hanging of Arab patriots in Beirut's Burj Square on August 15, 1916.[4]

The last few years of Ottoman rule in Lebanon and Syria are known as the "eyyam-atrak" the "days of the Turks." This term usually carries dark connotations, being associated with famine, the hanging of the martyrs in Burj Square, and Cemal Pasha's reign of terror. All these events are usually described from the perspective of the local population; as such they have a very important place in the formation of what has come to be recognized as the "collective memory" of a people. Leila Fawaz astutely points out that many Arab autobiographers who mostly wrote for their family circles, nonetheless "refer to shared experiences, myths, and recollections of the past" that were handed down over generations.[5] But how did the "atrak" themselves see their position in Lebanon, Syria, Palestine, and the Hijaz in the final years of the Great War?

This book will attempt to address this question based on Ottoman memoirs written by eyewitnesses to the last years of Ottoman rule. It aims to be a critical annotated edition of the memoirs contained within

---

4   Salim Tamari, *The Year of the Locust. A Soldier's Diary and the Erasure of the Ottoman Past* (Berkeley, Los Angeles and London: University of California Press, 2011), 5.

5   Leila Fawaz, *The Land of Aching Hearts: The Middle East in the Great War* (Cambridge Massachusetts and London: Harvard University Press, 2014), 235.

it, cross-referencing them and putting them in a historical context. The memoirs will be cited *in extenso*, given that the aim is to provide a reference work for readers who do not read Turkish, and given that most of these texts are only available in Turkish.

In all five of the memoirs cited in this work, at the time of writing the authors had shared a similar recent past. In the late 1890s a secret society had formed among young Ottoman officers, doctors, lawyers, and intellectuals whose aim was to bring an end to the despotism of Sultan Abdulhamid II (r. 1876–1909) and restore the constitution of 1878. This secret society would ultimately be named The Committee of Union and Progress (CUP) and would eventually come to be dubbed the Young Turks.[6] The CUP eventually spread to include a very broad spectrum of the late Ottoman elite and would lead the Revolution of 1908 which restored the constitution. A counter coup in April 1909 led to the deposition of Sultan Abdulhamid. The last free elections of 1912 were followed by a military coup in 1913, after which the empire was effectively ruled by the CUP. The leadership of 1913 would ultimately be winnowed down to the infamous ruling Triumvirate of Enver Pasha, Talat Pasha, and Cemal Pasha. When the clouds of war started to gather in Europe, the leadership of the Young Turks saw the war as an opportunity to recover lost territory and build a strong state. As elegantly put by Mustafa Aksakal: "The new Ottoman leadership of the twentieth century viewed Great Power diplomacy as a fixed game: the Great Powers were the House, and you could not beat it by playing by the rules."[7] Diplomacy had had its day, the only solution was military. After shopping around for allies among the European powers, the Young Turks signed an alliance with Germany on August 2 1914. The Ottoman Empire entered the war on November 2.

The commonly accepted, official narrative in the early years of the Republic of Turkey was that the Young Turks dragged the Ottoman Empire into the war and thus to its destruction, or that they had been tricked by

---

6   There is an extensive literature on the Young Turks and the CUP. A few of the better known works are the following: Feroz Ahmad, *The Young Turks: The Committee of Union and Progress in Turkish Politics 1908–1914* (Oxford: Oxford University Press, 1969); Şükrü Hanioğlu, *Preparation for a Revolution: The Young Turks, 1902–1908* (New York: Oxford University Press, 2001); Şükrü Hanioğlu, *The Young Turks in Opposition* (New York: Oxford University Press, 1995).

7   Mustafa Aksakal, *The Ottoman Road to War in 1914: The Ottoman Empire and the First World War* (Cambridge and London: Cambridge University Press, 2008), 9. The CUP would also be referred to as the "Ittihadists" (*Ittihatçılar*).

the Germans. A new generation of historians has now completely revised this position. Notably, Mustafa Aksakal and others have shown that the Ottoman Empire's entry into the war was the result of a conscious decision which was backed by almost all of the Ottoman elite rather than a small coterie of Young Turks.[8]

Many people within the Ottoman Empire in the years leading up to the war were obsessed with the loss of the Balkan Provinces (Rumeli) and the belief that they were besieged by enemies. The Balkan Wars (1911–1913) were a particularly traumatic memory as many of the Young Turk cadres were from the Balkans. They particularly resented the fact that the European powers were not at all concerned over the aggression meted out by the Balkan states toward Muslim populations. This feeling hovers like a shadow in all the memoirs cited in this book. Hüseyin Kazım, whom we will meet below, was one of the core group that founded the CUP. In a small pamphlet written in 1914 he condemned the Albanians for being responsible for the "Balkan Alliance" (Balkan İttifakı).[9] Falih Rıfkı was a fiery young writer for the official CUP newspaper *Tanin*. Rıfkı would bemoan the loss of Rumeli, which he felt was the true home of the Turks, and lament over his belief that they would always be strangers in the Arab lands: "The air of Lebanon is a hundred times more foreign for us than the air of Dobruca." Münevver Ayaşlı, who was from Salonica, would grieve over the loss of her beloved home town. Naci Kıcıman would agonize over the "Anatolian lads" who were being sacrificed to defend the Arabian desert.

The official publication of the Turkish General Staff castigated the Arabs as cowardly and disloyal. All of our authors were writing and publishing in the intellectual *milieu* of the Kemalist republic, whose attitude to the loss of the Arab lands I will define below as the "good riddance syndrome."

The most important central actor in the creation of this negative image of the "atrak" was undoubtedly Cemal Pasha. One of the Young Turk triumvirate, together with Enver and Talat, Cemal Pasha had been appointed the Commander of the Fourth Army District (essentially Syria, Palestine and Lebanon) where he enjoyed almost dictatorial powers.[10] One of his

---

8   Ibid., 57–92.
9   Ebru Boyar, *Ottomans, Turks and the Balkans. Empire Lost, Relations Altered* (New York: Tauris Academic Studies, 2007), 40, 91.
10 The exact date of his appointment is unclear. On November 18, 1914 he sent Enver a telegram where he signs himself as "Commander of the Fourth Army." On December 13, 1917 he left Damascus for good. My thanks to Talha Çiçek for this information.

close aids would ironically refer to him as "Viceroy of Syria" although the Ottoman high command had no such official rank.[11] During the three years (1914–1917) in which he ruled Syria with an iron fist, Cemal set up a reign of terror and became infamous for the trial and execution of some forty Arab nationalists whom he accused of sedition. Recent scholarship has somewhat revised this negative image of Cemal but the image of the "iron fist" and the "reign of terror" still prevails. Thus Cemal Pasha came to symbolize much more than the executioner of the Arab patriots, he became a figure symbolizing the "four hundred years of decadence" of Turkish rule, "which was judged before the tribunal of nascent Arab nationalism."[12]

Although there is a renewed interest in the Ottoman history of the Great War and much of the new historiography uses memoirs, there is hardly any writing on the memoir literature that can be called content analysis.[13] On the Turkish side, until recently the prevalent discourse has been what I will refer to as the "stab in the back syndrome" whereby the Arabs are seen as seditious traitors who collaborated with the enemy to bring down the Empire. This resulted in an entire generation of political actors in the young Turkish Republic whose attitude to the loss of the Arab provinces can be summed up as "good riddance." Particularly in the years after the abolition of the Caliphate in 1924 the theme of "Arab treason" became the dominant narrative and was featured as such in school textbooks:

> . . . The descendant of the Prophet Sharif Husain . . . chose to accept the gold of the enemy. . . . and exchanged the honor of Islam for a Kingdom under the protection of the English. He actually entered into competition with the

---

11 Falih Rıfkı Atay, *Zeytindağı* (Istanbul: Pozitif Press, 1932), 91–92. The word he uses is "Visrua" which is actually not a Turkish word. A German officer was to refer to him as "Vizekönig," see Talha Çiçek, *War and State Formation in Syria: Cemal Pasha's Governorate During World War I 1914–1917* (London: Routledge, 2014), 3. This is an excellent book that combines European and Ottoman sources and should be considered the most current work on this topic. As such it has been used extensively in this study. See also Ali Fuad Erden, *Birinci Dünya Savaşında Suriye Hatıraları* [Syrian Memoirs during the First World War] (Istanbul: İş Bankası, 2003), 95: "Everyone feared Cemal Pasha. . . ."

12 Youssef Mouwad, "Jamal Pacha, en une version libanaise. L'usage positif d'une légende noire." In *The First World War as Remembered in the Countries of the Eastern Mediterranean*, ed. Olaf Farschid, Manfed Kropp, Stephan Dahne (Beirut: Orient Institut, 2006), 425–446.

13 For a recent useful overview of the historiography, see Ömer Turan, "Turkish Historiography of the First World War," *Middle East Critique* 23, no. 2 (2014): 241–257.

enemies of Islam for the shedding of the pure Turkish blood, with the desert and town Arabs in his train. . . .[14]

The early republican press frequently referred to Islam as "an Arab religion." Mustafa Kemal endorsed the publication of a treatise entitled, *There is no Religion, Just Nationality: My Turkishness is my Religion.*[15] Thus Arabs became in a very real sense the "essential other" for the nascent Turkish Republic:

> In order to fortify Turkishness as the basic historical consciousness of the new citizen, the "traitorous Arabs" who had "stabbed the Turks in the back" became the ideological cement for the new radical westernizing ideology.[16]

This mindset is reflected in four of the five memoirs used in this volume. Falih Rıfkı with his scathing irony about how "foreign" the Arab lands were for Turks, Ali Fuad with his firm conviction that the "Arab officers were planning to poison the Turks in their sleep," Naci Kıcıman with his frequent references to "barelegged Arabs who were spilling the blood of Anatolian lads," and finally Münevver Ayaşlı, who treats the population of Beirut very like a British *memsahib* would have treated Indian subjects of the British *raj*, are all imbued with some aspect or other of the mentality described above. The one exception is Hüseyin Kazım, who places the blame for the loss of Arab lands squarely on the shoulders of corrupt and incompetent Ottoman officials.

The five memoirs used in this book were each chosen for a specific purpose. Falih Rıfkı was Cemal Pasha's close aid and an eyewitness to his policies in the region. Moreover, he also represents a typical example of the post-imperial Turkish mindset regarding the Ottoman past. From his texts, I chose *Zeytindağı* in particular because it is beautifully written, and is therefore a pleasure to translate.

Ali Fuad was Cemal's "nuts and bolts man" who actually administered the Fourth Army zone. His memoir was chosen because Ali Fuad was an

---

14 Talha Çiçek, "Erken Cumhuriyet Dönemi Ders Kitapları Çerçevesinde Türk Ulus Kimliği İnşası ve 'Arap İhaneti'" [The Construction of Turkish National Identity in the Light of Early Republican School Textbooks and "Arab treason"], *Divan* 17 (2012): 169–188. Çiçek is quoting a school history textbook from 1931.

15 Şükrü Hanioğlu, *Ataturk: An Intellectual Biography* (Princeton: Princeton University Press, 2011), 63. The work in question is Ruşeni Barkın, *Din Yok Milliyet Var: Benim Dinim, Benim Türklüğümdür.*

16 Çiçek, "Erken Cumhuriyet," 181

atypical example of a Turkish officer of the time: he was a hard-headed realist and a dreamer who likened himself to the legendary figure of the French Revolution, Saint-Just.

Hüseyin Kazım appears in these pages because he was an exceptional character. A member of the Ottoman elite, the son of a legendary long-term governor of Trabzon, and a founder member of the CUP who fell out with his erstwhile comrades. He was also exceptional in that he was the only one of the five who abstained from taking an active part in the politics of the republican era.

Naci Kıcıman's memoir was chosen because it is both a memoir and a biography. The memoir is as much about Naci Kıcıman himself as it is about his legendary commander, Fahreddin Pasha, the defender of Medina. It is also a typical example of the "stab in the back syndrome," which will be explained below.

I chose Münevver Ayaşlı because of the fact that her memoir is one of the very few eyewitness accounts of the last days of the Turks in Syria written by a woman. Furthermore, her memoirs were written decades after the events and yet represent a remarkable feat of memory judging by their impressive accuracy.

The memoirs that I have used fall into the category of what Philipp Wirtz refers to in his insightful book as "post-Ottoman memoirs," given the fact that they were all written and published in the context of Kemalist Turkey. As he points out, memoir writers often wrote as a result of the urge to "bear witness," or "to set the record straight."[17]

Some comments on the use of memoirs and the concept of "collective memory"

There is an extensive literature on autobiography, describing its impact on the structure of collective memory and its contribution to the formation of collective identity.[18] It would be beyond the scope of this study to attempt

---

17 Philipp Wirtz, *Depicting the Ottoman Empire in Turkish Autobiographies. Images of Past World* (New York: Routledge, 2017), 23, 33.

18 David Middleton and Derek Edwards, eds., *Collective Remembering: Inquiries in Social Construction* (London: Sage Publications, 1990); Dorthe Bernsten and David C. Rubin, eds., *Understanding Autobiographical Memory. Theories and Approaches* (Cambridge: Cambridge University Press, 2012); James W. Pennebaker, Dario Paez, Bernard Rime, eds., *Collective Memory of Political Events* (New Jersey: Mahwah, 1997); Paul Connerton, "Seven Types of Forgetting," *Memory Studies* 1, no. 1 (2008): 59–71; Robin Ostle,

an exhaustive theoretical treatment of the subject. I will limit myself to a few very brief observations that will have a direct bearing on the memoirs discussed here. In the words of the pioneering *doyen* of collective memory studies Maurice Halbwachs:

> Collective memory differs from history in at least two respects. It is a current of continuous thought whose continuity is not at all artificial for it retains from the past only what still lives or is capable of living in the consciousness of the groups keeping the memory alive. . . . It provides the group a self-portrait that unfolds through time, since it is an image of the past, and allows the group to recognize itself through the total succession of images.[19]

The memoirs studied here are indeed a very good reflection of the "self-portrait" of the late Ottoman personages and their "images of the past."

Memoirs as a historical source for the last years of the "atrak" in the Arab lands are indeed indispensable, with the proviso that they be used without any illusions as to their "objectivity." Memoirs are by their very nature subjective, and demand, in the words of one of major thinkers of the subject, some form of "autobiographical pact" between the author and the reader whereby the reader will be free to "look for differences (errors, deformations etc.)" with the historical record.[20]

Everyone thought they were making history or at the very least providing testimony for future generations. In a recent study on genocide denial in Turkey, Müge Göçek notes: "The main limitation of memoirs as a historical source is that it is hard to move beyond the personal idiosyncrasies of individuals in general and their political orientation in particular."[21] Yet it is precisely those "idiosyncrasies" and "political orientations" that are my concern here.

As Philip Dwyer has pointed out, the actual act of writing down what is remembered can transform what was in fact a subjective impression into a "historical reality." "In this manner, memoirists become mythmakers,

---

Ed de Moor, and Stefan Wild, eds., *Writing the Self: Autobiographical Writing in Modern Arabic Literature* (London: Saqi Books, 1998).

19 Maurice Halbwachs, excerpt from "The Collective Memory," in *The Collective Memory Reader*, ed. Jeffrey K. Olick et al. (Oxford: Oxford University Press, 2011), 139–155.

20 Philippe Lejeune, *Le Pacte Autobiographique*, accessed January 12, 2017, www.edisc1plinas.usp.br/pluginfile.php/1896026/mod_resource/content/1/lejeune_pacte autobiographique-pacte_1.pdf.

21 Müge Göçek, *Denial of Violence: Ottoman Past, Turkish Present, and Collective Violence Against the Armenians 1789–2009* (Oxford: Oxford University Press, 2015), 54.

creating records that not only influence the manner in which readers see the past, but also how historians interpret the past." All five of the memoirists in this volume were very self-consciously writing for posterity. All five texts to be cited here were, again to echo Dwyer, "remembered, restructured, and filtered by time." As he points out, what the writers of the memoirs think is worth remembering shapes the "cultural memory" of the future. The writers of the memoirs used in the present volume are very much a product of the "cultural memory" of the Kemalist state.[22]

All five memoirs analyzed in this book have a political agenda. Some memoirs are indeed in self-conscious dialogue with one another. Hüseyin Kazım specifically states that he wrote in order to "expose the lies of Cemal Pasha." It is important to know when the memoirs were written, and the historical context in which they were published. All memoirs also have a projected public, an audience for whom they are intended.

Falih Rıfkı's *Zeytindağı* was first published in 1932. Meanwhile, Falih Rıfkı had taken the surname Atay and gone on to write books and articles of a panegyric nature lauding Atatürk as a godlike leader. *Zeytindağı*, therefore, is very much a product of an early republican mindset which saw separation from the Arab lands as a blessing. Falih Rıfkı was very close to Cemal Pasha and was an eyewitness to some of the period's key events. Yet, Rıfkı is extremely cynical regarding what he calls "Ottoman Imperialism." Rıfkı refers to Enver in extremely negative terms as an "empty head covered in pomaded skin" yet always refers to Cemal with the utmost (if sometimes somewhat grudging) respect, reflecting the various cliques and clientele networks that had evolved around the Enver–Talat–Cemal triumvirate. The Palestine front was the last stand of the Ottomans in the Arab lands. The critical battles waged between the Ottomans and the British in this area were to mark the collective memories of the last generation of Ottomans.

The political climate at the time of the memoirs' publication is also significant. For example, although Falih Rıfkı fitted in fine with the *air de temps* in the heyday or Kemalism, it is no wonder that Hüseyin Kazım's memoirs were published only after his death in 1934, given the unabashed anti-Kemalism of the writer. Hüseyin Kazım is an exceptional figure in many ways. Firstly, unlike almost all the civilian and military officials on the Palestine–Syria front, he did not join the nationalists in Ankara, nor did he go on to

---

22 Philip Dwyer, "Making Sense of the Muddle: War Memoirs and the Culture of Remembering," in *War Stories. The War Memoir in History and Literature*, ed. Philip Dwyer (New York: Bergahn, 2017), 1–27.

hold prominent positions in the new Turkish state. After returning from Beirut, he became a member of the penultimate Ottoman parliament when he was an MP for the province of Aydın. In 1920, he was elected to the post of Deputy Speaker. In 1921 he was part of the Istanbul government's official delegation in the Bilecik negotiations that attempted to find some middle ground between Istanbul and the nationalists in Ankara. The negotiations failed and the Istanbul delegation was "invited" to come to Ankara. Hüseyin Kazım recounts feeling that he was treated as a hostage. In fact, he was very critical of Mustafa Kemal and the new regime, going so far as to state in his memoirs that Kemal created "a new form of oppression and despotism called the republic."[23] He wrote two versions of his memoirs, one that ends in 1929 and another, ending in 1930. The second text was written specifically to answer accusations against its author. He openly refers to Mustafa Kemal's epic speech, the *Nutuk*, where Kazım was, as he states, falsely accused of being a defender of the sultanate. His self-defense is scathing, going so far as to refer to the iconic text as "a masterpiece of lies and distortion" (*şah-eser-i kezb-u tahrif*). It is therefore no wonder that his memoirs were only published after his death in 1934.[24]

Ali Fuad [Erden] states in the introduction to his memoirs that he "waited forty years which is two generations" before publishing his writing. He was clearly concerned about protecting the name of Cemal and others who were involved in the last days of Ottoman rule in Syria. He clearly states that "Cemal Pasha was my Commander and will always be my Commander."[25] Münevver Ayaşlı was writing some forty years after

---

23 Hüseyin Kazım Kadri, *Meşrutiyettden Cumhuriyete Hatıralarım* [My Memoirs from the Constitutional Period to the Republic], ed. Ismail Kara. (Istanbul: Dergah, 2000), 123.

24 Ibid., 190, 223. In 1927, Mustafa Kemal delivered a mammoth five-day parliament speech, the *Nutuk* (October 15–20), which amounted to an apologia of everything dealing with the founding of the republic. In this speech there are three negative references to Hüseyin Kazım. See footnote 35 by the editor, Ismail Kara. For one of the rare critical evaluations of *Nutuk* see Hülya Adak, "National Myths and Self Narrations: Mustafa Kemal's *Nutuk* and Halide Edib's *Memoirs* and the *Turkish Ordeal*," *South Atlantic Monthly* 102, nos. 2/3 (2003): 509–528.
The memoirs of Kazım, one the leading commanders of the Anatolian resistance and an opponent of what he saw as Kemal's dictatorial inclinations, were in large part a rebuttal of the *Nutuk*, to the point where one prominent late-Ottomanist called it the "anti-Nutuk." See Erik Jan Zürcher, "Young Turk Memoirs as a Historical Source: Kazım 'Istiklal Harbimiz," *Middle Eastern Studies* 22, no. 4 (1986): 562–570.

25 Philipp Wirtz, *Depicting the Late Ottoman Empire in Turkish Autobiographies*, 22–34. Wirtz rightly points out the importance of "forewords" or "introductions" as key to understanding the context of a late Ottoman memoirs.

the events she described and thus her text is very much imbued with the conservative world view of a first-generation republican woman. Her somewhat facile snobbery is interesting as she makes her judgments less along ethnic lines but focuses more on class. Thus, the Lebanese merchants are "unctuous and toadying" while the Sursocks are very "convenable" (*kibar*) and it is a sign of her family's social standing that Linda Sursock "would come for coffee" at Ayaşlı's home.

I have used the memoirs as sources for a study of intellectual, not military, history. In this regard (particularly in relation to the memoirs of Kıcıman and Erden), I have not translated large tracts of detailed military operations. I am more interested in passages that illustrate the mindset of the actors involved. Also, there is much repetition which I have chosen to omit.

Another point that needs clarification is the manner in which I have handled the actual process of translation itself. Jay Winter refers to the ways in which Henri Barbusse's novel *Le Feu* (1916) was "sanitized" in its English translation in 1917, where references to soldiers as "victims and executioners" was softened because "language codes precluded direct translation and silenced the difficult moral judgement...."[26] I have tried to avoid euphemistic censorship and sensationalism while striving to give the actual "flavor" of the Turkish original.

Turks and Arabs: an uncomfortable symbiosis

In the memoirs covered for this book, I came across a contradictory worldview regarding the Arabs and Arab lands in the memoirs of Ottoman individuals who were in the Arab region during the last years of the Empire. The contradiction lies in the constant reference to the "loss" of the Arab lands, yet they all express a deep sense of alienation and an ever present feeling of "them" and "us." Yet the "us," although essentially meaning Turks, remains ambivalent, sometimes including the Muslim Arabs and even the Christians.

Halil Halid Bey was one of the staunchest defenders of Turkish-Arab brotherhood, waxing lyrical about the special relationship between the two races and declaring that

---

26 Jay Winter, "War Memoirs, Witnessing and Silence," in Dwyer, *War Stories*, 27–47.

. . . the Arab and the Turk cannot live without each other. . . . The Arab race was a like a diamond that had been broken and scattered into a thousand pieces. It was the Turks who first realized how valuable they would be if united. After they became united as brothers in religion they came to the Arab lands and helped unite all the pieces. Verily, the crown of the Turkish sultanate was emblazoned and glowed with the brilliance of all these pieces of the diamond that was united.[27]

There is a very clear idea of the "otherness" of the Arabs, which is some-times expressed in downright racist stereotyping. For example, Falih Rıfkı uses the phrase "hair of the Arab" (*Arap saçı*) meaning "to make some-thing tangled and confused."[28] Rıfkı's disparaging references to the Arabs of Medina who had made a vocation out of exploiting pilgrims, and his conviction that Istanbul was the true Muslim city that had made worship into an art form, are very similar to the language one hears today from Turkish *hajis* returning from pilgrimage. When *Zeytindağı* was written, Turkey was firmly looking west and the "Orient" was a thing of the past. In subsequent editions of *Zeytindağı*, Rıfkı's attitude would become even more severe: "Ottoman history has been a world of lies. Lying is not shameful in the Orient."[29] Evidently, by the time he wrote and published *Zeytindağı*, Falih Rıfkı had moved much closer to the official line of Turkish Kemalist nationalism.

Yet, some Ottoman officials had a very self-critical view of the Turkish presence in Arab lands. Hüseyin Kazım was a very distinguished example. While he served as the Vali (Governor) of Aleppo, Kazım observed that the Ottoman officials collaborated with the local notables to create an alli-ance of "mutual interest" in order to exploit the local population. In Aleppo Kazım became something of a local celebrity. Appointed as Vali in 1910, he became the nexus of what can be called the "Hüseyin Kazım Affair." Seen by the emerging liberal middle class of Aleppo as the new reformist Vali

---

27 Çerkeşşeyhi Zade Halil Halid, *Türk ve Arap* [The Turk and the Arab] (Cairo: n.p., 1912, reprinted edition, Istanbul: Melissa Press, 2016), 61–62. Halil Halid was an interesting figure. After teaching Turkish to British diplomats at Cambridge for over ten years, he became a devoted propagandist for the Young Turk regime. He later served as the Ottoman Consul in Bombay.
28 See below, p. 12.
29 Falih Rıfkı Atay, *Zeytindağı*, online edition, accessed March 11, 2017, www.kitapsevenler.com, 7–8.

replacing Fahreddin Pasha, an Ottoman military man of the old school, Kazım came to be known as "our Vali / *Walina.*"

Unusually for an Ottoman official, he spoke fluent Arabic. On the occasion of his triumphant return from Istanbul, where he had gone to defend his reformist policies,

> A large crowd greeted him at the train station. Troops in formation and a band made up of the students from the College de La Terre Sainte serenaded his arrival. Refusing to board a carriage, Hüseyin Kazım walked to the governorate building with the procession stopping to deliver two speeches on the way.[30]

There followed a flurry of telegrams to and fro between Aleppo and Istanbul, with which the traditional notables of the city did their best to assure his downfall. They ultimately succeeded and he has recalled in 1911. In a letter to a friend shortly before his recall Kazım stated the following:

> . . . As far as I can see the government made two big mistakes here. Firstly it did nothing to confirm its existence, and secondly it did not even think about pleasing the people. . . . Since I have been here I have tried to win over the people. . . . I think that to a certain extent I have succeeded in making them more hopeful towards the state. Now everyone has understood that there is a government that defends the weak, is in favor of justice, and is trying to heal old wounds.[31]

Yet, even with Hüseyin Kazım there is an undertone of a belief in his entitlement to rule. With reference to Cemal Pasha's oppressive rule in Syria, Kazım states on at least two occasions in his memoirs that it was because of Cemal Pasha's cruelty that Syria was "lost."[32]

It is difficult to know what to make of the episode in his memoirs where he recounts how he was approached by some Beirutis who declared that they were prepared to go to Jerusalem to tell General Allenby that "they wanted to remain under Ottoman rule." There is no mention in any literary source

---

30 Keith David Watenpaugh, *Being Modern in the Middle East: Revolution, Nationalism, Colonialism and the Arab Middle Class* (Princeton: Princeton University Press, 2006), 110. We will meet Fahreddin Pasha below in the section on the siege of Medina.
31 Ismail Kara, "Halep'den Mektup Var" [There is a letter from Aleppo], *Derin Tarih* (January 2017): 3–6.
32 Hüseyin Kazım Kadri, *Meşrutiyettden Cumhuriyete Hatıralarım*, 139, 143.

of such a proposal. On the other hand, Kazım is not given to invention; if anything, his memoirs are somewhat given to understatement.[33]

Hüseyin Kazım's most remarkable achievement was his idea to compile an encyclopedic work, *Lubnan: Mubahis Ilmiyya wa Ijtimaiyya* (*Lebanon: Scientific and Social Research*), published in August 1918 and prepared under the protection of the *Mutasarrıf* Ismail Hakkı Bey, probably at the instigation of Hüseyin Kazım who had very close relations with him.[34] This multi-authored work, comprising articles by Arab, American, and Turkish authors, stands as an enigmatic piece of scientific compilation of knowledge concerning a very broad spectrum of subjects. People, geography, religions, agriculture, and monuments are all covered in twenty chapters. The editor and author of two of the articles was Father Louis Sheikho, a Jesuit priest with no reason to love the Turks, as he and his order had been the target of systematic harassment by Cemal Pasha and Azmi Bey, the Vali of Beirut, who deeply distrusted the Jesuits as a result of their well-known pro-French leanings.[35]

The enigma that surrounds the work lies in its timing. The volume was approved by Cemal at the end of 1917 when Baghdad and Jerusalem had already fallen (March 11 and December 9) and published in August 1918, literally weeks before the Allied occupation of Beirut. What was the aim of such a work? Carla Eddé's hypothesis regarding this issue is as follows:

> This body of knowledge was nothing other than a continuation of the war by other means, even if these means had to be adapted to the changing conjectures of war for the main protagonists. [They] were the Ottoman officials, and the local actors' ideologies of the Town [Beirut] and the Mountain with all their permeability and nuances.[36]

---

33 Ibid., 142–143.
34 Carla Eddé, "Le Savoir Encyclopedique ou la Continuation de la Guerre par d'Autres Moyens," paper presented at the symposium *La Première Guerre Mondiale au Proche Orient: Experiences, Savoirs, Memoires*, Université St. Joseph, Beirut, November 3–4, 2014. Quoted with the permission of the author. The work was in Arabic and Turkish.
35 Christian Tautel and Pierre Wittouck S. J., eds., *Le Peuple Libanais dans La Tourmente de la Grande Guerre 1914–1918 d'après les Archives des Peres Jésuites au Liban* (Beirut: Presses Universitaire St. Joseph, 2015), 63. A diary entry by Father Shiekho for February 2, 1917 reads: "The Turks, if they are victorious, are determined to crush the Christians in their empire. They are prepared to use any means necessary to re-establish their wounded authority in Syria and Arabia. Cemal Pasha is travelling the country and striving to revive Muslim fanaticism."
36 Eddé, "Le savoir encyclopedique."

It is likely that Hüseyin Kazım served as the go-between in linking Sheiko and Father Antoine Salhani, another Jesuit, with Azmi Bey and Ismail Hakkı Bey.[37] Kazım, apart from writing the Preface, contributed two articles to this gargantuan task by writing both "Islam" and (as he was a trained agronomist) "A scientific overview of agriculture."

Were the Ottomans hoping that they would be able to keep Lebanon as part of the Empire after the peace treaty? Was the volume intended as a document for posterity? Was it intended to serve as a blueprint for a future independent state of Lebanon? Eddé's hypothesis regarding the issue is that "[t]his encyclopedic work turned out to be a work of propaganda for both the Ottoman Empire and the specific identity of Lebanon."[38]

It is also a very important document that is very evocative of what I have referred to above as the "uncomfortable symbiosis": an Ottoman Turkish former governor, who has chosen a life of contemplation and retreat in Lebanon, befriends a circle of Jesuit fathers, who have been harshly victimized by his own government, and convinces them to contribute to an encyclopedic work on a land that will soon be "lost" to the Turks. Hüseyin Kazım stated in the Preface to the volume:

> The government of Lebanon, in publishing this work, brings Lebanon to the attention of the world and exposes to the world the magnificent scenery that is typical of this Mountain, blessed with beautiful flora and fauna. The aim [of the government] can be summed up briefly as twofold, to know itself and to make itself known. This was a plan that was neglected until now. The government of Lebanon wanted to see with its own eyes the regions of this

---

37 Eddé, "Le savoir encyclopedique"; Henri Jalabert S. J., *Jesuites au Proche-Orient Notices biographiques* (Beirut: Université de Saint Joseph, Faculté des Lettres et Sciences Humaines, 1987), 168–69, 210–211. As Jalabert describes, "Pere Louis Sheikho (1859–1927): When the war of 1914 led to the expulsion of the Jesuits from the University [St. Joseph], his services to the entire culture of the Orient earned him, with the friendship of an important member of the Young Turk Party, former Vali of Aleppo, Hüseyin Kazım Bey, the right to work in the Bibliotheque Orientale which was thus saved from pillage and ruin, together with the famous remark [about him] by Cemal Pasha during the bloody trials of the military tribunal, 'He is the Sultan of the Arabic language.'" Antoine Salhani (1847–1941) was also an accomplished Arabist. The articles contributed by Sheikho were entitled, "Lebanese People and their Religious Affiliations. A Brief Account of Lebanese History from antiquity to the Arab Period." He also contributed an article on Beirut. Both Sheikho and Salhani rejected a draft article on foreign schools because it contained anti-French remarks, see Eddé, "Le savoir encyclopedique."

38 Eddé, "Le Savoir Encyclopedique."

land, splendid and historic, and then to care for them with all of its heart. That is what caused it to prepare this book. ... Generally speaking, this book comprises all the studies which will find favor with all the Lebanese of all walks of life.[39]

With these words Hüseyin Kazım was elegantly summarizing the symbiotic feeling of not really belonging, yet belonging very much. Why would a government that was about to abandon Lebanon publish a multi-authored volume, prepared in record time? Perhaps, as put by Kazım himself, "to know itself and to make itself known."[40] The alternative explanation may have been that even in the last months of the war they expected to be at Germany's side during the peace negotiations. This will be discussed in the last section of this introduction.

Turkish attitudes towards Arab soldiers in the Ottoman armed forces as reflected in the memoirs

According to Mehmet Beşikçi, whose book remains a leading reference point on the issue of Ottoman military mobilization in the Great War, statistics regarding the proportion of Arab troops in the Ottoman forces are "fragmentary." In the Yıldırım Army Group, formed in the last year of the war, the deputy chief of staff noted in a report that 66% of the troops were Turkish and 26% were Arab. In his evaluation of the proportion of Arabs in the Ottoman forces, Beşikçi extrapolates from the general proportion of the population of each ethnic group in the Empire to their proportions in the armed forces: "out of about totally 23 million people in 1914, the approximate ratios of major groups would be as follows: 47 percent Turks and Anatolian Muslims, 37 percent Arabs, 8 percent Ottoman Greeks, 7 percent Armenians and 1 percent Jews."[41]

Arab troops were sent to distant fronts such as Gallipoli and Eastern Anatolia. Yet, the attitude of the Ottoman high command toward Arab

---

39 *Lubnan*, Preface (*Dibaje*). Yet it is interesting that there is no mention of the volume in his memoirs.

40 Ibid. Ismail Kara, who edited his memoirs, claims that "[after] the armistice in 1918 when the Ottoman state lost Syria, he refused the position of Vali of Beirut which was offered to him by the locals and returned to Istanbul." *Meşrutiyetten Cumhuriyete Hatıralarım*, 24. This is not mentioned in the memoirs.

41 Mehmet Beşikçi, *The Ottoman Mobilization of Manpower in the First World War: Between Voluntarism and Resistance* (Leiden: Brill, 2012), 253.

troops was often disparaging. A recent official publication from the Turkish General Staff Military History Department declares:

> The Turk who by nature possesses many of the military virtues, is perfect, brave, undemanding, dauntless, obedient, submissive and genuinely loyal. As for the Arab, he is far from being this valuable. Arab troops never carried out, were unable to carry out, the duty expected of them. . . . From the point of view of purity, loyalty, determination, readiness to sacrifice their lives, resilience and courage they were inferior to the Turks. The nucleus of the Turkish army was made up of heroic children of the Anatolian plateau. . . . The Muslim Arab units were not suited to the needs of warfare, either defensive or offensive. For this reason, all Arab units needed to be reinforced by Turkish units in a proportion of 1/3.[42]

General Liman von Sanders, commander in chief of the Palestine front, had a more moderate view as to the relative capacities of Turkish and Arab soldiers:

> The Turkish soldier, particularly the Anatolian, is excellent fighting material. Well looked after and sufficiently nourished, properly trained and calmly led these men will accomplish the highest aims. A large part of the Arabs may be made into good usable soldiers, if from the very beginning of their service they are treated with strictness and justice.[43]

Thus, even in the German general's estimation, the difference between Turkish and Arab soldiers was patent.

Regarding the military units in the Fourth Army district, the official military record notes that in January 1917, the Fourth Army Command had asked for "10,000 reinforcement troops of Turkish blood" (*Türk soylu ikmal eri*). In Mount Lebanon, it was stated, "[i]n the 43rd Division in Mount Lebanon the battalions were made up of 670 soldiers. They were all Arabs from the zone of Beirut."[44] These records amount to an official account of

---

42 *Birinci Dünya Harbinde Türk Harbi, IV. Cilt., 1. Kısım., Sina Filistin Cephesi, Askeri Tarih ve Stratejik Etüt Başkanlığı* [*The Turkish War in the First World War*, vol. IV, part 1: *The Sinai and Palestine Fronts, Directorate of Military History and Strategic Studies*] (Ankara: Genelkurmay Başkanlığı Harp Tarihi Dairesi, 1979), 336.

43 Liman von Sanders, *Five Years in Turkey* (Annapolis: United States Naval Institute, 1927), 191. "Liman Pasha" served for five years as the head of the German military mission in the Ottoman Empire.

44 *Birinci Dünya Harbinde Türk Harbi*, 483–484. The official military history gives the proportion of Arab troops in all units.

the military collective memory of World War I. All statements about the Arab troops, such as the above, are anonymous, but they are footnoted with references to the documents in the official archives of the Directorate of Military History and Strategic Studies (ATASE).

Another curious feature of these volumes is their similarity to the memoirs of Ali Fuad cited below. Regarding the situation of the Fourth Army, the records state:

> The GHQ was in a very critical situation, it was like a buoy floating in a sea of rebellion. . . . In the summer of 1915 nearly all its effectives had been sent to other fronts. All that was left in Syria was the 23rd Division and the coast guard. All of them were Arabs. Most of their officers were Arabs. . . . Propaganda was rife among the Arab officers and it was heard that the Turkish officers were to be killed one by one in the night and the revolutionary committees would take over, declare the independence of Syria, and join with the French.[45]

The image of a "buoy floating in a sea of rebellion," and the Turkish officers murdered in their sleep is an almost verbatim repetition of Ali Fuad's memoirs.[46] It is highly likely that the anonymous retired officers who compiled these volumes used contemporary memoirs like those of Ali Fuad and Cemal Pasha in their work.

While the surrender of the British forces under General Townsend was being negotiated in Kut in Mesopotamia in April 1916, the Ottoman General Halil Pasha stated that in the matter of the exchange of prisoners, "he would insist on exchanging Britons for Turks, Indians for Arabs."[47] Evidently the Turkish commander had the same racial sliding scale in mind as the British.

Many of the soldiers of the famed 19th Division in Gallipoli who were "ordered to die" by Mustafa Kemal were Arabs. Together with their Turkish counterparts, they stemmed the critical Anzac offensive on April 25, 1915. Most of them did die. It is interesting that in the preface of Edward J. Erikson's famous book, we meet the same mindset seen above:

---

45 Ibid., 692.
46 See below, p. 98.
47 Neil Faulkner, *Lawrence of Arabia's War. The Arabs, The British, and the Remaking of the Middle East in WWI* (New Haven, CT: Yale University Press, 2016), 93.

> This book is about the Turkish Army, although it carries the title *A History of the Ottoman Army in the First World War.* . . . Although it is true that . . . many of the subject peoples, such as Kurds and Arabs, served in the army, the essence of the Army was Turkish. . . . That is why, in this book, the term Turkish Army is used instead of the more proper term Ottoman Army. . . .[48]

On February 25 Lieutenant Colonel Mustafa Kemal telephoned divisional headquarters and declared:

> Please Sir, we must ask [a favor] from the Commander Pasha [The Minister of War, Enver Pasha]: The regiments numbered 72 and 77 that were given under my command are all Arabs. . . . Some of them are Yezidi and Nusayri, who are against the war. Their [military] training is also limited. Let them take these [regiments] back and return my two previous regiments that were composed of genuinely Turkish boys (*halis Türk delikanlıları*).[49]

The request was refused and the 77th Regiment lost 700 men (nearly its entire force) in the first day of battle.

In October 1915, Cemal Pasha, partly to combat the ill will engendered by the executions of the Arab patriots in Beirut, arranged for a goodwill tour for some thirty prominent Arab intellectuals from Syria. The aim was to show Arab-Turkish solidarity in the war effort. Mustafa Kemal took impish pleasure in exposing this delegation of Syrian literati to enemy fire during a visit to their Arab brethren in the trenches. His aide wrote with glee how

> [the] dignitaries in the group became alarmed and panicked as a result of violent explosions, followed by the whistling sound of shrapnel flying through the air. Immediately they turned pale. Instinctively they looked to their horses. . . . When they pronounced the word *yallah* [let's go!], the second wave of bombardment had already started, and this time the shrapnel was coming pretty close. It was looking for the man whose number was up. . . . After our guests left, my commander [Mustafa Kemal] had a good laugh

---

48 Edward J. Erikson, *Ordered to Die: A History of the Ottoman Army in the First World War* (Connecticut: Greenwood Press, 2001), xvi.

49 Ayhan Aktar, "A propaganda tour organized by Djemal Pasha: The Arab literati's visit to the Gallipoli Front, 18–23 October 1915," in *Syria in World War I: Politics, Economy, and Society*, ed. Talha Çiçek (New York: Routledge, 2016), 61–86.

when I described to him how the code-word *yallah* had an accelerating effect on them.[50]

It is remarkable that the same disparaging superiority is seen in the memoirs of Falih Rıfkı, Naci Kıcıman, and Ali Fuad, which will be discussed below.

There is at least one memoir written by an Arab officer in the Ottoman army that gives the lie to the image of "Arab unreliability" or "Arab cowardice." Abdallah Dabbous was from a well-to-do Beiruti family and fought as an NCO in a machine gun unit in the Ottoman forces.[51] In the battles for Amman in March–April 1918 he took part in a critical fight in the village of Shunet Nimrin. He would have been part of the Ottoman 48th Division under the command of Colonel Iskender Bey who defended the village from April 30 to May 4.[52] Dabbous gives a very cool headed account of the engagement, where the hill of Nimrine changed hands several times:

> We received the order to go back to our initial position the hill of Nimrine. During the afternoon our enemies started to show up, one thousand men on their horses. Here we recognized that we are not more than victims and that our end had come. When the troops approached we opened fire. This situation continued until sunset. The commander ordered us to retreat and stop firing.[53]

Dabbous's unit then took part in the final days of the retreat towards Deraa during which they camped at a village called Ramla, some two hours from Deraa, where they were surrounded by the enemy:

> The luckiest troops made their way to Deraa but our troop met with the Australian army on the way. We made for the sand hills above the village and began to open fire. The enemy successfully surrounded us and we became like a point in a circle. We were out of bullets and 40 men were killed, so it was useless to stay and continue the fight. I gave the order to pull back and we regrouped in the square of the village. We were almost 200 soldiers. I told

---

50 Ibid.
51 Abdallah Dabbous, *Muzakkerat Abdallah Dabbous* [The Memoirs of Abdallah Dabbous] (Beirut: n.p., 1993). My thanks to his great-granddaughter, Sara Itani, for bringing this source to my attention. My thanks also to Sara Itani and Theresa Mikhael for the translation of the passages cited here.
52 Faulkner, *Lawrence of Arabia's War*, 396.
53 Dabbous, *Muzakkerat Abdallah Dabbous*, 135. This would have been the New Zealand Mounted Rifles. See also Faulkner, *Lawrence of Arabia's War*, 395.

the officers to come and told them that we faced a danger worse than the foreigners. Those Bedouin look at you with hatred and they are waiting for you to show weakness so they can start their extermination.[54]

As most of his superior officers were either killed or wounded, Dabbous was put in charge of what was left of his unit. When they were surrounded by Bedouin, Dabbous ordered his troops to mount the machine gun and fire over the enemy's heads. He then called out to them,

> "You the Arabs! I am going to give you one minute to leave and go back to your homes." Here I ordered the soldiers to start firing over their heads. The Bedouin were so afraid that they ran to their homes. The soldiers started celebrating.[55]

Nonetheless, Dabbous and his superiors eventually decided to surrender and met up with the British cavalry:

> Two horsemen began to approach us slowly, and when they were fifty meters from us they signaled us to put our guns down. As they came up I told them I could speak English so they felt safe and we continued on our way.[56]

Eventually, after Dabbous and his men were taken prisoner, he was summoned to the tent of the commanding officer:

> I entered a luxurious tent where you can find newspapers, a radio, a telephone. . . . The officer [asked me], "Are you the officer of these non-unified troops?" I replied, "No, I am not, I am the leader of a machine gun company, and the commander of these troops is in the building beside us and we do not know if he is going to live or if he is going to die. He said, "What brought you here so you have caused the death of 40 of your soldiers and 40 of ours? If you had surrendered, you would have saved them." I said, "I am an Arab and a soldier in the Ottoman army, and as an Ottoman I am doing my duty like the Turks and the rest of the population." He said, "Would this prevent you from joining the Arab Army? I think they need a man like you who is fluent in English and also an experienced machine gunner."

---

54 Dabbous, *Muzakkerat Abdallah Dabbous*, 136–137. His account is accurate as the Turks definitely preferred to surrender to the British rather than Arabs. See also Faulkner, *Lawrence of Arabia's War*, 446.
55 Dabbous, *Muzakkerat Abdallah Dabbous*, 138.
56 Ibid., 139.

I said, "No Sir, I cannot fight against the Ottomans after a long and harsh time fighting for them."[57]

In fact, very few Arab officers defected to the British or the Sharifian forces. The majority remained loyal to the end, serving with distinction on various fronts. This was due to "a mix of professionalism, camaraderie, suspicion of British and French intentions, lack of confidence in the opportunistic leadership of the Arab Revolt, and antipathy towards its feudal-tribal social base and reactionary program."[58] The initial British effort, soon after the outbreak of the Arab Revolt, to "turn" Arab Ottoman prisoners of war, officers and enlisted men, was a complete failure. On August 1, 1916 the first group of prisoners brought from India arrived in Jeddah. Upon their arrival they refused to get off the ship stating that they would not fight against the Turks. They were sent back to Egypt. Reginald Wingate, the Governor General of the Sudan referred to the episode as a "fiasco." A few months later, in November, the British had to force Ottoman prisoners on board ship at Bombay at bayonet point. However, later in the war a core of ex-Ottoman Arabs would join the Arab Army.[59] Some, like the key commander Jafar Al Askari, would have a critical role in training Arabs as regular troops.[60] Al Askari was taken prisoner by the British in 1916 and after he decided to join the Sharifian cause, he was set the task of "turning" Arab prisoners of war to the Arab side. In his memoirs he recorded that he did not have much success. Arab officers were not inclined to change sides as many feared for their families, or they were in camps where they were mixed in with Turks, "[whose] presence acted as something of an antidote to my exhortations-my eloquence was of no avail."[61]

In fact, the great majority of the Arab officers in the Ottoman army stayed loyal right to the end. Recent research has shown that the received wisdom of mass treason is simply incorrect. "The Ottoman Arab officers

---

57 Ibid., 140. The officer who spoke to Dabbous was, most likely, Major General Chayton, the New Zealander in command of the Anzac troops. See Faulkner, *Lawrence of Arabia's War*, 439.

58 Faulkner, *Lawrence of Arabia's War*, 186.

59 Eliezer Tauber, *The Arab Movements in World War I* (London: Frank Cass, 1993), 104–105.

60 Jafar Al Askari, *A Soldier's Story. From Ottoman Rule to Independent Iraq: The Memoirs of Jafar Al Askari* (London: Arabian Publishing, 2003).

61 Ibid., 111.

did not desert *en masse*. Instead, most of them fought until the very end."[62] This was due to a mix of professionalism, a feeling of shared destiny with Turkish officers, and a long period of training in Ottoman military academies. In fact, some Arab officers actually volunteered to fight in Mustafa Kemal's forces against the Greeks in the war of 1919–1922.[63]

Among the other ranks, given the brutality of Cemal's regime, the rate of Arab desertion from the Ottoman armed forces remained low. The massive desertions predicted by the British Arab Bureau in Cairo never materialized. According to British sources, out of a total of 7,233 Ottoman deserters and prisoners in 1917, 64 percent were Turks, 27 percent were Arabs.[64]

The *Harb Mecmuası* (The War Gazette) was a heavily illustrated propaganda magazine that was published with the aim of garnering support for the war effort among the Turks on the home front.[65] Eyal Ginio has shown that the photographs of Arab soldiers contained within the magazine portrayed them as loyal, courageous, and ready to follow the lead of their Turkish officers. Moreover, units like the camel corps (*hecinsuvar alayı*) received special emphasis as they preserved the traditional Bedouin way of life, that of riding camels, and yet had been taught to combine this traditional skill with the use of sophisticated weaponry while facing the British. "This was clearly presented as an accomplishment by their Ottoman officers and instructors."[66] Thus, for the home front (or whoever else who could read Turkish), the Arab soldiers were presented in a way that was the very opposite of the way they were actually seen by their Turkish officers at the front.

Some officers did, however, develop a feeling of genuine respect for their Bedouin fighters. In *Ateş ve Güneş*, the book that Falih Rıfkı wrote immediately after his return from Syria and which served as the first draft of *Zeytindağı*, we see a much more moderate tone regarding Arabs. In the section taken from the notebooks of an unnamed officer, the Bedouin are

---

62 Mesut Uyar, "Ottoman Arab Officers between Nationalism and Loyalty During the First World War," *War in History* 20, no. 2 (2013): 527–544.

63 Beşikçi, *The Ottoman Mobilization of Manpower*, 256.

64 Ibid.

65 Eyal Ginio, "Presenting the Desert to the Ottomans during WWI; The Pespective of the *Harb Mecmuası*," *New Perspectives on Turkey* 33 (2005): 43–63.

66 Ibid., 59. See Plate 9 in this volume depicting the officers of the Ottoman Camel Corps.

portrayed as loyal and courageous fighters. The unnamed officer recounts how he came to make the acquaintance of a Bedouin sheikh:

> At first I was not much impressed by his appearance. But when he spoke he was so brave, so frank, and inspired such confidence, I did not hesitate to share my plan [of action] with him.

The same officer also recounted how he had the Sheikh read a passage from the Qur'an to fortify the morale of his troops before they went into action. The Bedouin fighters went on to acquit themselves very well during the attack on the Suez Canal, inflating animal skins to support them as they could not swim.[67]

In the final months of the war, and as the Arab Revolt gathered momentum, the discord between Arab and Turkish troops became discernible. Liman von Sanders noted in his memoirs:

> The [Turkish] troops disliked to receive Arab soldiers though they might be well trained, because they no longer trusted them, since the Arab movement in favor of the British was progressing.[68]

The Holy War "Made in Germany"[69]

On November 14, 1914, The Shaikh ul Islam of the Ottoman Empire officially declared a Holy War (*jihad*).[70] As the Sultan was also officially the Caliph of Islam and at least nominally the leader of the (Sunni) Muslim world, the Ottoman state had a pivotal role in the world of Islam. The declaration was made largely at the instigation of Germany, where many decision makers believed that a declaration of Holy War on the part of their Ottoman ally would lead to mass uprisings of Muslims in the empires of Britain, France, and Russia. Yet, it soon became evident that the mass upheavals would not occur and that even among Arab Ottoman troops Muslim solidarity was thin on the ground. A leading German who participated in the Suez Canal Campaign commented that the performance of the Arab troops was "a squalid fiasco." Yet, the same observer later stated,

---

67 Falih Rıfkı Atay, *Ateş ve Güneş* [Sun and Fire] (Istanbul: Pozitif Press, 2009), 69, 72, 73.
68 Sanders, *Five Years in Turkey*, 218.
69 This term was coined by the famous Dutch orientalist Snouck Hurgronje in his book *The Holy War "Made in Germany"* (New York: Putnams and Sons, 1915).
70 Eugene Rogan, *The Fall of the Ottomans* (New York: Basic Books, 2015), 52.

"we did not have any Muslim deserters."[71] In the Arab lands of the Ottoman Empire, it was felt that shared religion would cement the already existing ties between Turks and Arabs. Cemal Pasha himself, although a totally secular individual, felt that "[t]he majority of Arabs would not hesitate to make any sacrifice in this great war for the liberation of the Muslim Caliphate."[72] In one of his numerous speeches before his reign of terror in Syria, Cemal called on the Syrian youth to support the holy war: "Together with the allies that we acquired almost by [accidental] good fortune we have not hesitated to declare *jihad* against those who have been the enemies of our religion for centuries."[73] The reference here to allies "acquired almost by good fortune" (*adeta tesadüfün bize verdiği müttefikler*) is very significant, because the Ottoman *jihad* was in fact a "selective jihad." As humorously put by Sean McMeekin, "Death to Infidels Everywhere! (Unless they be Germans, Austrians, Hungarians, Americans or—possibly—Italians)."[74]

In fact, the *jihad* seems to have had not much effect in the Arab lands. Quite to the contrary, the call to arms and military conscription (*seferberlik* or *safarbarlik*) came to be synonymous to ruin in much of the Arab lands, and the term became an integral part of the negative stigma of the *eyyam atrak*.[75] The Arab troops that were taken into the Ottoman armies were there because they had no choice, not necessarily out of a feeling of Muslim brotherhood.

The execution of the martyrs and Cemal Pasha's reign of terror

Together with the famine and the *safarbarlik*, the other key marker of the *eyyam atrak* was the execution of the martyrs by Cemal Pasha in Beirut and Damascus in 1915 and 1916. In Beirut on August 21, 1915, and in Damascus and Beirut on May 6, 1916, Cemal ordered the hanging of thirty-two Arab patriots. The notorious courts martial at Aley were nothing more than show trials, with few acquittals and death sentences *in absentia*. Some death sentences were reduced to imprisonment, and some of

---

71 Sean McMeekin, *The Berlin-Baghdad Express: The Ottoman Empire and Germany's Bid for World Power* (Cambridge: Harvard University Press, 2010), 172, 177.
72 Jamal Pasha, *Memoirs of a Turkish Statesman* (London: Hutchinson & Co, 1922), 144.
73 Cemal Pasha, *Hatıralar* (Istanbul: Iş Bankasi Yayınları, 2008), 245.
74 McMeekin, *The Berlin-Baghdad Express*, 123.
75 Laila Fawaz, *A Land of Aching Hearts* (Cambridge, MA: Harward University Press, 2014), 161–204.

the accused were released after being subjected to torture: "the aged and venerable Shukri Pasha al-Ayyubi was flogged day after day within inches of his life."[76] All of the victims were prominent men, intellectuals, journalists, poets, or politicians. Among the executed there were Christians as well as Muslims. The wide spectrum of victims meant that the event would become part of the unifying foundational legend of the Lebanese state, as the hatred of Cemal would prove ecumenical. Youssef Mouawad has shown that the commemoration of Martyrs Day (May 6), beginning in 1934, was initially a bid to unite Muslims and Christians in Lebanon.[77] This event was to become a watershed in Arab-Turkish relations as it became clear to most of the Arabs of the empire that the end of the road had been reached as far as loyalty to the Turks was concerned. In the memorable words of George Antonius, "Jamal's savagery burned all bridges between Turks and Arabs."[78]

Tarif Khalidi sums the situation up wonderfully:

> Perhaps no single political event of the war could compare with the impact of the public hangings of prominent nationalists in 1915–1916. The shock waves were felt throughout Greater Syria. . . . Anger, horror, sullen resentment were directed at Jamal Pasha. . . . This widespread anger would soon be transformed into the realization that the days of the empire were numbered.[79]

Jafar Al Askari, whom we have met above, declared that when he heard of the execution of many of his friends he immediately decided to join the Arab Revolt: "I made up my mind there and then to seek revenge, and to make every effort to join the Sharif of Makkah at the earliest possible opportunity."[80]

A contemporary Arab notable, Salim Salaam, was to make the following statement to a high Ottoman official immediately after the war:

> You know what Cemal Pasha did to us in Syria. It was not enough for him to inflict persecutions, imprisonment and torture on us, but beyond this he

---

76 Antonius, *The Arab Awakening*, 202.
77 Youssef Mouawad, "1915–1918: La Grande Famine du Mont Liban," *Historia: Une Histoire du Liban des Phéniciens a Nos Jours* (December 2016–January 2017): 444–445.
78 Antonius, *The Arab Awakening*, 190, 192.
79 Tarif Khalidi, "The Arab World," in *The Great World War, 1914–1945*, vol. 2: *The Peoples' Experience*, eds. J. Bourne, P. Liddle, I. Whitehead et al. (London: HarperCollins, 2001), 298. See also Fawaz, *The Land of Aching Hearts*, 242.
80 Al Askari, *A Soldier's Story*, 30.

had sent a great part of our men and women and children into unknown Anatolia. Therefore we hate him, and we want to take revenge by any possible opportunity.[81]

One of the leading figures who was arrested, Mohammad Jafar El Safa', a prominent *alim* (scholar) from Jabal Amel, wrote extensively about the persecutions of Cemal Pasha. As to the reason for Cemal's acts, he writes:

[O]ne was that Jamal felt that the Free Arabs were inclined to revolution because of their traditional hatred for the Turks, and because of the great misery of the country because of the civilian and military misadministration before and during the war. Another version was that Jamal Al Saffah, because of his nature was inclined to murder and repression and was looking for an opportunity to terrorize the Secret Arab Association.[82]

First and foremost, in the memoirs of Cemal Pasha, it is clear that the perpetrator of the executions was entirely unrepentant and attempted to justify his actions. Cemal maintained that he was convinced that a large-scale uprising was being planned in Syria and Lebanon. The French Consul in Beirut, Georges Picot (of Sykes–Picot fame) had neglected to destroy incriminating documents before he left at the beginning of the war. A member of the embassy staff informed the Ottoman authorities of the hidden compartment in the embassy which was broken into and the documents confiscated. These documents formed the basis for the prosecution of the Arab patriots for "treason."[83] One of the leading figures in this somewhat scandalous breech of diplomatic protocol, as the consulates were under the protection of the neutral American consul, was the notorious CUP hitman (*fedai*) Kuşcubaşı Eşref Bey. In his personal papers Eşref recounts proudly how he and his staff were responsible for finding the "evidence" to convict the accused men. The documents seized amounted to some thirty-one boxes.[84] Cemal maintained in his memoirs that he refrained from using the

---

81 Christoph Schuman, "Individual and Collective Memories of the First World War" In *The First World War as Remembered in the Countries of the Eastern Mediterranean*, ed. Olaf Farschid et al. (Beirut: Orient Institute, 2006), 246–263. This statement is all the more remarkable as Salim Salaam was one of the few Lebanese notables who was actually seen as above suspicion by Cemal.

82 Mohammad Jaber El Safa, *Tarikh Jabal Amel* (Beirut: Dar el Nahar, 1918), 213.

83 See Fawaz, *The Land of Aching Hearts*, 243–249, and Rogan, *The Fall of the Ottomans*, 292–296.

84 Benjamin Fortna, *The Circassian. A Life of Eşref Bey, Late Ottoman Insurgent and Special Agent* (London: Hurst, 2016), 49, 172–173. This is a fascinating account

evidence, the documents seized from the French Consulates in Beirut and Damascus, because he hoped that the nationalists could be won over to the Ottoman cause: "The policy I desired to see pursued in Syria was a policy of clemency and tolerance. I left no stone unturned to create unity of views and sentiments in all the Arab countries."

Cemal went on to state that although he had ample evidence against the suspects he refrained from pursuing them, hoping that they would see the light and rally to the banner of Islam.[85]

In 1913 an Arab Congress had met in Paris to discuss the future of the Arab provinces. The Ottoman government had sent official observers to the meeting. During private meetings with French officials, when Turkish officials were not present, some of the Arab delegates had made compromising declarations regarding willingness to come under French rule. These were among the documents later seized by Cemal during the war and used as evidence against the Arab patriots. "Yet a unified opposition to Istanbul did not exist and did not materialize before the Great War."[86]

Yet suspicion of just such an opposition was rife even well before the war. Mahmud Nedim Bey, one of the leading Young Turks recounts a conversation in 1909 with Talat where Talat told him that he had grave suspicions about the activities of the Arab intellectuals in Istanbul: "We are not so foolish as not to see what they are after. What gets on my nerves the most is that they show us a smiling countenance, seemingly sincere and loyal, they take us for fools and laugh at us behind our backs. . . . No matter how much they smile at us, they are our opponents. . . ."[87]

Mahmud Nedim Bey also mentions a conversation with Abdul Hamid al Zahrawi in Istanbul before the war where he stressed that he saw the need for reform in the Arab provinces, but counseled patience and moderation.

> I told him, "you must not threaten us. When you want something from the government you seem to be threatening us, your attitude is almost military. You seem to be relying on the Syrians."

---

based largely on the personal papers of this highly controversial figure. Eşref Bey was a founding member of the Special Organization (*Teşkilatı Mahsusa*) that was the Ottoman intelligence service. It was also infamous for its role in the perpetuation of the Armenian Genocide. Fortna pithily refers to Eşref as having "transferable skills."

85 Jamal Pasha, *Memoirs of a Turkish Statesman*, 201.

86 Fawaz, *A Land of Aching Hearts*, 24–25.

87 Mahmud Nedim Bey, *Arabistan'da bir Ömür: Son Yemen Valisinin Hatıraları* [A Lifetime in Arabia: The Memoirs of the Last Vali of Yemen] (Istanbul: ISIS Press, 2001), 177–178.

> Zahrawi told him that they had lost patience with the government and that they "were running out of time."[88]

Hasan Kayalı, in his classic book on Turkish Arab relations during the Great War stated that by ordering the executions Cemal was not overreacting to "sensational revelations" and that he was "convinced that a nationalist movement in Syria was a real, if not an imminent threat."[89] As such it had to be nipped in the bud.

Recent research in the Ottoman archives has shown that Cemal wrote to Talat as early as the beginning of May 1915 informing him that he was planning to do away with Abdul Hamid al Zahrawi and the other Arab nationalists well *before* the courts martial at Aley even began. Zahrawi, who was a member of the Ottoman Senate, was in Istanbul at the time that Cemal decided to go after him. He wrote to Talat, asking him to send Zahrawi to Syria, but Talat hesitated, fearing that Zahrawi's arrest would cause an uprising. However Cemal insisted that he wanted to take this opportunity to "finish him off." Talat relented and Zahrawi was sent to Syria. Cemal used a supposed uprising that was being prepared in Sur and Sayda by Abd al Qarim al Khalil and Rida al Sulh as an excuse to persecute the Arabists. He referred to them using insulting language, telling Talat that he would prevent any uprising by, "breaking the heads of these accursed (*mel'un*) people." In his letter, Cemal declared to Talat that

> Finally, during the Entente's campaign in Gallipoli, they [the Arabists] assumed that the collapse of [the Ottoman] government was imminent and they began to propagandize in the vicinity of Sur, Sayda and Merc Uyun. So I put my hands on their shoulders (*işte o zaman onların omuzlarına ellerimi yapıştırdım*).[90]

Talat was right to fear an uprising over the arrest of Zahrawi. In a book published before the war, Khairallah Khairallah, a prominent Christian intellectual, lauded Zahrawi to the skies stating that he was a fine example of an Arab leader who was always ready to oppose the government. As for his

---

88 Ibid., 182.
89 Hasan Kayalı, *Arabs and Young Turks: Ottomanism, Arabism and Islamism in the Ottoman Empire 1908–1918* (Los Angeles: University of California Press), 194.
90 Çiçek, *War and State Formation in Syria*, 44–45.

popularity, Khairallah stated, "For the people it was more than sympathy and esteem, for them [Zahrawi] was a cult figure."[91]

How real was the danger of the conspiracy in Sur? One of the movement's early participants was Mohammad Jafar El Safa' who stated in his memoirs: "The *ahrar*, the free people among the Arabs, took the opportunity of anger against the government and the fact that it was occupied with the war and set about working for the awakening of the Arab Movement in Syria." From his account it appears that such a movement did indeed exist,

> On 18 October 1914 the *ahrar* designated as delegate for Sayda and Sur and Jabal Amel, the martyr Abd al Quarim Al-Khalil. . . . He was among the best of the young Arabs in education and merit and national zeal. He enjoyed a distinguished reputation in the Jabal Amel. He had little experience and great temerity. He was not completely aware of the traditional conditions of the country and the situation of the *zuama* (local feudal lords) of Jabal Amel. He was over hasty and out of dedication created a cell of the Association [of the Arab Revolt] in Saida, composed of a category of persons who were uninformed and unreliable. Some disclosed his secret and turned against him from one day to the next. Some out of ignorance and stupidity and others out of malice and yet others out of treason and pro-Turkish sympathies."[92]

In fact, Al Khalil was betrayed to Cemal by several informants, including members of his close circle. It is doubtful that the Arabists in Syria had enough mass support or a definite plan. According to "celebrated German orientalist" Martin Hartmann, who was attached to the German army, "the Arabist movement was not strong enough to drag its members into a revolt against the Ottoman government."[93]

George Antonius's view is that there was in fact a plan, largely prepared by the secret society *Al Ahd*, to stage a rising but fact and rumor merged to such an extent that uncertainty prevailed:

> Military intelligence is seldom at its best in following up political clues; and the General Staff of the Fourth Army was no exception; while it had an ear for rumors, its nose failed to pick up their scent. The information was substantially true, but it could not be traced home to any of the plotters,

---

91 K.T. Khairallah, *La Syrie, Territoire, Origines Ethniques et Politiques, Evolution, Esquisses: La Vie Sociale et Littéraire, la Vie Politique en Syrie at au Liban* (Paris: Ernest Leroux, 1912), 128.

92 Jaber El Safa', *Tarikh Jabal Amel*, 212.

93 Ibid. See also Çiçek, *War and State Formation in Syria*, 47.

and Jemal was disturbed and it made him anxious and vindictive but bewildered.[94]

As a result, Cemal cast his net far and wide, pursuing the innocent as well as the "guilty." He justified his acts by claiming that the only troops he had at his disposal were Arab and if these had mutinied he would not have been able to save Syria:

> I decided to take ruthless action against the traitors. . . . [As the courts martial proceeded,] the wide range of their plotting simply astounded me. At this time the only troops in Syria were Arab regiments, and if these had mutinied I should have nothing with which to quell the revolt. The battle at the Dardanelles was raging in all its fury, and it was out of the question to take a battalion let alone a division from that front.[95]

He defended his decision to order the executions without reference to Istanbul by the extensive powers granted to him by wartime conditions:

> After reading the proceedings of the courts martial and obtaining the views of the Judge Advocate General, I confirmed the sentence of death, and it was carried out the following day at Beirut.[96]

It is remarkable that the Turkish official military history of the First World War echoes Cemal's words:

> Because most of the troops in the region were Arabs, if these were to mutiny the army would be left with nothing. That is why the Fourth Army, in order to save the future of Turkism and Arabism, did not hesitate to punish them in exemplary fashion by carrying out their sentences in Beirut. Some local and foreign sources who have been deceived, link the Arab Mutiny to the hanging of the Syrian and Lebanese traitors. This is wrong. Sharif Husain's mutiny had nothing to do with the hanging of the traitors.[97]

Thus in an official publication which appeared in the 1970s the Arab patriots are seen as "traitors." A better example of the longevity of the "stab in the back syndrome" could not be wished for.

---

94 Antonius, *The Arab Awakening*, 186.
95 Jamal Pasha, *Memoirs of a Turkish Statesman*, 213.
96 Ibid.
97 *Birinci Dünya Harbinde Türk Harbi*, 336, 338.

In his memoirs Ali Fuad Erden gives a detailed account of how Colonel Şükrü Efendi, the chief judge on the tribunal in Damascus, came to him with the result of their deliberations and the suggested sentences. He asked Ali Fuad to intercede with Cemal in order to approve the sentences. Out of the twenty accused only four had received the death penalty. Cemal personally changed all the sentences to death by hanging, brutally overriding the decision of the court.[98] Yet, Ali Fuad also stated, "A few days later Cemal Pasha would approve these convictions in the name of the Turkish nation and he would order their carrying out, again in the name of the Turkish nation."[99] Thus, it was "the Turkish nation" that hanged the Arabs.

Indeed, it seems that Cemal actively cultivated his image as the source of terror. Falih Rıfkı was to witness how Cemal seemed to take pleasure in flaunting the evidence in the face of the accused. One of the few instances in *Zeytindağı* where Rıfkı comes close to criticizing his commander is found in his description of how Cemal took pleasure in humiliating his victims.[100]

It is clear that Cemal was determined above all else to make an example of the hanged men. He repeatedly turned down pleas for clemency, even from Talat who interceded for Zahrawi, and from Sharif Husain who warned that the death penalty would lead to a situation where "blood will cry out for blood."[101] There is little doubt that the execution of a whole generation of Arab intellectuals by Cemal Pasha was what earned him his title of "The Blood Shedder" (Jamal al-Saffah). Yet this was not his only title. Aziz Bek, Cemal's head of intelligence in the Fourth Army district, compiled a whole string of flattering epitaphs that the people of Syria used for him: "Jamal al Zalim! (The oppressor!), Jamal al Taghiya! (The tyrant!), Jamal Mutawi' al bilad! (He who starved the people!), Jamal Hatik al-a'rad! (Violator of women's honor!)"[102] The people of Syria felt humiliated because they saw the hangings as "collective punishment." It has been estimated that Cemal sent thousands of Syrians into exile; indeed, he bragged about this, telling Falih Rıfkı, "everywhere there are those who I sent there."[103]

---

98 Ali Fuad Erden, *Birinci Dünya Savaşında Suriye Hatıraları*, 325; see below, p. 129.
99 Ibid., 275.
100 Falih Rıfkı Atay, *Zeytindağı*, 37.
101 Rogan, *The Fall of the Ottomans*, 295.
102 Fawaz, *A Land of Aching Hearts*, 241.
103 Ibid., 245.

Among the close observers of Cemal Pasha's iron rule in Syria and Lebanon was the President of Syrian Protestant College (today the American University of Beirut), Dr. Howard Bliss. The United States did not join the war until 1917 and the position of the college was delicate. Cemal deeply mistrusted the American staff of the college and suspected that it was a hotbed of Arab nationalism. Howard Bliss was to admit that, "Among the people of Syria there has always been a strong feeling of opposition to the Turkish regime, and Constantinople has always suspected the loyalty of this province. It now believes that Syria is a hot bed of sedition." Bliss admitted that some of the graduates and students of the college were associated with the "Arab movement" but insisted that it was unfair on the part of the Turks to make this a basis for a general charge of seditious activity against the college. Soon after the first executions Bliss was to pen one of the most accurate assessments of the Young Turks' state of mind:

> . . . The group of men in control of the Empire are determined, able, unscrupulous, and violent men. They are flushed with unexpected success. They will go just as far as in the direction of desperate measures as they dare. They are playing for high stakes. They must win or lose everything.[104]

The martyrs became a foundation legend in Syria and Lebanon in the years after the war and came to epitomize the idea of the "dark days of the Turks." As shown in the seminal work of James Gelvin, "The initial attempts to create meaning from the executions ordered by Jamal Pasha were made by those who participated in the Arab Revolt and their supporters who worked with the Arab government." Memorial ceremonies were carried out and patriotic plays were produced featuring "Jamal Pasha the Butcher."[105] Nicolas Z. Ajay, somewhat exaggeratedly, compares, "[T]he feelings of the Lebanese toward the Turks, [which are] somewhat akin to that of the Armenians and Greeks toward the Turks."[106]

Yet Gelvin is critical of the "myth of the executions" as "a critical boundary in the history of the evolution of the Arab movement" which has

---

104 American University of Beirut Archives, Howard Bliss Collection, Box 16 AA 2-23-2 16-6, "The Syrian Protestant College and the Ottoman Government: A forecast of some of the more or less remote contingencies in the course of the war's progress," a seventeen-page report dated February 1916.

105 James L. Gelvin, *Divided Loyalties: Nationalism and Mass Politics in Syria at the Close of Empire* (Berkeley: Cambridge University Press, 1998), 256.

106 Nicolas Z. Ajay, "Political Intrigue and Suppression in Lebanon during World War I," *IJMES* 5 (1974): 140–160.

become "commonplace among historians of 'Arab nationalism.'" He points out that even after the executions, "Jamal Pasha was frequently feted and celebrated by Damascenes, many of whom would later figure prominently in nationalist activities."[107]

Gelvin's analysis tallies with Rıfkı's and Fuad's accounts of base flattery even after the executions. However Gelvin tends to minimize the collective horror and terror that the executions *did* create. Self-seeking flattery or compliance as a means of self-preservation can be easily combined with a secret loathing toward the cause of the suffering.

As we see in the memoirs of Anbara Salaam, she refers to Cemal Pasha as "a monster" because he had hanged her fiancée. Nonetheless, at the behest of her father Salim Ali Salaam, she is made to be present at a social function where she is obliged to make a speech in Cemal Pasha's presence, even receiving his compliments. Salaam notes in her memoir, "the words of congratulations I heard for my speech felt like a series of stabs at my heart."[108]

There were also prominent locals who out of self-interest or genuine Ottoman patriotism supported Cemal Pasha. One of the most prominent was Emir Shakib Arslan, a Lebanese Druze aristocrat who remained a committed Ottoman loyalist to his dying day. He established himself as Cemal's right hand man and, "an intermediary between Jamal Pasha and the Arab populace." Arslan came to be hated as a collaborator and this stigma followed him to the end of his days.[109]

Another prominent supporter was Shaikh As'ad al Shukairi, who became infamous for issuing *fatwas* in support of the executions. He was later to be roundly condemned as a collaborator. Salim Al Ya'qubi was another important personage who backed Cemal, a leading religious scholar and poet, in 1916 Al Ya'qubi, issued a *fatwa* condemning Sharif Hussein. He retained his pro-Ottoman sympathies even after the Allied entry into Syria.[110]

107 Gelvin, *Divided Loyalties*, 176.

108 Anbara Salaam Khalidi, *Memoirs of an Early Arab Feminist: The Life and Activism of Anbara Salaam Khalidi*, trans. Tarif Khalidi (London: Pluto Press, 2013), 70

109 William L. Cleveland, *Islam Against the West: Shakib Arslan and the Campaign for Islamic Nationalism* (Austin: University of Texas, 1985), 31: "Arslan quickly established himself as an intermediary between Jamal Pasha and the Arab populace." As Cemal did not speak Arabic, his speeches would be translated by Shakib Arlan or As'ad Shukairi.

110 Salim Tamari, "Muhammad Kurd Ali and the Syrian-Palestinian intelligentsia in the Ottoman campaign against Arab separatism," in Çiçek, *Syria in World War I*, 37–60.

In order to justify and legitimize his policy of terror, Cemal Pasha published a book giving the official line on the courts martial at Aley and the subsequent executions. Published in Arabic, Turkish and French, the "Red Book," as it came to be called, remains a masterpiece of propaganda.[111] The point that is adamantly hammered home in the introduction and several times in the text is that "[o]ne cannot insist enough on the essential point: the trial carried out by the court of Aley was in no way a matter of nationalism; it was a simple matter of high treason." Cemal very ably played on the Arab sense of honour by declaring:

> . . . those individuals who have received the just punishment for their acts have soiled the good name of the Arabs in the eyes of statesmen of the enemy countries and have made them believe that this race has no morals or character and would yield themselves up to the first invader to occupy their lands.[112]

The introduction took pains to point out that the plotters were only a small group who "abused the good faith of the Arab nation, the great mass of whom, proletarians, bourgeois and aristocrats remained outside their movement." The Red Book stressed that the courts martial "only tried and condemned some two hundred individuals, as many Muslims as Christians" ostensibly proving that the movement was a very restricted one.[113]

Another important aspect of the Red Book was its justification for the policy of exile.[114] In describing the various categories of individuals who were exiled, the "second category" after the actual families of the condemned, are the "feudal class" who had oppressed the population, exploited their servitude, and had moreover,

> always opposed the efforts of the government which was trying to assure an equitable partition of the land and to defend the right of the population to enjoy the fruits of their labour. They always tried to oppose all the efforts of the government to uplift the working man.[115]

---

111 *La Vérité sur la Question Syrienne. Publié par le Commandement de la IV ème Armée* (Stamboul: Imprimerie Tanine, 1916). Although Cemal does not clearly appear as its author, the publication clearly reflects his views as seen in the Turkish and English versions of his memoirs.

112 Ibid., 7–8.

113 Ibid., 9.

114 Cemal Pasha exiled some 5,000 Syrians to Anatolia. See Çiçek, *War and State Formation in Syria*, 51; Rogan, *The Fall of the Ottomans*, 291. Rogan gives the number of deported at 50,000 this is probably and exaggeration.

115 *La Vérité*, 154.

Even more brazen than Cemal the friend of the working man was Cemal who "did not deport but simply transported these families. . . . Nothing changed, a compatriot who was Syrian became a compatriot who was from Bursa."[116]

The end of Lebanon's autonomy

The country which is today Lebanon was divided into two administrative units during Cemal Pasha's rule of the Fourth Army district: The *Vilayet* (Province) of Beirut, established in 1888, and the *Mutasarifiyya* (autonomous province) of Mount Lebanon. The *Mutasarrıfiyya* had an autonomous status regulated by the *Réglement Organique* of 1861 which had come into force following its signature by the Sublime Porte and the ambassadors of the Great Powers. Although it was officially part of the Ottoman Empire, it was overseen by a Christian governor called the *Mutasarrıf*, who was appointed by the Ottoman Sultan, but with the approval of the signatory Great Powers. He had to be an Ottoman Christian. The special status of the *Mutasarifiyya* did indeed allow for considerable autonomy from direct Ottoman rule. Cemal Pasha never officially abrogated the *Mutasarifiyya* but in 1915, after the last Christian *Mutasarrıf* Ohannes Pasha Kouyoumdjian was forced to resign, a Muslim *Mutasarrıf* was appointed, *de facto* ending Lebanese autonomy.[117]

The first Muslim *Mutasarrıf* was Ali Münif Bey, a close associate of Talat Pasha. He wrote his memoirs in the late 1940s.[118] Although he dedicated only a short chapter to his period as *Mutasarrıf*, it is a remarkable source. The most striking statement Münif makes is his assessment of his relations with Cemal Pasha:

> The only difficulty I experienced during my duties in Lebanon was Cemal Pasha. As he was alienating the population with his ruthless measures, I was seeking to mend the damage and win back their affection. In fact this was one of the reasons why I had been sent to Lebanon as governor.[119]

---

116 Ibid., 156–157.
117 Engin Akarlı, *The Long Peace: Ottoman Lebanon 1860–1920* (Los Angeles: University of California Press, 1993). See also the memoirs of Ohannes Pasha Kouyoumdjian, *Le Liban. A la Veille et au Début de la Guerre: Mémoires d'un Gouverneur 1913–1915* (Paris: Centre d'histoire arménienne contemporaine, 2003).
118 Taha Toros, ed., *Ali Münif Bey'in Hatıraları* [The Memoirs of Ali Münif Bey] (Istanbul: ISIS Press, 1996). The memoir was first published as a serial in the *Akşam* newspaper in 1955.
119 Ibid., 71.

Münif stated that the main source of conflict between the two men arose over the issue of the military intervention in the Mountain and the fact that the Pasha was not sensitized to "the traditions and legal practices of Lebanon." Yet he maintained that over time they developed a friendly relationship.

The official *ferman* (Imperial order) declaring Münif as *Mutasarrıf* began by announcing, "The privileges of Jabal Lubnan have been abrogated!" It went on to declare that the autonomous status of the *Mutasarıfıyya* and the appointment of a Christian *Mutasarrıf* with the approval of the foreign powers was to end forthwith.

Yet, the new governor attempted to soften the blow by declaring in a speech that the previous practices would be continued and that the Mountain would not be subjected to conscription. Münif stated in his memoirs that "because I was aware of the sensitivities of the local population," he had prepared his speech with great care. He confidently declared that "[t]he people of the Jabal were content, they became even more affectionately attached to their Muslim *Mutasarrıf* [than the Christian ones]."[120]

Indeed, a contemporary Lebanese writer, Lahad Khater, gives a very balanced view of the short tenure of Ali Münif Bey (September 25, 1915–May 15, 1916).[121] On the positive side, it is stated that he administered "with wisdom and rigor," that he prevented military intervention in the affairs of the Mountain, and that he shut out the old coteries of opportunists that clustered around previous *Mutasarrıfs*.[122] However, on the negative side he was implicated in a company formed by a leading Beiruti that monopolized the wheat market, "The wheat was sold on the black market at exorbitant prices, which greatly aggravated the famine and enriched [Ali Münif] enormously. This was the price that was paid by the souls who perished."[123]

In mid-May 1916 Münif was appointed the Vali of Beirut and held the position until mid-1918.[124] The position of the last Christian *Mutasarrıf* of Lebanon, Ohannes Pasha Kouyoumdjian, a highly sophisticated Ottoman diplomat, who was an Armenian Catholic, became more and more difficult.

---

120 Ibid. See below Falih Rıfkı's account of Cemal Pasha's speech on the new status of Lebanon.
121 Lahad Khater, *Ahd al Mutasarrıfin fi Lubnan* [The Period of the *Mutasarrıfs* in Lebanon] (Beirut: Editions Lahad Khater, 1982).
122 Ibid., 203.
123 Ibid. The Beiruti in question was Alfred Sursock, a close associate of Cemal Pasha.
124 Ibid., 204.

The Administrative Council of the *Mutasarıfıyya* was abolished on May 15 and its legally elected members were replaced by men who were chosen by Cemal and Münif. This was the last straw for Kouyoumdjian, who presented his resignation to Cemal.[125] Thus ended the fifty five years of the "Long Peace" of the *Mutasarrıfıyya* period.[126]

Kouyoumdjian had become convinced that Cemal had indeed singled out Lebanon for special treatment. At his first meeting with the *Mutasarrıf*, Cemal made a point of enumerating a long list of grievances against the Lebanese. As proof he brandished a book by a Syrian author, declaring vehemently:

> I will use their own testimony against them. In nearly all the pages of this book, there is clear evidence that the Lebanese, more particularly the Maronites, are traitors and criminals acting against their sovereign. . . . It is high time that we clamped down on these unfaithful infidel subjects and make them realize that there is no other salvation other than sincere submission to Ottoman rule.[127]

The book in question, written by Khairallah Khairallah, a prominent Christian intellectual, did indeed make open references to France as the "traditional protector of the Maronites" since the time of the medieval kings of France. Cemal may well have objected to statements such as, "The Turkish intellect lacks prestige and assimilative power. Its misfortune is the fact that it is faced by an intellect [the Arab] that is superior to it socially and morally. This means that the Turkish element can never prevail without tyranny."[128] The message of the book was clear, Syria and Lebanon were to come under French protection.[129]

There is little doubt that in Cemal's risk analysis for Lebanon, the greatest danger he saw were the Maronites. It was well known that they were pro-French and were demonized to the extent that even in the official archival publication of the modern day Turkish chiefs of staff we read the following remarkable words:

---

125 Ohannes Pasha Kouyoumdjian, *Le Liban*, 148, 150. Cemal did not accept his resignation, referring him to the Grand Vizier Said Halim Pasha. Kouyoumdjian was accorded three months leave "for reasons of health."

126 Akarlı, *The Long Peace*.

127 Ohannes Pasha Kouyoumdjian, *Le Liban*, 113.

128 Khairallah, *La Syrie*, 119.

129 Kais M. Firro, *Inventing Lebanon* (New York: I. B. Tauris, 2003), 23.

The Maronites were sincere enemies of Islam. They were being supported from the outside. In Lebanon a sect called the "Holy Warriors" had been created. Every one of them who killed a Muslim was paid a salary of four *liras* if he was a bachelor and eight *liras* if he was married. Of course these monies were provided by the French and the British who generously showered their gold for propaganda purposes."[130]

This reference to a sort of sect of "Maronite Hashisheen" is repeated almost verbatim from Ali Fuad's memoirs cited below.[131] Curiously, it is also included (down to the exact amount paid for each death) in Rıfkı's *Zeytindağı*.[132] Evidently, the negative stigmatization of the Maronite population as the atavistic enemy became an enduring racial stereotype.

Both Cemal and Ali Fuad sincerely expected a Maronite backed French landing in Lebanon. In both Cemal's and Fuad's memoirs Lebanon is depicted as the "weak spot" on the Syrian coast. There is frequent reference to the "thirty thousand rifles in Mount Lebanon." What is even more interesting is that the same concern is voiced verbatim in the official history of the Turkish military, "It was imperative to keep in mind the thirty thousand rifles in the hands of the people of the Mountain who were pro-French."[133]

As Cemal was about to order a search for weapons in the Mountain, Kouyoumdjian intervened and declared that the people of the Mountain were indeed armed, but that these arms were purely for their own protection. As to the possibility of an armed rising against the Ottomans, he declared, "Unless they are driven to despair, the Lebanese will not rise. They have neither the courage nor the means to do so. They will move only if the enemy lands. Even then these prudent mountaineers will only join them if they are in sufficient numbers."[134]

Cemal claimed that he did not order to search for arms because:

. . . it was certain that, whoever took in hand the business of disarming them, several illegal acts were bound to occur and many innocent people would be unnecessarily disturbed. Under the pretext of house searching the

---

130 *Birinci Dünya Harbinde Türk Harbi*, 690.
131 Ali Fuad Erden, *Birinci Dünya Savaşında Suriye Hatıraları*, 22.
132 Falih Rıfkı Atay, *Zeytindağı*, 30.
133 *Birinci Dünya Harbinde Türk Harbi*, 107
134 Ohannes Pasha Kouyoumdjian, *Le Liban*, 97.

properted classes among the inhabitants of Lebanon were bound to suffer immense material damage.[135]

Cemal instead set out to harass the Maronite Patriarch Elias Howeyk who was known for his pro-French inclinations. He considered exiling the Patriarch to Anatolia but was prevented through the intervention of the Papal Nuncio in Istanbul, Monseigneur Dolce, and the Austrian government. Cemal humiliated the Patriarch, who traditionally never left his seat in Bkirké, by obliging him to visit him in Sofar.

When Cemal sent his personal car to fetch Patriarch Howeyk, Rıfkı was to make the snide comment, "The Maronites considered the Patriarch to be a god. It was amusing to see a god riding in a motorcar."[136] Rıfkı seemed to have a somewhat exotic view of Maronite beliefs. The Maronite Patriarch was not regarded as a god. One of the Jesuit fathers wrote in his diary that Cemal summoned the patriarch and gave him "two-days grace" to present himself, ostensibly to talk about famine relief. On the issue of the motor transport, Father Joseph Mattern wrote: "We are told of a rapprochement between his Beatitude the Patriarch and the Commander Cemal Pasha. They met in Damascus and travelled together by car as far as Jounieh. It seems that the Commander is in no way convinced of the Ottomanist sentiments of the Maronite nation. His Beatitude attempted to prove him wrong."[137] One of the measures that the Maronites disliked the most was that Cemal Pasha removed the hitherto autonomous status of the Maronite patriarch making him an Ottoman official.[138]

The patriarch arrived in Sofar on July 25. According to Antoine Yammine, a Maronite priest who wrote one of the earliest accounts of Cemal's rule in Syria, Cemal was surprisingly affable, receiving the patriarchal delegation with great pomp and circumstance. He even arranged for a considerable amount of provisions to be sent to the visiting prelate's flock.

---

135 Jamal Pasha, *Memoirs of a Turkish Statesman*, 202–203.
136 Falih Rıfkı Atay, see below, p. 50.
137 Tautel and Wittouck, eds., *Le Peuple Libanais dans la Tourmente de la Grande Guerre 1914–1918*, 35. See diary entry of Joseph Mattern for July 22, 1915. The Jesuit fathers, who were French nationals, had to leave Lebanon. Those who were either Lebanese nationals or nationals of Germany or Austria were allowed to stay. The work cited here is a compendium of the diaries of several Jesuits who were in Lebanon throughout the war.
138 Çiçek, *War and State Formation in Syria*, 91. Çiçek gives the date of the patriarchal visit as July 27.

There was, however, a price to be paid. According to Yammine, Cemal prevailed upon the patriarch to issue a public statement that would be published in the French press, declaring that all was well in Lebanon and that "[t]he myth that the authorities were deliberately organizing the famine by blocking the entry of food [to the Mountain] was a monstrous invention." The declaration also stated that the men who were executed had been proven to have undertaken traitorous activities, and that "all civilized states take such rigorous measures in similar circumstances." Yammine stated that the patriarch should not be held responsible for making the declaration because he had been forced to make it "in order to save the surviving members of his flock from a tiger thirsty for blood."[139]

Howeyk was later to be criticized by the Maronite community for making this declaration "[and showing] weakness at one point of his protracted confrontation with the man who symbolized Turkish rule."

Archbishop Abdallah al-Khuri, who had been the go-between between Cemal and Howeyk, would publish in 1922, in the Jesuit founded newspaper *al Bashira*, a defense of the actions of the Patriarch; "In Al Khuri's narrative, the statement of good treatment from Jamal that the Patriarch would now sign was the latter's response to the existential crisis of Maronites in general that was now forcing him to negotiate and concede."[140]

After the war Patriarch Howeyk presented an official declaration to the Paris Peace Conference roundly condemning Cemal and the Turks in general for "atrocities and executions committed in Lebanon." In this document he demanded that Turkish officers and officials of all ranks should be tried as war criminals.[141]

Carla Eddé has given a detailed account of how Beirut and Mount Lebanon were "liberated" twice in October 1918. A few days after the departure of the Ottoman troops, Shukri Pasha al Ayyubi, the representative of

---

139 Antoine Yammine, *Quatre Ans de Misère: Le Liban et la Syrie pendant la Guerre* (Cairo: Imprimerie Emin Hindie, 1922), 61.

140 Dennis Walker, "Clericist Catholic Authors and the Crystallization of Historical Memory of WWI," in *The First World War as Remembered in the Countries of the Eastern Mediterranean*, ed. Olaf Farschid, Manfed Kropp, and Stephan Dahne (Beirut: Orient Institut, 2006), 91–127.

141 Elias Hoyek (Patriarche), "Les Revendications du Liban. Mémoire de la Delegation Libanaise a la Conference de la Paix," *La Revue Phenicienne* (Noel 1919): 24–288; Antoine L. Boustani, *Histoire de la Grande Famine au Mont-Liban (1914–1918): Un Génocide Passé sous Silence* (Beirut: Presse Chemaly et Chemaly, 2014), 86–87.

Emir Faisal, arrived in Beirut on October 6. Although the Arab forces and Shukri Pasha were well received, there was some tension between them and the local notability regarding the division of power.[142] It was finally decided that Shukri Pasha would preside in the Grand Sérail, which had long been the seat of the Ottoman Vali, and Omar Al Dauk, a prominent Sunni notable of Beirut and to whom the last Ottoman Vali had handed over the administration, would be installed in the Petit Sérail which had been the seat of the municipality. Salim Ali Salaam, another wealthy Sunni who had represented Beirut in the last Ottoman parliament and was dedicated to the Arab cause, represented the local notability at the celebration of their liberation. Dauk refused to attend. "In the presence of an enthusiastic crowd, the Sharifian flag was raised over the Grand Sérail, and the *hutba* was read in the name of Sharif Husain at the Friday prayer."[143]

However, this jubilation was not universal. Shukri al Ayyubi had also taken possession of the Mountain by occupying the palace of Baabda, the seat of the *Mutasarrıfiyya*. This worried the Christian Lebanese. The Pasha tried to appease them by appointing Habib Pasha al Saad as the governor, Habib Pasha had been the president of the last Administrative Council dissolved by Cemal. Yet the anxiety of the Christian Lebanese increased when Habib pledged allegiance to Emir Faisal. The fact that both Beirut and the Mountain had declared in favor of the Sharifian side was intended to weaken the claims of the French. This show of united support for Emir Faisal was meant to enforce the claim to Arab independence. Yet, this measure actually worked in favor of the French. Sharif Husain had been obliged to cede Mount Lebanon to the French, who now complained that the Arabs had trampled on their "rights," obliging the British to come to their ally's aid. When the French in Lebanon asked the British to intervene in their favor the British could not refuse. On October 4, a French naval squadron was ordered to occupy Beirut and French marines landed the next day and immediately started to distribute food. On October 8, the occupation troops arrived. Allenby ordered the lowering of the Arab flag and sent Shukri Pasha away.[144] The second "liberation" had ended the first, which had lasted only two days.

142 Carla Eddé, *Beyrouth: Naissance d'une Capitale* 1918–1924 (Paris: Actes Sud. Sinbad, 2009), 44.
143 Ibid., 44.
144 Ibid., 45.

The Great Famine

Together with the execution of the martyrs, the famine of the war years stands out starkly in the collective memory of the Arab lands in the last years of Ottoman rule. The famine was particularly disastrous for the population of Mount Lebanon. The death toll varies between 80,000 and 200,000. The widely held view is that Cemal deliberately starved the Maronite population in order to keep them weak and unable to rebel, as he knew that they were pro-French. A frequently repeated dictum is that Enver Pasha supposedly told Cemal, "we have done away with the Armenians by the sword. We will reduce the Christians of Lebanon by hunger." This statement is attributed to a Maronite priest who was working for French intelligence, and it was used extensively in French propaganda. A recent, somewhat controversial, book by Antoine Boustani openly contends that Cemal's actions against the Maronites amounted to genocide.[145] This view is contested by Joseph Mouawad who states that the land blockade imposed by Cemal Pasha on grain imports to the Mountain was the main cause of the famine. Mouawad tends to be skeptical regarding the intelligence report mentioned above. He does, however, qualify what happened in more moderate terms, refusing to call it genocide, "given the evidence at hand," but he does declare that it was "a crime against humanity."[146]

There were several factors that led to the famine. Grain and other food-stuffs were regularly requisitioned by the army. Local merchants also speculated and hoarded. The Allied blockade of the Syrian and Lebanese coast was also a major factor and an invasion of locusts in 1915 ruined crops.[147]

Even George Antonius, who has no love for the Turks, does not claim that Cemal deliberately organized the famine. He declares that the famine was due to several reasons, mismanagement, defective transport, currency depreciation, and, "above all . . . profiteering and a dastardly collusion, for which no epithet would seem too strong, between Turkish officials and certain Syrian merchants."[148]

---

145 Boustani, *Histoire de la Grande Famine.*
146 Mouawad, "1915–1918: La Grande Famine du Mont Liban."
147 There is extensive literature on the famine. Linda Schilcher, "The Famine of 1915–1918 in Greater Syria" in *Problems of the Modern Middle East in Historical Perspective*, ed. John Spagnolo (Reading: Ithaca Press, 1992), 229–258; Eddé, *Beyrouth: La Naissance d'un Capital;* Tamari, *The Year of the Locust;* Fawaz, *A Land of Aching Hearts*, 88–93, 96–100.
148 Antonius, *The Arab Awakening*, 203.

In his declaration to the Paris Peace Conference Patriarch Elias Howeyk stated in no uncertain terms that "the population of Lebanon was decimated by a famine systematically organized by the enemy." He claimed reparations and demanded that the "Turco-German" enemies be made to stand trial for the "atrocities" such as the famine "which had wiped out one third of the population."[149]

The famine is also reflected in the memoir literature. Of particular importance in this regard are the memoirs of Cemal Pasha. In the Turkish version of his memoirs, Cemal devotes an entire section to the famine, answering specific accusations that he had deliberately used the famine as a weapon of war to weaken potential opponents. In a deliberate effort to clear himself of blame, he resorts to very flowery language:

> In my capacity as Army Commander I was in no way responsible for the provisioning of the population. But to see the suffering of all my beloved citizens was becoming unbearable. That was why I sometimes even supplied grain from army stores at the risk of exposing the army to starvation. . . .[150]

In his memoirs, Cemal blames the usual suspects: local speculators, Sharif Husain, the Entente blockade etc. Cemal also stated that he wrote the section on the famine to answer the "slanderous lies" of the American Ambassador Morgenthau and the Dragoman of the Russian Embassy Mandelstam.[151]

On the issue of American aid and whether he would allow representatives of America or the Entente to supervise of the distribution of food:

> I answered, it suffices that the supplies come, if they want I will set up a distribution committee consisting of representatives from America, Italy, Britain; I will even allow the distribution by representatives of the Entente. As long as these supplies arrive here and the people are saved from hunger. Because I have grown weary of having to witness the death in the streets of all these innocent citizens. . . . The Entente powers were telling the people (of Syria): "so you are dying of hunger anyway, at least start an uprising in

---

149 Hoyek, "Les Revendications du Liban," 239–240.

150 Cemal Pasha, *Hatıralarım* (Istanbul: İş Bankası, 2006), 341.

151 The issue of the famine does not appear in his *Memoirs of a Turkish Statesman*, which is curious considering that he was addressing principally his foreign detractors such as Morgenthau and Mandelstam. Henry Morgenthau, *Ambassador Morgenthau's Story* (Ann Arbor: Gomidas Institute, 2000); André Mandelstam, *Le Sort de l'Empire Ottoman* (Lausanne and Paris: Librarie Payot: 1917), 337: "The new national project [planned in 1916] was the extermination of the Syrians by famine."

your country and throw the Turks out. Then we will give you everything you want. Far fewer of you will die during the uprising that from hunger." I had been charged with the sacred duty of defending six centuries of Ottoman presence in Syria and four centuries of attachment to the Caliphate. But these gentlemen forgot that it is not an easy thing to start an uprising in the lands that I govern.[152]

It is worth noting that in Hüseyin Kazım's memoirs we find the only direct reference in the memoir literature in Turkish to Cemal's admission that if the Christians died of hunger, this was not a bad thing. Kazım bears witness to his statement, "May the wretches perish, we will thus be rid of them!"[153] Kazım, one of the last Turks to leave Lebanon, and who witnessed the Allied occupation, was summoned by the British authorities and specifically questioned on the famine and the government's responsibility for it. The famine also looms large in the memoirs of Ali Fuad Erden, who castigates the rich and powerful in Beiruti society for their indifference to the suffering of the poor.[154]

From mid-1916 onwards, Cemal was prevailed upon by Talat and Enver to moderate his rule of terror in Syria in order not to run the risk of "the Sharif being elevated to the status of a hero who would save the Arabs from the Turkish tyranny." The Arab Revolt was well under way and they wanted to keep their options open with a view to bringing Sharif Husain back into the Ottoman fold.[155] Although Cemal had planned a third wave of executions he was told to put them off.[156] This relative moderation was also reflected in Cemal's efforts to alleviate the horror of the famine by opening up soup kitchens and undertaking other forms of relief. Yet, for many it was a question of too little, too late. Father Louis Sheikho, whom we met above, wrote in his diary on May 5, 1916:

[Cemal Pasha had ordered that] a committee be formed consisting of the superiors of various convents and other religious houses to come to the rescue of the hungry. Yet we often hear these words attributed to Cemal

---

152 Cemal Paşa, *Hatıralarım*, 343
153 Huseyin Kazım Kadri, *Meşrutiyettden Cumhuriyete Hatıralarım*, see below, p. 70.
154 Ali Fuad Erden, *Birinci Dünya Savaşında Suriye Hatıraları*, see below, p. 135.
155 Çiçek, *War and State Formation in Syria*, 61–65. The Ottomans were negotiating with Faisal as late as May 1918.
156 Ibid., 60.

Pasha regarding the ravages of the famine in Lebanon: he said, "as long as the Lebanese do not eat each other they can still praise God."[157]

At the beginning of 1917, according to Anbara Salaam, "for some reason I cannot fathom, the Ottoman authorities began to initiate relief operations." She and a few other ladies from the Beirut elite set up a committee to carry out relief work.[158] The mobilizing of the Beirut ladies for charity work by Azmi Bey (the governor of Beirut) is also mentioned by Bayard Dodge of the Syrian Protestant College, who somewhat caustically remarked,

> He himself organized some of the wealthy ladies of the higher circles of society and started many charities. . . . He did interest the selfish leaders of Beirut society and forced them to give time and money to the poor. A number of wealthy women who had never thought of doing anything unselfish proved themselves capable workers and saved hundreds of lives.[159]

By mid-1917, Cemal Pasha and Azmi Bey, as well as the *Mutasarrıf* of Mount Lebanon, Ali Münif Bey, seem to have actively undertaken relief work. On April 13, 1917 Cemal sent the following cipher telegram to Istanbul:

> I am copying to you the telegram I have sent to the Vilayet of Beirut concerning the provisioning of Mount Lebanon. . . . I have estimated that until the next harvest at least one hundred and fifty thousand liras are needed for the provisioning of the poor of Mount Lebanon. I propose to raise this money by putting up as a gage the property and enterprises of the Maronite Church. The money thus raised will not be given to the Maronite Patriarchate but will be put at the disposition of a special committee constituted by the Vilayet of Beirut for the purchase of grain from the army stores.
>
> I have read the letter from the Maronite Patriarchate [speaking of] the great suffering of the people of the Mountain where every day hundreds of children are dying of hunger and asking for the army to provide relief. This letter was brought by a special commission of three lay personages and a bishop.[160]

---

157 Tautel and Wittouck, *Le Peuple Libanais dans La Tourmente de la Grande Guerre*, 63.
158 Khalidi, *Memoirs of an Early Arab Feminist*, 71–72.
159 American University of Beirut Archives, Howard Bliss Collection, Box 18 AA2-3-2. Report on the Abeih and Suk al Garb soup kitchens, by Bayard Dodge. Dodge was Howard Bliss's son-in-law and an active participant in relief work.
160 Başbakanlık Osmanlı Arşivi (BOA), Ottoman Archives, DH-I-UM 20/2, Commander of the Fourth Army Cemal Pasha to Grand Vezirate, 30 Mart 1333 (April 13, 1917).

Cemal instructed Azmi Bey to "receive the commission [from the Patriarchate] cordially and carry out with them extensive consultations about what can be done . . . for the provisioning of the Mountain."[161] Azmi Bey was also very active in setting up soup kitchens. He wrote to Istanbul on March 26:

> I thank you for the two thousand liras for the provisioning of the poor. In the past four months in the city of Beirut sixty thousand poor have been fed. They are given free of charge, bread and a meal. Three thousand children are being fed and educated in orphanages. . . . Two thousand liras are sufficient funds for only one week for this charity work. I am about to open more soup kitchens for the feeding of thousands of poor from the Mountain who, as of tomorrow will be unable to find even a mouthful of bread. Thousands are dying each day. The government which is obliged to help must send fifty thousand liras.[162]

Anbara Salaam appreciated Azmi Bey's efforts, "Azmi Bey was the person we resorted to for all our needs. He was a hardworking man in touch with every issue, large and small, that concerned the city and its inhabitants. . . ."[163]

The soup kitchens and other relief works were inadequate given the scale of the famine. The funds sent by Istanbul were utterly insufficient. Indeed, competition over scarce resources seems to have developed between Azmi Bey and Ali Münif Bey. Bayard Dodge commented: "[A]t the beginning of the new year, that is January 1917, a new development occurred. The Governor of Mount Lebanon disregarded the strict attitude of his neighbor, the Governor of Beirut. . . . Perhaps his conscience was bothering him, because it was he who had been one of leading spirits in cornering the wheat market. . . ." Regarding Azmi Bey, Dodge stated that he had done a great deal to offer succor to orphans and the poor, setting up hospices, work houses, and soup kitchens: "His plans sounded splendidly and many persons sang his praises at first, but after a while the hospices became run down, the children were very much underfed and the citizens of the city turned against the Governor in a most bitter way."[164]

---

161 Ibid. There are some twenty documents in this file, all dealing with soup kitchens and orphanages.
162 Ibid. Governor of Beirut Azmi Bey to the Ministry of Interior. 13 Mart 1333 (March 26, 1917).
163 Khalidi, *Memoirs of an Early Arab Feminist*, 73.
164 American University of Beirut Archives, Howard Bliss Collection, Box 18 AA2-3-2.

Azmi Bey wrote:

> [For charity work] we are spending ten thousand liras a month. It is without doubt that the population of the Jabal was more than three hundred thousand before the war. Forty five thousand of these have moved to Beirut. Fifty thousand have gone to Jabal Druze [Hauran]. This year some seventy thousand have died. This leaves [in the Mountain] a maximum of two hundred thousand. In Beirut we have a population of one hundred and fifty thousand. . . . There is no doubt that Ali Münif Bey is favoring the Jabal. . . .[165]

Azmi Bey constantly complained that he had insufficient funds for relief work and requested that the ten thousand liras provided be increased to twenty thousand a month. Talat Pasha personally cabled him, stating: "Given the present state of the treasury for now it is not possible to increase the sum and you are requested to make do with the money sent."[166] What is striking about these documents is the frank and open admission that thousands were dying of hunger and Azmi Bey's sincere statement that seventy thousand people had died in the Mountain within a year.

The issue of famine relief and charity work was taken in hand at the highest levels of state. On July 1, 1918, Enver Pasha wrote,

> [The following sums] have been sent to the Yıldırım Army Group command. Twenty thousand liras for the poor of Beirut and Mount Lebanon, two thousand five hundred liras for the orphanage at Antoura, forty-two thousand liras for the poor of Damascus. This makes a total of sixty-two thousand five hundred liras. Any monies spent from these sums must be accounted for every three months.[167]

There are two interesting things about this document. The first is that just months before the Ottoman surrender on October 30, 1918 the government was sending funds for relief work in Syria and no lesser a personage than Enver Pasha himself had taken the matter in hand. At the very least, this complicates the "famine as genocide" thesis. The second is the order

---

165 BOA DH-I-UM 20/2, Governor of Beirut Azmi Bey to the Ministry of Interior, 22 Mart 1333 (April 4, 1917).

166 BOA.DH.ŞFR 75/2 1 Nisan 1333 (April 14, 1917), Minister of Interior Talat Pasha to the Fourth Army Command.

167 BOA DH. ŞFR. 88/163, cipher from Minister of War Enver Pasha to Vilayet of Syria, 18 Haziran 1334 (July 1, 1918). The Yıldırım (Lightning) Army Group was the last desperate plan on the part of Enver to recover Baghdad. It was later diverted for the defense of Palestine. Rogan, *The Fall of the Ottomans*, 342–343.

to "provide accountability every three months." Evidently, Enver at least (who admittedly was not the most realistic of men) believed that all was not yet lost. However, the monies being quoted in the letters were in Ottoman paper money that was greatly devalued at the time. The total of sixty-two thousand five hundred liras was pittance compared to the enormity of the crisis.[168]

It is worth asking the question why the Ottoman authorities in Syria decided to undertake humanitarian work in 1916. One possible answer is that the Allied press, particularly the French, had started a vociferous campaign against Cemal Pasha, declaring that he was deliberately starving the Christians. Hüseyin Kazım states in his memoirs that Cemal started the famine relief after damning articles appeared in the French press. He referred particularly to an article in *Le Temps*. Although Kazım did not give the precise date, articles such as the one below began to appear in mid-1916:

> The Tragic Situation in Lebanon. For nearly four months the Turks have started a massacre of the Lebanese population.
>
> [For Cemal Pasha] the time was ripe for the execution of his plans for the extermination of the Christians of the Orient. . . . The eyewitness who visited Lebanon spoke of nearly 80,000 victims up to 10 May, when he left. The mind boggles at the ravages of the double plague, that of the Turks and of the famine which has struck Lebanon.[169]

A few months later, the same paper ran a story entitled, "The Turks are starving Lebanon," which stated that the visit of Enver Pasha to Syria had resulted in a "veritable calamity" for the population. Enver, the article claimed, had given strict orders that no grain was to be allowed into the Mountain. As a result, thousands were dying, and the roads "are covered in cadavers." A delegation of notables had gone to Ali Münif Bey, the *Mutasarrıf* of Lebanon to ask him to address the situation. Ali Münif told them to mind their own business: "This is a matter for the government not private individuals. When the Lebanese start devouring each other only

---

168 By mid-1918 the rate of the paper lira to gold was 4.5 paper liras to one gold lira, thus 62,000 liras does not amount to much. It should be recalled that Azmi Bey stated that he was spending 2,000 liras a week for famine relief work in Beirut alone. See footnote number 97. My thanks to Şevket Pamuk for this information. See also Şevket Pamuk, *A Monetary History of the Ottoman Empire* (New York: Cambridge University Press, 2000).

169 *Le Temps*, June 27, 1916, accessed February 7, 2017, www.gallica.bnf.fr/ark:/12148/bpt6k2425894.

then will you be able to claim there is a famine." What is remarkable here is that the famous statement "when the Lebanese eat each other," which is commonly attributed to Cemal, is here reported as having come from Ali Münif.[170]

Almost a year later the influential French journal *L'Orient Arabe* ran an article based on the testimonies of American missionaries who had recently left Syria, stating that "numerous cadavers in the streets have become a common sight." The article did, however, state that four or five soup kitchens had been opened at the initiative of Omar Da'uq and Münif Bey. The governor of the *Mutasarifiyya* had openly told the American relief committee that "every day he was registering one thousand deaths." The article also mentioned war profiteering as a cause for the famine. The first reason given for the famine was, "the well-known aim of the Turkish government to kill the Arab element which is defying it, or at least to reduce it to a condition where it can do no harm."[171] It is worth noting that this article coincides with the efforts mentioned in the documents above to create soup kitchens and work houses and to generally alleviate suffering.

The last days in the overall context of the Great War

What was going through the minds of the Young Turk leadership at this time? How could they be making what were clearly long term, or at least medium term, plans up to the last few months before the collapse? What were they counting on? Here it is important to do a synchronous evaluation of events in the Ottoman theater and those of the Western Front. In 1917 the war was going badly for the Entente. On April 17, French forces failed to take Arras and the mass slaughter of repeated futile offensives led to a mutiny among the troops. In the same year, the British offensive was bogged down in Flanders. In late spring German submarine warfare came close to knocking Britain out of the war. Britain was shaken by several mass strikes by an increasingly radicalized labor force. Most stupendous of all, the Russian front collapsed and an armistice was signed on December 17, followed by treaty at Brest-Litovsk on March 3, 1918.[172]

---

170 *Le Temps*, November 6, 1916.
171 *L'Orient Arabe*, October 20, 1917.
172 Michael S. Neiberg, "1917: Global War," in Winter, *The Cambridge History of the First World War*, vol. 1, 110–132.

Brest-Litovsk was indeed a game changer. "The Treaty of Brest-Litovsk represented an enormous success for the Ottomans." The Bolshevik seizure of power and the collapse of the Russian Caucasus Army on the eastern front released a great number of veteran troops that Enver now wanted to use to retake Baghdad and Palestine from the British. Talat was to negotiate in person at Brest-Litovsk and when the news of the revolution reached him he was to declare that peace was at hand as the Allies would now have to come to terms. "Futher, he emphasized, only negotiations could end the war."[173]

The Ottomans thus secured their 1877 frontiers with Russia and the peace with the Bolsheviks enabled the transfer of thousands of troops to other fronts, notably Palestine. "The Young Turks were thus prime beneficiaries of the Treaty of Brest-Litovsk."[174]

It must also be recalled that in the same year the Gaza front was holding firm and by April 1917 it was being said among the British ranks that "Gaza was another Gallipoli."[175] Interestingly, the Gaza-Gallipoli equation was also made by Ottoman troops defending the region. When an officer asked one of them whether he thought the British would come again after the Second Battle of Gaza, a seasoned veteran of Gallipoli replied, "No, Effendi, they will not, they have seen our regimental insignias," meaning that the enemy had seen that they were up against the foe who had already defeated them.[176]

Even after Allenby's breakthrough at Beersheba on October 31, 1917 and the decisive victory at Gaza on November 6–7, although in full retreat, the Ottoman army was not broken.[177] Their German ally was winning on the Western Front and nobody thought the end of the war was close.

After the fall of Jerusalem on December 9, 1917, the Ottoman forces made "an astonishing recovery."[178] In May 1918, Küçük Cemal sent Shukri Pasha Al Ayyoubi to Emir Faisal to sound him out on possible negotiations, promising his father full autonomy on the condition that he abandon claims to independence. Faisal by this time had no reason to trust the

---

173 Michael A. Reynolds, *Shattering Empires. The Clash and Collapse of the Ottoman and Russian Empires 1908–1918* (Cambridge: Cambridge University Press, 2011), 162, 189, 190.
174 Rogan, *The Fall of the Ottomans*, 357.
175 Faulkner, *Lawrence of Arabia's War*, 255.
176 Falih Rıfkı Atay, *Ateş ve Güneş*, 99.
177 Faulkner, *Lawrence of Arabia's War*, 342.
178 Rogan, *The Fall of the Ottomans*, 329.

CUP. Indeed, the Ottoman authorities in Istanbul "were optimistic about the outcome of the war" and planned to replace Sharif Husain after the war with Sharif Ali Haidar. [179]

Just months before the armistice, in July 1918, Enver was instructing his subordinates to provide quarterly accounts of their spending for relief work. Just before he left Syria, Cemal sponsored and published two encyclopedic works on the Vilayet of Beirut and the *Mutasarrıfıyya* of Mount Lebanon. Even well after the American entry into the war, Dr. Howard Bliss was writing to Cemal Pasha, who had long since left Syria, in the most affectionate terms on May 20, 1918, telling him that the College remembered him fondly,

> [F]or all you have done for the cause of education in Syria and of course your many favors to our College. . . . We are looking forward to the next autumn when we hope to resume our work on October 9. We miss Your Excellency very much but it is a great comfort to know that although you are far away and occupied with many great affairs Your Excellency does not forget us and that in you we have a strong, just, and constant friend.[180]

Evidently, the good doctor was still hedging his bets in case the college had to contend with a world where the Turks retained control of Beirut. Again, we have to shift our gaze to what was happening on the Western Front. In the spring and early summer of 1918, the German spring offensive seemed likely to succeed.[181] At the very least the leadership of the Young Turks may have thought that they could secure a place at the table for a negotiated peace which would allow them to keep some of their Arab provinces. The much belated efforts to provide famine relief can also be seen in this light. Bad press in the west would not look good if the Ottoman state was to take its place at the negotiating table. The recall of Cemal in 1917 and his replacement with Mersinli [Küçük] Cemal Pasha, who was much more

---

179 Çiçek, *War and State Formation in Syria*, 64, 65.
180 American University of Beirut Archives, Howard Bliss Collection, Box 18, AA 2-3-2, May 20, 1918, Howard Bliss to His Excellency Ahmed Djemal Pasha Minister of Marine Constantinople. The United States broke off diplomatic relations with the Ottoman Empire but never actually declared war against it, hence the college was allowed to continue teaching. The very same Howard Bliss waxed lyrical after the fall of Jerusalem just five months previously, crowing, "Jerusalem has been redeemed." See Plate 10: Cemal Pasha's visit to the Syrian Protestant College in 1917.
181 Christoph Mick, "1918: Endgame," in Winter, *Cambridge History of the First World War*, vol. 1, 133–171.

favorably regarded by the Arabs, can be seen as an attempt to repair the damage done and possibly win back Arab favor after the war. Some Arab intellectuals actually felt that, "Mersinli was expressly appointed by Istanbul in order to control the damage towards the Ottoman state brought about by the actions of Ahmad Cemal."[182] There is evidence that Cemal Pasha had high ambitions for his political future after the war. A group of influential CUP members, "[h]aving come to the conclusion that the Ottoman Empire had lost the war, believed that what was needed was a new policy under a new grand vizier, namely Djemal Pasha." It was hoped that because Cemal had a reputation as a relative moderate in the eyes of the victors he might procure more lenient peace terms.[183]

Although, as Sean McMeekin has shown in his admirably documented book, the Turkish-German alliance was stretched to breaking point in the final two years of the war, it is an overstatement to declare, as he does, that "[f]or Berlin, the Turks were no more than a tool to exploit the resources of the Orient—a tool which was now long past its expiration date."[184] By his own admission, the Germans actively encouraged Enver's push into eastern Anatolia and the Caucasus in the aftermath of Brest Litovsk. As the Russian armies collapsed in the spring of 1918, the Germans endorsed the stipulation in the final treaty of Brest-Litovsk that "Russia shall do everything to in her power to guarantee a speedy and orderly return of the East Anatolian provinces to Turkey." In less than two months the Ottoman Third Army had reversed all of the Russian gains of the last three years. Thus the Ottoman Empire secured a return to the pre-1877 borders with Russia with the blessing of the Germans.[185] Ultimately, in the Caucasus, the Ottoman forces were almost too successful for the taste of their German allies and the Turco-German competition for the possession of the oil rich Baku region actually led to skirmishes between the Ottoman "volunteers" and the Germans.[186]

But in 1917 and well into 1918 the Germans had certainly not given up on the Ottomans. No lesser a personage than Erich von Falkenhayn, the

182 Salim Tamari, "Arabs, Turks, and Monkeys. Ottoman Ethnographic Mapping of Palestine and Syria," in Salim Tamari, *The Great War and the Remaking of Palestine* (Los Angeles: University of California Press, 2017).
183 Talha Çiçek, "Myth of the Unionist Triumvirate, The Formation of the CUP Factions and Their Impact in Syria during the Great War," in Çiçek, *Syria in World War I*, 9–36.
184 McMeekin, *The Berlin-Baghdad Express*, 333.
185 Ibid., 330. The Ottoman provinces of Kars, Ardahan, and Batumi had been ceded to the Russians by the Treaty of Berlin in 1878.
186 Reynolds, *Shattering Empires*, 217.

ex-commander in chief of all German armies, was sent to take command of the The Yıldırım Army Group in 1917. The Yıldırım Army Group, was originally designated for the recapture of Baghdad, but diverted, at the insistence of Liman von Sanders, for the defense of Palestine, was almost entirely staffed by German officers. A "full German infantry division" was sent to the Palestine front, and the Germans committed "£5 million in gold—extremely scarce resources in mid-1917—to ensure Yıldırım had the resources to succeed"[187] Despite (admittedly serious) mutual tensions, the Germans and the Turks fought tooth and nail to stem the British advance. If the Ludendorf offensive had succeeded in the spring of 1918 (as it very nearly did) the Turks would have quite probably demanded some *quid pro quo* in the Arab provinces from their German allies.

They certainly would have felt that they deserved to be fairly treated by Germany, as much to the world's surprise, Germany's major ally in the Great War had turned out to be not Austria-Hungary (whose defeats at the hand of tiny Serbia and Russia had in fact made it a liability), but the Ottomans. It were the Ottoman troops that had helped stem the Russian advance into Galicia and hence onto Vienna. The victory at Gallipoli had indirectly contributed to the advent of the Russian revolution by denying sea access to Russia and any potential support from the Entente. The victory at Kut-al-Amara had gained the Ottoman Empire tremendous prestige in the Muslim world.[188] Even the two attempts against the Suez Canal, although they failed, pinned down tens of thousands of British and colonial troops in Egypt, troops that could otherwise have been invaluable on the Western Front. McMeekin himself admits that "[i]n the annals of the First World War, the successful Turko-German Sinai desert crossing has to count as one of the greatest achievements."[189]

Curious interludes: Anglo-American attempts to make a separate peace with the Ottomans

One of the most ambiguous (and understudied) grey areas of the Great War remains the possibility of a separate peace between the Ottoman Empire and the Entente. It appears that as early as mid-1916, after the victories of

---

187 Rogan, *The Fall of the Ottomans*, 342–343. "The Yıldırım Group was to be organized along the lines of a German army group."
188 Ibid., 267: "With a loss 13,309 in total Kut was the British armies' worst surrender ever."
189 McMeekin, *The Berlin-Baghdad Express*, 174.

Gallipoli and Kut-al-Amara, the Germans were worried that Istanbul would make a separate peace. German emissaries reassured Berlin that Enver and Talat had told them that they would continue the war to its end.[190] Later in the war, attempts were made by American and British diplomats to separate the Ottoman Empire from her German ally. In May 1917, according to the suggestion of Henry Morgenthau, the former US ambassador to the Sublime Porte, President Wilson, "approved a secret mission to sound out the the Ottoman government for a separate peace."[191] Morgenthau told Secretary of State Robert Lansing that conditions were ripe for such a plan as Enver, Cemal, and Talat were "heartily sick of their German masters." He proposed that he should go to Switzerland where he would meet "two members of the Ottoman Cabinet." His local man was Arshag Schmavonian, who had been Morgenthau's Armenian *dragoman* in Istanbul. Morgenthau told Lansing that Schmavonian was in constant touch with the Ottoman authorities and that he should accompany him on his mission.[192]

Secretary Lansing sounded out the British Foreign Secretary Balfour who was in Washington. Balfour replied that although he had nothing definite to go on, he was aware that the Ottomans were "nibbling." However Balfour stated that as Switzerland was "simply overrun with spies, Morgenthau should proceed to Egypt from where he could easily establish contact with the Ottomans. His ostensible cover was that he would be travelling to Egypt to investigate the conditions of the Jews in Palestine.

This bizarre plan came to nothing. It seems that Wilson changed his mind as a result of the determined intervention of the Zionist lobby, led by Justice Brandeis. Documents in the archives of the American University of Beirut originating from Special Agent William Yale, the American liason officer attached to the British Expeditionary Force in Egypt, show that the Zionists were very much opposed to a separate peace with the Ottomans that would endanger their plans for a Jewish homeland. Morgenthau was waylaid in Gibraltar where he was met by leading British Zionist Chaim Weizmann and the French Zionist Weil. Weizmann would later recount

---

190 Ryan Gingeras, *Fall of the Sultanate. The Great War and the End of the Ottoman Empire, 1908–1922* (Oxford: Oxford University Press, 2016), 131

191 Nevzat Uyanık, *Dismantling the Ottoman Empire. Britain, America and the Armenian Question* (London: Routledge, 2016), 62. It must be recalled that at this point the United States had not entered the war. The United States would ultimately break off diplomatic relations with the Ottomans but would never declare war against it.

192 Ibid., 63. *Dragomans* were the official translators attached to foreign missions in the capital.

his cloak and dagger mission to Yale. According to Yale, Morgenthau had exceeded his instructions and had his knucles rapped in no uncertain terms by President Wilson. Yale also stated that Bogos Nubar, the leader of the Armenians nationalists, had told him in Paris that the famed Schmavonian was "the creature" of the Young Turks and was widely mistrusted by the Armenian community. Yale also pointed out that the British had been against the plan from the outset but did not want to offend Wilson by opposing his "pet plan."[193]

William Yale recorded in his private papers that in 1920 he had a memorable conversation with Dr. Chaim Weizmann on an Italian cruise ship bound from Trieste to Alexandria where the two men had a fortuitous meeting. He declared that he was "so astonished" by what Weizmann told him that he was "able to recall it word for word." Weizmann stated that he had been sent by Balfour with the specific instructions to scuttle Morgenthau's "secret mission." He and Weil told the ex-Ambassador that the Zionists in Britain and America were very much against a separate peace with the Ottomans because they wanted a Jewish homeland under British, not Turkish, rule. He even threatened that if the attempt were to go ahead Wilson would lose the support of the Zionist lobby in America and Britain. Yale recorded that Weizmann told him,

> On your national holiday, the Fourth of July, in Britain's greatest fortress, with British sentries facing outside the windows, three Jews decided whether or not to make a separate peace with the Turks.[194]

Morgenthau's ill-fated "secret mission" was followed by a British initiative in December 1917 to "detach the Ottoman Empire from German domination." What worried the British was the unravelling of Russian power in the Caucasus which would grievously threaten British interests in Iraq and Iran if Germany was allowed to fill the vacuum. Since the United States was not actually at war with the Ottoman Empire, Lloyd George felt that a "proper American" should be found to undertake such an approach. He had in mind Morgenthau's successor as US ambassador, Abraham Elkus.

---

193 AUB Archives Bayard Dodge Papers. AA 2-3-2-19-4. This is a remarkable hand-written document which is clearly a draft that William Yale would later include in his papers. It is entitled "Ambassador Henry Morgenthau's 'Special Mission' of 1917 by William Yale."

194 Ibid., 11.

The plan came to nothing because of the rapidly changing conditions in the region.[195]

Although neither of these plans for a separate peace came to fruition, the Ottomans must have been aware of their existence, particularly as Morgenthau's so-called "secret mission" was no secret at all. The *New York Times* published an article that stated that Morgenthau was on his way to make a separate peace with the Turks, and US Ambassador in Istanbul, Abraham Elkus, stated that "it was well known everywhere that Ambassador Morgenthau was on his way."[196] The Ottomans must have been enheartened by such an attempt that they must have perceived as a strengthening of their eventual bargaining position.[197]

The end is well known. The Palestine front collapsed as Allenby stormed through Palestine in September 1918, and the German breakthough in the Western Front was halted the same summer.[198] In the end, the German and Ottoman surrenders occurred at almost the same time. The Mondros Armistice (October 30, 1918) narrowly preceded the surrender of Germany (November 11).

Two of the writers featured in this book actually witnessed the very last days of the Turkish presence in Beirut. Hüseyin Kazım recounts in detail how some eight hundred Turkish families were stranded in Beirut after the Allied occupation and how he entreated the Allied authorities to procure a ship to evacuate them. Münevver Ayaşlı also saw the arrival of the British troops as they awaited evacuation. Hüseyin Kazım thanks Omar Bey Dauk, the head of the Municipality of the city, profusely for his help in alleviating the dire conditions of the last Turks in Beirut. Dauk declared that he was put in charge personally by the last Ottoman Vali of Beirut, Ismail Hakkı Bey. On October 1, 1918 Omar Dauk announced that Ismail Hakkı Bey had handed him a letter, declaring as follows:

> To all officials in general: In consequence of the proclaiming of the Arab Government, the city has faced an accomplished fact; therefore the administration of the government has been handed over to the head of the

---

195 Uyanık, *Dismantling the Ottoman Empire*, 76.
196 AUB Archives. "Ambassador Henry Morgenthau's 'Special Mission.'" 12.
197 No doubt, much more research is required on the issue of separate peace proposals to the Ottomans. I have not been able to access the Ottoman archives on this issue.
198 Rogan, *The Fall of the Ottomans*, 373–380.

Municipality. As a result of this state of things your offices have lapsed. I therefore make these changes known to you and bid you to act accordingly.[199]

Regarding the Turkish families who had remained in the city, Dauk Bey made the following declaration:

In view of the fact that the Turkish officials and their families, and the rest of the strangers constitute for us a trust everyone should take care to provide for their ease and security such as it is demanded by the Arab Government.[200]

So ended four hundred years of Ottoman rule in Syria.

What follows is an attempt to glimpse the mindset of some of the Ottomans who witnessed the twilight of the Empire in the Arab lands.

Notes on names, spelling, transliteration, and choice of passages translated

The family names of the authors used in this book would have been taken following the adoption of the Surname Law of 1934. Thus Ali Fuad took the surname Erden, Falih Rıfkı became Atay, Naci Kaşif would adopt the name Kıcıman, Hüseyin Kazım would adopt the name of his father, Kadri. Münevver Ayaşlı used her married name in her writings. In this book, I have used the name the actor in question would have called himself/herself at the time.

I have endeavored to consistently use the Turkish version of the name if the person is Turkish, hence Cemal, not Jamal. For Arab names I adopted the Latin spelling used by recognized works such as George Antonius's *Arab Awakening*.

In the choice of passages translated, I focused on sections of text that illustrate the mentality of the writer. I have left out long discussions of detailed military campaigns and skirmishes, except when they have a direct bearing on the mentality of the actor. I have translated the original subheadings in Turkish, sometimes I have felt the need to add another sub-heading for the sake of clarity, for example, Tripot [Tripod. Gallows. The hanging of the Arab martyrs]. The main body of the text which consists of

---

199 American University of Beirut Archives, Howard Bliss Collection, Box 18 AA 2-3-2 18-6. In English translation in the file.
200 Ibid.

translations has not been put in quotation marks. My interventions in the main text appear in brackets and are in italics.

Each of the following five chapters aims to reflect the perception of the last days of the Ottoman Empire in the Arab lands through the prism of the five actors mentioned above. All of the perceptions are *ex post facto*, that is to say, they are heavily colored by the postwar ambience of republican Turkey. Thus, Falih Rıfkı Atay is scathing about the "waste" of men and resources for what he later came to see as a lost cause. Ali Fuad Erden, a professional soldier, sought to position himself as an observer and not a military historian. Hüseyin Kazım Kadri is indeed trying to set the record straight by stating at the very outset of his memoirs that he is writing "not as a historian but as a witness." Naci Kıcıman sees himself as an intermediary, a go-between the events of the siege of Medina and his much revered commander Fahreddin Pasha. Münevver Ayaşlı, who is writing some forty years after the events is positioning herself as a very late Ottoman *avant la lettre*.

Chapter 1

Falih Rıfkı Atay

Falih Rıfkı [Atay][1]

[*Falih Rıfkı was a talented young journalist writing for the Tanin, the official newspaper of the Committee of Union and Progress (CUP). When war came, he was taken into the army as a reserve officer. His brilliant prose drew the attention of the Young Turk leadership, leading to his appointment as personal secretary to Talat Pasha. When Cemal Pasha was appointed governor general of Syria, he asked for Rıfkı to be attached to his staff as head intelligence officer. He took up his post in Jerusalem in February 1915. Rıfkı was Cemal Pasha's aide de camp throughout Cemal's governorate of Syria (1914–1917). He was a very close aide whom Cemal trusted completely, and Rıfkı traveled with Cemal everywhere he went. Rıfkı's memoirs were published for the first time in 1932. He had written a previous version, Ateş ve Güneş (Fire and Sun) in 1918 while he was fresh from his return from the front.[2] Much of the material from this work was subsequently included in Zeytindağı. Rıfkı later became a fervent Kemalist, writing several panegyric works lauding Kemal and his regime.[3] He was a member of parliament (1923–1950) and came to be known as one of Kemal's closest supporters. By the time Zeytindağı was published he was firmly in the camp of the "stab in the back syndrome" regarding the Arab ex-subjects of the late Ottoman Empire.*]

---

1   Atay was the surname adopted by Falih Rıfkı after the surname law was passed in Turkey in 1934. All the names that appear in brackets in this text refer to similar names that would have been taken by the writers of the memoirs cited in this volume.

2   Falih Rıfkı Atay, *Ateş ve Güneş* [Fire and Sun] (Istanbul: Pozitif Press, 2009).

3   Falih Rıfkı Atay, *Zeytindağı* [Mount of Olives] (Istanbul: Pozitif Press, 1932, subsequent editions 1956 and 2014); Falih Rıfkı Atay, *Çankaya. Atatürk Devri Hatıraları* [Çankaya. Memoirs of the Ataturk Era] (Istanbul: Pozitif Press, 2009).

ZEYTİNDAĞI

In the last days of the Great War I had written *Ateş ve Güneş* (*Fire and Sun*) in a few days. In the general feeling of defeat, I observed that the epic heroism and suffering of the Turkish army was forgotten. It had become fashionable to swear at the army. In the beginning of the book *Fire and Sun* I had stated that "we should distinguish between the war strategies of the government and the war of the army and the people. How can we put in the same frame a commander who makes the wrong decision and the officer and soldier who die for that decision?"[4]

Because now it is possible to talk about both, I am publishing *Zeytindağı*.

Those of us who are approaching our forties now, we are the last youths of the Ottoman Empire. Children who are three, five or seven years old today have become the youth of the New Turkey and they bear no trace in their memories of the Empire. I am writing precisely because I want to show them the images of the last years of the Sultanate in Syria, Palestine and the Hijaz.

This is neither a history nor a memoir: in these pages you will read a series of unordered and haphazard notes that attempt to portray an era.

For our fathers Nish was as close as Istanbul. We thought that if we abandoned Vardar, Tripoli, Crete, and Medina the Turkish nation could not survive. The Europe of our children ends at the Marmara Sea and Maritza River.

Collapse and Redemption, these two epochs that have never been encompassed in one century in the history of any nation, two events, only one of which is the most important era. This is the story of those who tasted the greatest sorrow and the greatest happiness in the space of some four or five years. Their story is worth reading.[5]

Zeytindağı is not a book about Cemal Pasha. However, any work on Syria in the Great War will inevitably refer to him. My judgement and evaluation of the personality and character of Cemal Pasha can only be determined after the elements of the big picture have been put together.

---

4   Falih Rıfkı Atay, *Zeytindağı*, 3.
5   Ibid., 3–6. Foreword to the 1932 edition.
     This foreword does not appear in the 1956 edition. The only other translations of passages from *Zeytindağı* into English to date are to be found in Geoffrey Lewis, "An Ottoman Officer in Palestine," *Palestine in the Late Ottoman Period*, ed. David Kushner (Leiden: Brill, 1986) 402–415. My translations differ from those of Lewis.

Nonetheless, in order not to be obliged to put forward a new description every day, I find it appropriate now to give a short description.

We hear from experts that Cemal Pasha was not a great soldier. I do not remember that he ever spoke of old and new military matters with any pleasure. It can also be said that he was not a great statesman: his appreciation of international affairs was basic. Cemal Pasha was an organizer and and general inspector, the like of which we seldom meet. When Marshall Allenby was marching into Syria he was right when he said, "At every step I come across Cemal Pasha." The Swedish traveller Sven Hedin has written that Cemal Pasha was the most Europeanized of the Turkish leaders. In administrative matters he tended to exaggerate police measures; he always gave undue importance to pomp and circumstance. In this respect he was a typical oriental. To this day I envy his capacity for work. I never saw him to be despondent, slack or lackadaisical. . . .[6] Until his last days, Cemal Pasha's intellectual capacity was so limited that he was capable of using the terms of Ottoman, Islam, and Turk interchangeably. . . . There is no doubt as to his patriotism. Just as he had unlimited ambition, it was just as impossible that he undertake any acts harmful to the nation. . . . We can say that with his death we have lost a valuable element. One of his greatest and severe critics was the Ghazi (Atatürk). Yet I remember that he felt very sorry for Cemal Pasha.[7]

Zeytindağı 1915

I had left Istanbul hearing and pronouncing Cemal Pasha's name like everybody else. In Adana the inflection grew lighter and the name became two names, The Great Cemal Pasha (Büyük Cemal) and Little Cemal (Küçük Cemal). The little one was a division general.

After we had gone beyond Aleppo, the P of "Pasha" was dropped and became B, and the words "Cemal Pasha" which [hitherto] had been used freely, loosely, like one would say "Ahmet Bey," became some sort of privilege, something that showed that one was close to him, that turned one into something mysterious.[8]

---

6   Falih Rıfkı Atay, *Zeytindağı*, 5.
7   Ibid., 6.
8   Ibid., 7. The reference here is to the rendering of the letter "p" as "b" in colloquial Arabic. The two Cemals in question are The Great Cemal Pasha, "Büyük Cemal," and "Little Cemal" or "Küçük Cemal," otherwise known as Mersinli Cemal Pasha.

The approach to the Fourth Army Headquarters, particularly after Damascus, becomes a vertiginous experience, as if one is approaching a temple. There is a feeling of terror. The name Cemal echoes with a resonance, resembling a name one would find in the Old Testament or the Bible.

The image of Cemal Pasha that I had known in Sirkeci, standing by the pool of the Military Academy, even then a little proud, [yet] still simple and likeable, was replaced by a man with lined features whom I would come to know anew.

Headquarters was in Jerusalem in the German hospice at Zeytindağı (the Mount of Olives). When I arrived in town all the money I had was two-quarter silver piasters. If I was not able to get billeted at Headquarters, I could not go back, nor could I stay at a hotel.

I ordered the carriage driver:

"To the headquarters of Cemal Pasha!"

The driver opened his eyes:

"What, Cemal Basha?!"

I pointed to the Mount of Olives. As the poor man replied *"Tafaddal!"* I felt that even the horses had greater respect for me.

A big, crushing, spotlessly clean German building! Everybody, officers and men, walking on tiptoe with, here and there the *shwesters* crossing to and fro in the broad corridors, serving in the refectory and the rooms.[9]

I was shown into the office of an aide. In his office there was quite a crowd aged between forty and seventy, with and without turbans. The aide, gazing at my reserve officer's uniform asked me:

"Who are you and what do you want?"

"I am Falih Rıfkı, whom His Excellency the Commander Pasha summoned from Istanbul.

He went in and emerged again:

"Please go in."

I was in a confused state of mind. What was to become of me? Where was I to go? How was I to find Cemal Pasha?

A big room: on the left the Old Town (Sharia) and the Sea of Galilee, on the right the city of Jerusalem, in front one can see Russian buildings and gardens called Moskofiye. Cemal Pasha is standing, signing papers, with his back to us in at the angle formed by the window looking out at

---

9   Ibid., 8.

Sharia and the window looking out at Moskofiye. We can only make out a small portion of his stern profile and his beard. Apart from me, there are three other officers present, with files of papers in their hands. He raised his head briefly, his gaze skimmed over me and focused on the second officer, and he commanded in an acid tone,

"Tell my aide to show in the notables of Nablus."

The entry of the crowd was a strange sight to behold. Standing on the threshold of a man who had the power of life or death, each one paused and said a brief prayer. Those who had not finished praying pushed back their friends who were pushing from behind. [Finally] there were some twenty of them lined up in front of the window looking out on the city of Jerusalem. The Commander did not even turn around to look at them. He was busy scrutinizing each page of the files awaiting his signature. He would occasionally jot down a note, a comment, and issue terse orders:

"What is this?"

"I cannot accept such an answer."

"Take this to the chief of staff."

As time wore on I felt that the Nabulsis were getting progressively paler. Each time Cemal Pasha uttered a word a tremor would pass through each turban, beard and robe. How long did this pose last? The Commander closed the file, taking hold of the arms of the armchair, he turned to the lines of the Nabulsis, and began addressing them in a commanding voice:

"Do you know the gravity of the crimes you have committed against your state?!"

The Nabulsis, twisting their heads and wringing their hands were saying things like,

"God forbid! (*Estagfurullah!*)"

With one glance the Commander stopped their grizzling, by shouting:

"Silence! Do you know what the punishment is for these crimes?"

The Nabulsis took on the color of men hanged, their lips were aquiver.

"It is hanging! Hanging! But be grateful that our Sublime Ottoman State is merciful. For now, I have decided instead to exile you and your families to Anatolia."

All the Nabulsi raised their hands thanking him profusely, almost as if they were prostrating themselves in prayer.

There was no end to the gratitude of the Nabulsi notables at being told that they were to be torn from their homes. The Pasha said,

"You may leave."

They stumbled out of the room as if they had been returned to life.

The show was over. Cemal Pasha dismissed the other officers, turned to me with his usual old smile that I knew well, and said:

"What can you do, this is how we do things here."

He then asked for the news from Istanbul.[10]

Headquarters

After the exiles of Nablus had left, Cemal Pasha sat me down next to him. His face was so different, it was as if a mask had fallen.

"What have you heard about the attempt to kill Talat Pasha?"

I had heard nothing. This attempt must have been the Enver/Talat fight that we would later hear about from the Great Ghazi.

After a few words of general conversation he called his aide:

"Take the gentleman to the chief of staff, he is to be attached to the cipher section."

Ali Fuad Bey (the present Director of the Military Academy Ali Fuad Pasha) was then the chief of staff. The aide introduced me and stated the wishes of the Commander. Ali Fuad Bey, without turning his head, [said] with a stern voice:

"No. He will be attached to the first section."

I was somewhat taken aback. Yet, the very next day I would come to learn that a half-civilian commander and a chief of staff who was a pure soldier were co-habiting at army headquarters.

Ali Fuad Bey was a strict disciplinarian. He was against any form of favouritism or anything that went against the strict hierarchy of command. As to the cipher section, it was more attached to the civilian rather than the military side of Cemal Pasha. There was an unending struggle between Cemal Pasha and Ali Fuad Bey over these half-civilians, and there was no reconciling Cemal Pasha's political and civilian administration with the mind of Ali Fuad Bey.

Ali Fuad Bey, like all those who were enemies of party faction rivalry, always remained a man of the law, of regulations, and respect for rank.

---

10 Ibid., 9, 10. Cemal Pasha exiled thousands of families, whom he considered dangerous to the state, to Anatolia. See Çiçek, *War and State Formation in Syria: Cemal Pasha's Governorate During World War I 1914–1917* (London: Routledge, 2014), 51: "On all occasions, he reminded the central government that the Syrians' exile to Anatolia was not temporary. They were sent there to be permanent residents."

Cemal Pasha, although he was the most Europeanized in mentality among the members of the war government, never forgot his own factionalism.[11]

I use the word "his own factionalism" because the truth was that the Committee of Union and Progress had been divided among a few leading figures.

In the Great War, it would not have been possible to label any one as an Ittihadist! Ittihadist meant the anonymous blank masses of the party. The label that was attached to an individual at the time was always "somebody's *man*." Cemal Pasha's man, Enver Pasha's man, Talat Pasha's man . . . I do not know [anyone] who was his own man.[12] Every man had his own men, such that as the groups got larger they became Cemal Pasha's team, Enver Pasha's team, Talat Pasha's team. . . .

On the Mount of Olives there were two groups, the officers of the Fourth Army and Cemal Pasha's men. The *man*'s importance could be told by his influence, which was often disproportionate to his rank or position. In the time of the Committee of Union and Progress these *men* made the best use of political power, but what the state and duty gained from these *men* is unclear.

Say, you are the chief counsellor of a minister. Ambassadors, governors, directors, everybody does their stint in the waiting room to see you. Just then a shabbily dressed personage enters without knocking. You speak to him with your hand on his shoulder. Those who are in your office look at each other with incredulous gazes, "Who is he?" The value of being the *man* lies precisely in obliging people to ask that question.

The man is called a civilian in the army; civilians call him a faction member (*komiteci*).[13] Merit, intelligence, rank, all of these are condemned to be overshadowed by the question of "Who is he?"

---

11 Falih Rıfkı Atay, *Zeytindağı*, 22–23. The Committee of Union and Progress was indeed a faction-ridden political organization. Although commonly referred to in the literature as the "Triumvirate," Enver, Cemal, and Talat had serious differences and each had his own network in the party. Talha Çiçek, "Myth of the Unionist triumvirate: The Formation of the CUP Factions and Their Impact on Syria during the Great War," in *Syria in World War I*, ed. Talha Çiçek (London and New York: Routledge, 2016), 9–35.

12 Falih Rıfkı Atay, *Zeytindağı*, 23. Here, Falih Rıfkı is reflecting the negative stigma that the term "Ittihadist" (*Ittihatçı*) during the Kemalist period when the official narrative was that the CUP had "dragged" the Empire into a war and to its ruin. Thus "Unionist!" as used here would be an accusation.

13 Ibid., 22. The word *komiteci* is derived from the Slavic word *komitaji* meaning variously, freedom-fighter, brigand, robber baron, etc. The Young Turks would be very inspired by the underground organization and the dedication of the Balkan *komitajis* that they

What I feared the most in the Great War was being branded with such a label: Enver Pasha's *man*, Talat Pasha's *man*. Is this some sort of specialization, some sort of science? No, all this is a sign of weakness on the part of the *main man* who is surrounded by a flock of parasites. Such irresponsible men have caused the decay of the Committee of Union and Progress. Yet, what personal power can replace the power of the state? The most brutal murderer is condemned by a judge with a shaking hand and he is hung by a gypsy. . . .

. . . I felt an affinity for the ideas of some of the Unionist leaders but their *men* alienated me. Although [this labelling] was what I had hated the most in the Armistice years, I was branded,

"Cemal Pasha's *man*!"

In real life I was one of the hard working officers of the Fourth Army and later [what became] the General Command of Syria and Western Arabia.

Ali Fuad Bey warmed to me somewhat because he came to like my style of work and writing. But my loyalty to Cemal Pasha regarding political and personal matters would continue to irk him.

I think the Commander and his chief of staff parted never having agreed on matters such as the Armenian issue, the Arab issue, and the issue of favouritism over trade in scarce goods. Ali Fuad Bey always intervened against the politics of pressure and terror.

Yet, it would have been easy for Cemal Pasha to rid himself of Ali Fuad Bey and find himself someone with whom he could work with more easily. It speaks favourably of the Commander that he chose to work with Ali Fuad Bey to the last day. Cemal Pasha was one of those leaders who does not sacrifice his men easily. He understood merit, would weigh the strengths and weaknesses, and would put up with many weaknesses for the sake of the strengths.

He had left all military matters to Ali Fuad Bey.[14]

---

fought against in the last days of Ottoman presence in the Balkans. They would later go on to adopt many of their methods. Şükrü Hanioğlu, *Preparation for a Revolution: The Young Turks, 1902–1908* (New York: Oxford University Press, 2001). The prevalence of factionalism and an unofficial command structure is born out by the career of the notorious Eşref Kuşcubaşı. Kuşcubaşı always proclaimed his total loyalty to Enver Pasha. His career and personality are a personification of the type of "man" described here by Falih Rıfkı. See Benjamin Fortna, *The Circassian: A Life of Eşref Bey, Late Ottoman Insurgent and Special Agent* (London: Hurst, 2016), 123.

14 Falih Rıfkı Atay, *Zeytindağı*, 23.

[Our empire. Falih Rıfkı on "Ottoman imperialism"]

I am sitting on top of the Mount of Olives. I am looking at the Dead Sea and the Mountains of Karak. Further off there is the whole left bank of the Red Sea, Hijaz, and Yemen. When I turn my head, the dome of the Church of the Holy Sepulchre blazes in my eyes; this is Palestine. Lower down there is Lebanon; Syria, stretching from the Suez Canal to the Gulf of Basra, deserts, cities, and flying above all of them, our flag! I am a child of this empire without borders.

The naked Christ was a carpenter's apprentice in Nazareth. When he travelled across the Mount of Olives he was riding a donkey that was his property. We in Jerusalem are living in rented lodgings. Beyond Aleppo, it is not just Turkish paper money that is not valid, neither is Turkish, nor the Turk.[15] . . . Just as Florence is foreign for us, so is Jerusalem. We walk in its streets as tourists. . . .

It is well-known that the Church of the Holy Sepulchre is divided up among Christian nations. Each part of its interior and every service to be performed in the church is the preserve of a different community. The only thing that these communities were not able to divide up is the key. That is why the key to the Church of the Holy Sepulchre is kept by a *hodja* [Muslim cleric].[16] In all of these lands we are doing the duty of this *hodja*: trade, culture, agriculture, industry, buildings, all of it is in the hands of the Arabs or other states. Only the gendarmes were ours, that is to say, not even the gendarme himself, only his uniform.

Where Ottoman rule is pure bureaucracy, the bureaucracy itself is pure Arab, or half Arab. I ran into no Turkified Arabs and very few Turks who had not been Arabized.

The Azms, who were Arab nationalists, were the grandchildren of the Kemik Huseyin of Konya.[17] All of the leading families of Aleppo had Turkish origins. Because all minorities in the Ottoman Empire had privileges and the Turkish element had no privileges, it was more advantageous to be a member of any Muslim minority rather than Turkish.

---

15 During the Great War Turkish paper money was, indeed, almost worthless as galloping inflation forced people to prefer specie.

16 Ibid., 25. *Hodja* is the Turkish generic term for religious scholar or learned man. The Church of the Holy Sepulchre is indeed parceled out between various Christian groups.

17 The Azm family were a leading Aleppine family, but it is very unlikely that they were from Konya.

Abdurrahman Pasha, who was descended from a Kurdish police sergeant, was rich because his father and grandfather stole taxes, and he was a senator because he had become Arabized. This Abdurrahman Pasha has only seen the full extent of his lands on a map.[18]

Perhaps there are those who still remember that a *hodja* from Eskişehir who had been Minister for Religion in the First Parliament, instead of saying "ve" he would say "vua."[19]

. . . In Syria, Palestine and the Hijaz, the answer to the question "Are you Turkish?" is inevitably "*Estağfurullah*! (God Forbid!)" We had neither colonized these lands nor had we nationalized them. In these lands the Ottoman Empire was nothing but an unpaid night watchman. If the *madrasa* mentality and the lack of awareness (*şuursuzluk*) had continued, there is no doubt that Arabization would have penetrated deep into Anatolia.[20] . . . Our imperialism, Ottoman imperialism, was an illusion built on the following principle: "the Turkish nation is incapable of building a state by itself. . . ."

The most beautiful building in Jerusalem was German, its second most beautiful building was theirs also, its largest building was Russian, all the other buildings were the property of the British or the French. All of them belonged to foreign powers.

The Druze whose beards smelled of spices, the Jews with plaited hair, the Bedouin with skin like leather, the Arabs in their robes, all stood aside in two facing ranks in the lands of Syria and Palestine as the Turkish Army marched between them onto the Canal, while they intoned, "Pass, my brave one, pass!"[21]

---

18 Abd al Rahman Pasha Al Yusuf was a pro-Ottoman notable who had vast landholdings in Syria amounting to some 100,000 hectares. Çiçek, *War and State Formation in Syria*, 152–153.

19 Rıfkı is referring to the difference in the pronunciation of the letter "v" pronounced "vé" by Turks and he is stigmatizing its pronunciation as "wua" in what he supposes is the Arab manner.

20 Falih Rıfkı Atay, *Zeytindağı*, 26. This is a typical example of what I have referred to as the "stab in the back" or "good riddance" syndrome that I described in the Introduction to this volume.

21 Ibid. Falih Rıfkı conveniently forgets that a large proportion of those troops marching to the Suez Canal were in fact Arabs conscripted into the Ottoman army. As a staff officer he would certainly have known this. Ignoring the Arab presence, and the implication that they were just passive onlookers, fits with the Arab stereotype that we find throughout Rıfkı's text.

Yet a handful of Turks held the whole region. We had filled the vast desert with buildings and gardens. We were too late. Neither Syria nor Palestine was any longer ours. Just as we had lost the Balkans physically, we had lost these lands in spirit. Not with a feeling of reality, but with a sense of history we wore ourselves out. Anatolia called out to be rebuilt from end to end, cities, villages, houses, and fields should have been enriched, and then, the Turks having become totally westernized, should have flowed from Aleppo to the Red Sea with technology and capital. Yet we only began to see civilization and population density when we crossed Anatolia and knocked on the doors of Aleppo.

. . . Aleppo is a big city, Damascus is big city, Beirut is a big city, Jerusalem is a big city, all are foreign to us. The air of Lebanon is a hundred times more foreign for us than the air of Dobruca.

Yet everywhere we saw we said it was,

"Ours."

Damascus was as much ours as our house, Lebanon as much ours as our garden. . . . There was no doubt that this feeling of possession and dominance was due to the blood that ran in our veins. In order to make ourselves understood to the hotelier, to the restaurant keeper, or even the postman, we were slowly learning Arabic.

The train leaving Damascus gets to Medina in three days and nights. We even refused to abandon Medina. A Turkey without Medina? This would mean the suicide of imperialism.[22]

What Medina? One day we were out to take the salute of a military unit that was going to pass down [south]. Despite the fact that there was rail transport, they had been marching since Adana. Some three thousand thin, pale, Turkish lads, in ragged uniforms, marched past us, worn-out and exhausted.

Do you know where they were going? To Aden!

. . . Cemal Pasha, who set out to conquer Egypt, while he was sitting in Lebanon, in Beirut, or Aleppo, was something like the commander of an occupation army.

We who are sitting in the German hospice on the Mount of Olives, the Austrian officer trying to climb onto his camel with a ladder, the camel frightened by the motor car, the Hungarian horse shying away from the

---

22 Ibid., 27. Falih Rıfkı is referring here to the long siege of Medina which is the setting for the memoirs of Naci Kıcıman discussed below.

camel, the infantry soldier from Sivas training in Lake Tiber to cross the Canal riding an inflated goatskin, and a strangled Arab voice:

"*Felyahya*! (Long live!)"

The art of empire is to draw on colonies and the ruled nations. The Ottoman Empire was a milk cow, reclining its huge body in Anatolia from Thrace to Erzurum, while its udders hung down into the mouths of its colonized nations and peoples who drank its milk mixed with its blood.[23]

"The hair of the Arab"

While the Fourth Army was in Syria, the Druze of Hauran never rebelled against us. Do you know why? The whole of Hauran is divided up among tribes; the sheikhs are not friends even with their own brothers. The only thing uniting the sheikhs of Hauran is shared interest [against] taxation, particularly the tax on livestock! When the tax collector gets to Hauran, all the Druze are united; when he leaves, they are again divided into a thousand pieces.

During the whole war we took no taxes, on the contrary, we drowned the Hauran in gold and decorations.[24]

In that vast land from Aleppo to Aden please do not think that there is an Arab Question. All the Arab Question consists of is *hatred for the Turks*. Remove this feeling and the affairs of Syria and Arabia will become like the hair of the Arab (*Arap saçı*), so tangled and twisted that you cannot make sense of it.[25]

There were those among the Muslim Arabs who were in favour of an Arab Caliphate. As for the Christians, although they were even greater haters of the Turks, they knew that the best government for them was the Ottoman government. Because once the Ottoman administration is gone they are certain to face the danger of oppression from the Muslim Arabs. Then, a foreign power will take over all the trade and resources of the land.

---

23 Ibid., 28.
24 Ibid., 29. The *ağnam* tax on livestock was one of the most important sources of revenue for the Ottoman state. The Druze were indeed given privileged treatment by Cemal Pasha. They were exempted from military service and taxation. Çiçek, *War and State Formation in Syria*, 209. Çiçek states that Cemal, "handled the Druze with kid gloves."
25 Falih Rıfkı Atay, *Zeytindağı*, 29. The racist trope of the "hair of the Arab" is a common Turkish saying used to express a feeling or situation that is hopelessly complicated and entangled. Italics in original.

Whereas the Turks were not in any way the rivals of the natives in trade or in the markets.

The Maronite Patriarch knows that if the French come, they will lose all their unearned privileges. What the Patriarch wants is to live under Ottoman administration, but under French protection.[26]

The issues of Christianity and Islam in Syria, Arabs and Jews in Palestine, Wahabism and Sharifism in the Hijaz were all more serious than the Turkish-Arab issue. Indeed, as soon as we left, the flame of factionalism was set alight throughout the Red Sea, the Mediterranean and in the desert.

At the beginning of the war, Lebanon was something like an autonomous state. The Ottoman government did not appoint the Maronite Patriarch. But, through the French, he constantly made declarations. The Maronites worship the Patriarch as a god. One-third of Lebanon belongs to Maronite pious foundations (wakf). They are committed enemies of Islam. In Lebanon there is a group called the Holy Warriors (Mukaddes Mucahit). Everyone who kills a Muslim becomes a Holy Warrior. If he is a bachelor he gets a salary of four liras, if he is married he gets 8 liras. Of the thirty-two thousand Muslim Druze of forty years ago, while we were there only some eight thousand remained.[27]

The Protestants favor the British, and the Orthodox favor the Russians.

In Palestine the Zionists had almost created a secret state. They had a flag and postal service; they would affix their own stamps to their letters which would be delivered by their own postmen.

It is not even appropriate to go into the names and issues of the countless tribes and sheikhdoms. One day's fact is negated by the sunset of the morrow. In the desert or semi-desert the only law is force and interest.

When a few foreign states get into the market for buying men, many a ready outstretched palm will they find. But it would be wrong to consider them the leaders of a serious movement. We made that mistake.[28]

Among the British, Russians, French, Italians, and the Ottomans, those who were the least informed about affairs in Syria, Palestine, and the Hijaz were the latter, that is to say, the true rulers of these lands. We went everywhere in a train of artillery and regarded the world through the eyes of a

---

26 Ibid., 29.
27 Ibid., 30.
28 Ibid. This is an oblique reference to Arab nationalism and the execution of the Arab leaders by Cemal Pasha.

corrupt official. Regarding the issue of how the Commander of the Fourth Army dealt with Lebanon, I will now quote from notes I took at the time:

> The whole of Lebanon is covered in flags. All of them have been drawn by amateurs, the crescent is wrong and the star is an awkward shape, but what a lot of Ottoman flags. The Lebanese girls have cut up all their red dresses and white underclothes to sew these flags. People playing *cirit* in the street, women dancing on camels, spears decorated with the plumage of beautiful animals, the whole of the African *phantasia*, the whole of the Druze folk wearing their long slitted robes and pantaloons, their heads covered with their *agel* and *kefiyya*, and then the evening feast . . . The table is strewn with wild flowers. Cold water rather than [alcoholic] drink, fresh *ayran*, I am surrounded by people dressed in the style of Istanbul of the Tanzimat years. They are all wearing black *stamboulines*, the classic *fez*, *effendis* decked out by the tailors and barbers of the time of Sultan Aziz, all of them thinking that if you are silent, you are thinking something against them, falling over each other to say something clever or to hit an elegant turn of phrase.

Then, the sound of a fork striking against a plate.
Cemal Pasha gets up to make a speech:

> "Gentlemen! Until today Lebanon suffered from a great ill. Lebanon was in pain. I have come to cure this ill. I hereby announce to you that from this day forward Lebanon is as Ottoman as Konya. There is no longer any trace of foreign privileges in this beautiful land of yours."
>
> Muslims and Christians, all those present began to intone prayers of praise to the Sultan to Enver Pasha and Cemal Pasha. Cemal Pasha had rescued them from their confusing (*mülevves*) state of half-independence. Those sitting and those standing up were as though drunk with pleasure from the good tidings brought by the Commander and the cold water and *ayran* provided by the municipality [of Beirut]."[29]

A French report states: "The Lebanese are incapable of rebellion. Once they asked us for weapons, we gave them weapons. Instead of staging an uprising they sold the weapons to the desert Arabs!"

In fearful and patient Lebanon, squeezed in between the sea and the railway, we had disentangled a small strand of the hair of the Arab.

---

29 Ibid., 31.

We used exile for Palestine, terror for Syria, and the army for the Hijaz. The calculating Jews awaiting the Balfour Declaration on the coast of Jaffa, did not even sacrifice a single orange, leave alone a single head. The Hijaz rose up; Syria remained silent.[30]

Üçayak (Tripod). [The Gallows. Executions of Arab Patriots]

There is no doubt that the last chapter of Ottoman history in Syria that will be remembered in the future will be the Court Martial of Aley. According to the decisions of this court, forty Arab nationalists were killed in Damascus and Beirut. Among those who were hung were senators like Abdul Hamid al Zahrawi, members of parliament like Shafik Al Muayyad, Abdulghani Uraysi, a first class journalist, and Rafiq Razzik Sallum, a poet. Some were politicians seeking their own interests, some were idealists.

At the time of the Balkan Wars, those who believed that the Ottoman Empire was about to collapse and who were seeking a new future in Syria met at a congress in Paris. The main organization that was involved in Arabist activities was the Decentralization Party (*Hizb al Lamarkaziyyah*).[31] Those who were imprisoned in Aley were members of this organization whose center was in Cairo.

They had been members, but when?

There is no doubt that the Decentralization Party was intriguing and working on starting an uprising in Syria when the Great War broke out. But did those who remained in Syria know about these attempts [those underway in Egypt]? Because in the meantime there had been a general amnesty. It would be impossible to condemn those who had been active in the party before the war.

But the Court Martial was convinced that the accused had collaborated with the party after the war [had broken out]. This was the crux of the matter.

It is up to the jurists to decide whether justice and the law were pushed beyond their limits at Aley. Why there was a need at the time for an intense reign of terror in Syria, this is a secret Cemal Pasha, who was killed on the streets of Tbilisi, had taken to his grave.

---

30 Ibid., 32.
31 Ibid., 33.

What a sad fate: there are many in Syria today whose notables were killed by Cemal Pasha, and yet they miss him. Cemal Pasha was killed by the Armenians, those same Armenians, whose lives the Pasha had saved in tens of thousands.[32]

Cemal Pasha believed that by applying a policy of terror and [infrastructure] construction as well as reform [all] at the same time, he could stop the current of Arabism. He never forgave those who managed to procure the highest honors and advantages from the Ottoman state and then proceeded to destroy its unity.

The belief that Istanbul was opposed to Cemal Pasha in these policies is wrong. Enver and Talat were actually with him on this. Neither of them wanted *treason* to go unpunished. But Enver Pasha interceded for Abdul Hamid al Zahrawi, and Talat Pasha interceded for Shafik Al Muayyad. There were also others from the CUP who interceded for some of the accused. Istanbul, to the very end, was to insist that the trials of Aley be repeated at the Ministry of War in Istanbul.[33]

One of the laws passed during the Great War gave the local commanders the authority to carry out the death penalty if they deemed it necessary for national defence. This ruling must have been authorized in order to deal with grave cases involving exemplary justice in the front lines. But because the letter of the law was very rigid, Cemal Pasha applied it to the court martial verdicts at Aley. He feared that if the files of the cases were to be taken to Istanbul everything would be overturned.

Thus, one morning, with a telegram *en clair* he announced to Istanbul that seven men had been executed in Damascus and the rest in Beirut. In this manner, he summarily resolved the matter.[34]

---

32 Ibid., 34. There is a view among some scholars studying the Armenian Genocide that among the Young Turk Triumvirate, Enver, Talat and Cemal, Cemal was the most moderate on the Armenian issue and that he did in fact save many Armenians who fell under his jurisdiction in the Fourth Army district. Hilmar Kaiser, "Regional Resistance to Central Government Policies. Ahmed Djemal Pasha, the governors of Aleppo, and the Armenian Deportees in the Spring and Summer of 1915," *Journal of Genocide Research* 12, nos. 3–4 (2010): 173–218. On Cemal's assassination, Eric Bogosian, *Operation Nemesis. The Assassination Plot that Avanged the Armenian Genocide* (New York: Little, Brown & Co., 2015), 12, 237.

33 Falih Rıfkı Atay, *Zeytindağı*, 34. Italics in original. Çiçek, *War and State Formation in Syria*, 45. Although Çiçek does point out that there were attempts to save this or that individual, "In view of the general attitude of the CUP against the Arabists, it is not surprising that the central government approved of Cemal's reign of terror."

34 Falih Rıfkı Atay, *Zeytindağı*, 34.

If the terror had not taken place, would there have been a revolt in Syria?

Was the revolt in the Hijaz the result of the terror?

Was the terror instrumental in the loss of Syria?

My belief is that the answer to all of these is negative.

Today's Turkish mentality is modern. It would be wrong to judge the Arab problem of those days with today's mentality. It should be taken into account that the CUP was never prepared to give up any of the rights and privileges of the Ottoman Empire. The CUP was the implacable enemy of all separatist nationalist minorities: Albanian, Armenian, Greek or Arab.[35]

Once, Cemal Pasha, writing to Enver Pasha about some suspicion surrounding the acts of the late Mahmut Kamil Pasha had said,

"If he is serving the country well in the front at Erzurum, let us leave him be."

I remember that Enver's answer to this cipher telegram was:

"No service to the country can absolve ill done to the country. If you have any documentary proof, let me know immediately."[36]

None of the convicted men believed that he was going to die. I remember when Abdul Hamid Zahrawi was shown into Cemal Pasha's presence. He was already angry at having been made to wait in the antechamber as a senator. He was a proud and arrogant man. His arrogance continued up to the moment that the Pasha showed him to a chair and read him a document dealing with his activities before the war; he turned yellow, asked for some water and managed to stammer: "Forgive me."

A similar scene was repeated with Shafik Al Muayyad who was brought to the headquarters at Damascus.

I was pained by something: How can anybody take pleasure at the sight of someone he is about to humble and kill as the man grovels and begs forgiveness at his feet?

I remembered one occasion when one of the exiles, who left the country because of his involvement in the Mahmut Şevket Pasha affair, had sent a telegram begging forgiveness from Cemal Pasha while he was still the Military Commander of Istanbul. I remember when I gave the telegram to Cemal Pasha, how he smiled into his beard and said,

"So many hundreds are moaning in Anatolia because of me!'

---

35 Ibid., 35.
36 Ibid. Mahmut Kamil Pasha was the commander of the Erzurum front.

I can still see how in order to hide the bitterness of his *gaffe*, he smiled and pretended to sigh.[37]

Those who died in Beirut were more young nationalists. They died bravely, with their heads held high, singing Arab nationalist marches.[38]

I heard the stories of those who had died in Damascus from Nurettin. Two stories in particular have always twisted my heart:

Shafik Al Muayyad had a full white beard. Thinking that this would constitute a sad sight after he was hanged, a gendarmerie officer from Damascus took a pair of scissors out of his pocket, seized the condemned man as he descended the stairs of the government building in his white execution tunic, and cut his beard. The memory of this murderous grooming has wiped out for me all the righteous and good aspects of the Arab cause, if there ever were any.[39]

Umar al Jazairi, who was quite nervous, was shouting as he climbed onto the scaffold. Someone shouted from below.

"Be silent or you will be held responsible! (*Sus! Mesul olursun!*)"

Umar was hanged having been frightened into silence.

Rafiq Razzik Sallum, who was a Christian, was a real idealist. He met death with a smiling face. He was to be hanged last. The other six had already become cold cadavers. As he approached the scaffolds he saw the only empty one and said:

"I think that is my place."

Later he became serious, contemplated the body in front of him, that of Abdul Hamid al Zahrawi and saluted him saying,

"O Father of Freedom, *marhaba!*"

He encouraged the trepident priest who was hesitant about approaching him and bid farewell to a Turkish friend he knew from the Law Faculty in Istanbul.

It is difficult to face death without hate and arrogance.

For another example, consider the story of Youssef Hani. No doubt, Youssef Hani was one of those who did not believe he was about to die even as the noose was placed around his neck. He was one of those elegant, rich, happy Syrians who would spend summers in Europe and the winters in

---

37 Ibid., 36. The reference here is to the assassination of Grand Vizier Mahmud Şevket Pasha on June 11, 1913.
38 Ibid.
39 Ibid. Nurettin was Falih Rıfkı's friend attached to Cemal Pasha's staff at Damascus.

Beirut. When war broke out he had remained in Beirut because he could not get out in time.

Youssef Hani was not an enemy of the Turks because he was a nationalist. He was because it was fashionable and did not do any harm. He accorded this title [of being anti-Turkish] no more importance than the necktie he wore.

A French document states:

> The Lebanese Christians are friends of France. As to the Lebanese Muslims they are the friends of the English because they do not like the Christians. The majority of the Arabs of Beirut like the French. Yet the Orthodox are attached to Russia. Why? Simply because they they want to feel allegiance to a flag more honorable and influential than the Ottoman flag.[40]

One day at the gaming table someone had brought a paper for Youssef Hani to sign. Until the Court Martial explained to him that the paper he had signed was a declaration of independence, Youssef Hani had no idea what he signed.

"Please," he was saying, "let me go. I am rich, a have a beautiful wife and child. I am one of those who only know pleasure and gambling. I know nothing else. That signature may well be mine. But how should I put it? I simply dashed out my signature like a poker chip."

Nurettin would tell us stories about this man when he came to Damascus.

"He had all of his suits brought to prison. I never saw him without perfectly ironed trousers. Every morning he would dress as if he was ready to leave right away, and make ready, and ask me, 'Am I staying here again tonight?'"

The Arab Question was no longer a matter of literature. At that time it was pointless to ask and seek forgiveness for such a crime.

Once as Cemal Pasha descended the stairs of his residence in Beirut, a pretty woman dressed in black and her child approached him. The child laid a bouquet of flowers at the Commander's feet and said,

"Forgive my father."

---

40 Ibid., 36–37. The references that Falih Rıfkı makes to "French documents" may well mean the documents seized from the French Consulate which were used as evidence against the accused in the Aley Tbunal.

On that day I saw the Commander's eyes water and his chin tremble. Because that woman in black, as she was going home, would see the cold white cadaver of her husband in a corner of the square. [41]

A Soirée (Bir Süvare)

That night the hot sun of Damascus set upon the white cadavers of the strangled. When we came to the hotel we found that the Commander was pale and white as death, pacing the living room in his ceremonial uniform, his belt adorned with his dagger.

On the mornings of death everybody shudders and shivers when they speak to each other.

Yet the next day all was forgotten. Do you remember the dirge by Musé? "If in Paris fifteen days is enough to forget everything, in the Orient this is not even fifteen hours. One should try not to die in the Orient. . . ."[42]

Quite the contrary, Damascus was preparing to give a big soirée honouring Cemal Pasha and the staff of headquarters. In a big cinema theater, composers, poets, orators, all of them were to express their thanks to the great man who had rescued Arabia from her naughty children.

Towards evening, Cemal Pasha summoned me and said:

"Go and look at the room and the people. Find out if it is a place worthy of my visit."

I went. What was I supposed to see? Plenty of turbans, plenty of jalabiyahs, and an equal number of pantaloons and shoes . . . For the great and the good in the Orient gilt and pomp are of the greatest importance.

Our Commander made a point of being always late to the trains, meetings, or feasts. He entered the cinema when everybody's expectations had reached their peak and settled himself in his loge.

Speeches, poems, odes, all for him, all competing to praise him. One would say, Allah, then the Sultan and then you; another, first Allah, then the Prophet, then you; finally one, not to be outdone, declared, first Allah, then you. The Arabic language was exhausted but the lies were not exhausted. Some said the same things in song.[43]

---

41 Ibid., 38.

42 Ibid., 39. This account is at variance with the account of Ali Fuad Bey. See below, p. 48.

43 Ibid. The excessive flattery that was lavished on Cemal so soon after the hangings is recorded by modern sources. James J. Galvin, Divided Loyalties. Nationalism and Mass Politics in Syria at the Close of the Empire (Los Angeles: University of California Press,

. . . Regarding Cemal Pasha, apart from his high rank and power that everyone knew, there were legendary rumors. In Syria it was said that when the Pasha was speaking to you, if he scratched his nose he was thinking of exiling you, if he played with his beard he was considering pardoning you. But beware, if he twisted his moustache, this could mean that you were a dead man.[44]

I have already said that one of the failings of Cemal Pasha was his fondness for pomp. For this he has even been the target of certain insinuations.

In Damascus lately we came to live in the Salihiyya quarter. On Fridays, well-dressed *hodjas* used to come to headquarters. The Commander, prayer beads in hand, would plunge deep into discussions about *suras* and *hadith* with the venerable *hodjas*. Then, his own car in front, followed by the *hodjas*, they would go to Friday prayer. In Istanbul they had dubbed these occasions *selamlık* and there was indeed a similarity with the *selamlık* of the Caliph.[45]

But his detractors gradually came to claim that these occasions showed that Cemal Pasha was setting himself up as the ruler of Syria and Arabia. I remember that Ismail Canbolad had been sent by these politicians as a covert inspector under the cover of some made up pretext. Because Cemal Pasha sensed the air of inspection in this visit, he had his aide meet Ismail Canbolad at the frontier of the Fourth Army zone and had him strictly escorted to his headquarters.

Leave alone patriotism and duty, a great deal of daring would be required for an attempt of this sort. The Commander of the Fourth Army was not a man to launch alone into such dangerous adventures.[46]

1998), 176: ". . . [E]ven after the executions, Jamal Pasha was frequently feted and celebrated by Damascenes, many of whom would later figure prominently in nationalist activities."

44 Falih Rıfkı Atay, *Zeytindağı*, 40.

45 Ibid. The *selamlık* ceremony was the occasion when after Friday prayers the Ottoman Sultan, who was also the Caliph of Islam, would receive petitioners and guests. On the *selamlık* ceremony see Selim Deringil, *The Well-Protected Domains: Ideology and Legitimation of Power in the Ottoman Empire 1876–1909* (London: I. B. Tauris, 2011), 23–24.

46 Falih Rıfkı Atay, *Zeytindağı*, 41. Ismail Canbulat was a leading militant activist of the CUP and he had come to Aleppo in November 1915 ostensibly to inspect the status of the Armenian convoys accumulating in Aleppo. Çiçek, *War and State Formation in Syria*, 121. One of the unsubstantiated claims made against Cemal Pasha was that he had contacted the Allies secretly, offering to have the Fourth Army zone secede from the Ottoman Empire in return for his recognition as ruler. This is highly unlikely given that the British and French sources do not cite any actual documents ostensibly emanating

Sheikh Es'ad (Shaikh Es'ad Shuqayr)

Those who happened to pass by the headquarters of the Fourth Army during the war will no doubt not have forgotten Sheikh Es'ad Efendi. . . . He spoke a weird Turkish and was a good speaker, mixing funny stories with a certain verve and elegance.[47]

We had heard from him why Abdulhamid had him exiled to Adana:

"I was gradually becoming one of the [court] favourites. At some point I made it known to the *harem* that I was an able fortune teller. This provoked the anxiety of the Palace and while I was expecting favor instead I was exiled. Sultan Abdulhamid had supposedly said, 'We have our Abulhuda, two Arabs are too many for the Ottoman state.'"[48]

Because he had been exiled by Abdulhamid, the CUP had made him a member of parliament. His seat in the parliament was next to a deputy from Baghdad who knew no Turkish. The delegate from Baghdad would sleep through each session of parliament and then when he woke up would ask Sheikh Es'ad Efendi: "O Sheikh, what happened today?" Sheikh Es'ad Efendi grew weary of the Baghdadi deputy. One day, after the session was over, when the deputy asked him the same question he replied,

"Oh, did you not hear? Today they gave each deputy a steamship for his province."

"What of Baghdad?"

"You were sleeping; because there were no further demands, you did not get one."

The deputy for Baghdad leaped up and started screaming,

"*Erbaa vaburat, lidditcleti velfirat!* (Four steamships for the Euphrates and the Tigris!)"

Ahmet Rıza decided that the deputy had gone mad and signalled the guards, who seized the deputy and took him to the fountain where they stuck his head under cold water. After this untimely shower the deputy

---

from Cemal and the Germans who were cognizant of the rumors did not take them seriously. Çiçek, *War and State Formation in Syria*, 113.

47 Falih Rıfkı Atay, *Zeytindağı*, 42. We will meet him again below in the memoirs of Ali Fuad Erden.

48 Ibid. Abulhuda Al-Sayyadi was an Aleppine sufi sheikh who had become a favourite of Sultan Abdulhamid II (r.1876–1909). He was active as a propagandist, writing tracts targeting particularly the Syrian Arabs emphasizing the legitimacy of the Ottoman Caliphate. Deringil, *The Well-Protected Domains*, 65.

effendi was taken to the Speaker. The *effendi* told them what happened. They laughed and told him that his friend was pulling his leg. The deputy form Bagdad grabbed Sheikh Es'ad in the lobby:

"O Sheikh, are you not ashamed to make fun of me?"

Sheikh Es'ad, assuming a serious countenance, told him,

"Fine, my Sheikh, do whatever you like, you are right. Let us say I lied to you and the others told you the truth."

When the deputy once again ran towards the office of the Speaker, Sheikh Es'ad escaped.[49]

During the Great War for some reason he had incurred the displeasure of Enver Pasha who had sent him to the desert. On his way, he was waylaid by Cemal Pasha who kept him by his side until his last days in Syria, to make him tell funny stories and make speeches.

Do you know what his official title was? The Mufti of Cairo! We were carrying him in our baggage in order to install him in this position when we entered Cairo.

One day, in Beirut, he was invited to a gathering where men and women, Christian and Muslim were present. Suddenly during the meal Cemal Pasha said to him,

"Rise up, o Sheikh, and make a speech."

"What does Your Excellency order me to talk about?"

"Talk about womanhood!"

"You are putting me in a difficult position, o Pasha. You know I am a pious Muslim. The ladies present here are Christians. Firstly, what should I talk about? Besides, I do not speak French, they do not know Turkish. Allow me to speak Arabic."

And he addressed the ladies thus:

"I had said that I am a pious Muslim. So I am. But there is one aspect of Christianity that has always made me jealous: the value and respect accorded to women! Christianity had even sent its God on the lap of a woman, and still depicts him thus."

In Sheikh Es'ad I saw a half-intellectual half-folksy wise man, who certainly had all the skills of a great orator.[50]

The last joke I heard from him was the following: after the Armistice the British had made the Sheikh prisoner and taken him to the prisoner of

---

49   Falih Rıfkı Atay, *Zeytindağı*, 43. Ahmed Rıza was one of the founders of the Committee of Union and Progress and he was the Speaker of the Second Ottoman Parliament.

50   Ibid., 44. It seems that Cemal Pasha used Sheikh Es'ad as something like a court jester.

war camp at Sidi Bashir. Dressed in a blue shirt and blue pantaloons, the Sheikh was living a sad life. One day, as he was sitting on the hot sand, he heard the plea of an Arab prisoner:

"Ya Allah! Ya Allah!"

He said,

"Don't call him, my son, don't call him. If he did take it into his head to come and save us, the British will take him prisoner and he will never escape. What's more, you will deprive the Muslims of their Allah."[51]

At the shrine of the Prophet [The visit of Enver and Cemal to Medina][52]

Enver Pasha, Cemal Pasha, a few high ranking officers and two officers from headquarters, the Mevlevis with their tall conical turbans, and an Armenian waiter, we are all going to Medina. We boarded the train in Amman.

The next morning we awoke in the middle of the desert. No more are we to see a single tree, nor town, all we will come across for hours are desolate train stations consisting of a well and a telegraph office. All day the same desert date palms that do not even provide enough shade for one head, Bedouin in dirty, torn clothes with faces even more dirty and torn, children begging for bread and money extending their bony, claw-like hands, a few flat hills and the next morning more desert.[53]

We arrived in Tabuk, our eyes burning having travelled through mountainous terrain consisting of yellow rocks and red rocks. A group of sheikhs ran out of a date grove to welcome us. One of the sheikhs was nine years old. The Chief Sheikh of the Bani Atiyya! This child with a round and intelligent face fixed us in a stony stare, leaning on a sword taller than he was.

Everyone except the sheikhs is naked. All have distended bellies like leather hanging down like a leather sack, their bodies look as though they have been greased and scalded.

Oh this desert, this sandless desert of thorns and rocks, an abandoned camel extending its yellow neck towards a bed of cacti, a woman and a child walking silently towards a copper colored mountain through a mass

---

51 Ibid. Sidi Bashir was one of the main prisoners of war camps in Alexandria.

52 Enver and Cemal visited Medina in February 16–19, 1916. The Mevlevi Batallions were made up of adherents to the sufi Mevlevi sect known for their performances as "whirling dervishes." During the Great War they marched playing their *ney*, a long flute and were used to fortify morale, in a fashion similar to bagpipers in the British army. See Plate 11.

53 Falih Rıfkı Atay, *Zeytindağı*, 45–46.

of thorns, Bedouins running scared from sounds and civilization, then night, empty and disorderly night, descending slowly on the desert, the night full of big and countless stars, and Enver Pasha sprinkling coins at each station!

Someone says:

"What are they going to do out here with bits of silver, press them into their flesh?"

Only Enver Pasha was spoiling the décor.

At the station of Madayin Salih we leave behind the restaurant car and the Armenian waiter. Because Christians may not enter Medina. In Medina the locals welcomed us dressed in silks.

The town of Medina consists of a few grey date palms. We are in the town of the Prophet, whose name since childhood we could not think of voicing aloud without titles like honorable (*hazretsiz*), may peace be onto him (*aleyhiselamsız*), without trembling with fear. I keep forcing myself in vain to feel old-fashioned piety.

In Medina this feeling is entirely lost. Medina is a nest of base charlatans who have made a trade of the remains of the Prophet. Every inhabitant of Medina seeks to sell to those simple folk who come from afar, the stones, the soil, and well water of this dirty shambles of a town, making them kiss it forty times before taking their money.

At the station festooned with tribal flags, we were met by a large crowd decked out in red, black, and green.

Women with veils revealing only their eyes, open and alert, their veils tied with a string over their noses are ululating wildly,

"Lü lü lü lü . . ."

The Mevlevis went first, Enver Pasha and Cemal Pasha in the middle, and the rest of us squeezed in with the common folk at the back. So we advance. Tears are streaming from Enver Pasha's holy eyes into his pomaded German moustache. As to Cemal Pasha, his thick beard is serving as a hairy mask totally shading all expression.[54]

---

54 Ibid., 47. Falih Rıfkı's attitude of assumed superiority towards the Bedouin is typical of the late-Ottoman "civilizing mission"; something I have commented on before in my previous work. See my, "'They live in a State of Nomadism and Savagery': The Late Ottoman Empire and the Post-Colonialism Debate," *Comparative Studies in Society and History* 45 (2003): 311–342; Ussama Makdisi has also provided parallel insights. See Ussama Makdisi, "Ottoman Orientalism," *American Historical Review* 17, no. 3 (2002): 768–796.

The weather is so hot and stifling that I chose to fall back from the crowd and board a cart. The passenger carts of the town of Medina are very like the garbage carts of Istanbul. It's only covering is a patched piece of cloth. Inside one squats on a hard seat and the thing is drawn by a single mule whose skeleton is clearly visible. The driver, mounted on the mule is a skeletal slave, who could not be thinner and still be alive. The roads are bad and tortuous, constantly winding, turning, and squeezing to avoid the sun.

The Arab of Medina plays with your money as if he constantly has his hand in your pocket. Why he takes it, when he takes it, how much he takes, you never know, you submit to his robbery and carry on.

Covered in dust and sweat, we arrived at the green domes of Rawza. The Prophet lies under this dome. His shrine was his home in life. Rawza is the mosque surrounding this shrine. In the last century, like everything else we have touched, here too we have smothered it in yellow paint, whitewash, and heavy plants.

It is a privilege to be able to enter the shrine. The keys to its doors are kept by tall Ethiopians. In any event, all the décor of Medina consists of is the cloth covering the coffin of the Prophet and these Ethiopians.

In Medina I completely understood that the true Muslim city which ennobles religion and makes it an art form, where true respect is shown to holy men, is Istanbul. Here the grave of the Prophet's uncle has become the shack of the water sellers and cups hang from his coffin.

First we lined up for prayer. One of Enver Pasha's aides was next to me. At some point an Arab bearing a water pitcher passed in front of us. As far as I knew if someone passes in front of you while you are praying the prayer is not valid. It seems that I forgot that this was not the case in Medina, and, also forgetting that the water of Zam Zam is in Mecca, thought the Arab was giving us water of Zam Zam. He gave me a cup of water. Taken aback, I lowered my hands and drank. As soon as I opened my hands to continue praying, the Arab seized my sleeve and demanded:

"Money!"

It turned out that the creature was selling water. I went through my pockets and could not find any change. I requested some from the aide next to me. I guess the aide was a religious man because first he saluted [the ritual turning of the head to right and left in ending the prayer—SD], then gave the Arab a few coins.

Today was Friday. Before the visit, a white-bearded, pale-brown tall speaker mounted the pulpit. His moustache was trimmed, he had a broad and clear forehead, in his hand he held an olive wood walking stick, he wore red shoes, a silk turban of silver cloth, and a yellow silk robe. He had a nervous voice, a voice that bore the entire fever ridden soul of hot Arabia. At one point he said:

"This Prophet . . . (*bu Nebi* . . .)"

That Prophet was right next to us and the speaker turned his chest heaving with emotion to the shrine. With a brusque gesture he pointed to the yellowed metal bars surrounding the shrine. Our nerves were stretched to breaking point. These words were Arabia, desert, naked mountain, the dark cave, and the Prophet.

The voice ceased.

After the sermon it was announced:

"There is going to be a visit!"

They covered us in shroud-like cloths tied up at the waist; they put some hard turbans on our heads. A lanky Ethiopian slid like a shadow among us, on his belt he bore silver keys hanging from silver hoops. The door opened slowly.

We entered among guides bearing candles. Under the dome beneath a cover of atlas cloth lay the Prophet Mohammad and the [Caliphs] Abu Bakr and Omar.

Swathed in musky incense, they placed Enver Pasha in one window alcove and Cemal Pasha in another and gave them each a metal bowl. It transpired that the greatest merit was acquired by standing in these alcoves and lighting one of the oil lamps brought down from the ceiling.

This place is the Prophet's home and his grave. One is overcome by many imaginings and dreams. Everyone is pensive and deep in thought. All of the Ethiopians converged on Enver as the commander in chief, bringing down lamps for him to light. Cemal Pasha felt neglected and did not like it. He had always had an acid voice. Because he had not spoken for a long time, he muttered hoarsely, indicating the lamps just above him:

"Well . . . who is going to bring these down?"

This bitter and hoarse voice swept away all the sanctity of the shrine, like wind dispersing fog, and all we were left with was a coffin covered in green cloth.

Scrawny hands of beggars were extended from every window, every tear in the curtain, the smallest hole. All the nerves in these hands squirmed and clenched as if squeezing money.

I returned to the hotel after having tread on the robe of an Arab standing in the doorway, picking at the scabs of his enflamed wound, for which I received a solid oath in the pure language of the Qur'an.[55]

The *Haji*

The Indian, the Bokharan, the Javanese . . . The silken robes of the notables of Medina brush against the greasy, rotten, stinking rags of these abandoned men. Asia, Africa, and Anatolia can be found begging in the streets and markets of Medina. . . .

. . . Tomorrow you will be surrounded by Arab brigands. The grandchildren of the Prophet will fire bullets at the green dome of the Rawza. We will get as agitated as if Istanbul itself was under attack and we will send you Turkish lads torn from the breast of Anatolia. You who are dying with your skin stuck to your bones, surrounded by the fire and starvation imposed on you by the grandchildren of the Prophet. The lads from Anatolia will defend the tombs of Mohammad, Fatima, Abu Bakr, and Omar, trying to chew fried locusts in mouths ridden with scurvy sores.[56]

All the way to Damascus, three days and three nights by rail, we will surround both sides of the railway with Turkish lads. We will pour Anatolian gold into Arab purses, Anatolian grain into Arab gullets.

This is no joke, we are practicing Islamic imperialism. You with your guts pierced by Arab daggers, scorched by the desert sun, you the brothers of those who froze on the ice mountain of Sarıkamış, are you not all the victims of a vacuous dream dreamed by the vacuous head covered in pomaded skin?[57]

The tomb of Christ

Like the dates of the Hijaz, the olives of Palestine can only be bought with money. The pilgrims coming to Jerusalem, suffering, twisting the greasy strand of hair stuck to their temples, are no happier than the Muslim *haji*

---

55 Falih Rıfkı Atay, *Zeytindağı*, 47–49.

56 Ibid., 52. The Ottoman troops besieged in Medina did in fact eat locusts. See the section on Naci Kıcıman below.

57 Ibid. The "pomaded face" is a reference to Enver Pasha. The defeat of Sarıkamış was the disastrous campaign of the Ottoman Third Army against the Russians in December 1914, when almost the entire army was destroyed. Eugene Rogan, *The Fall of the Ottomans* 114: "Of the nearly 100,000 soldiers sent into battle only 18,000 returned."

coming to Medina toying with a loose thread from the rotten cotton of his robe. The hungry of Jesus, like the hungry of Mohammad, are both condemned to misery.

Yet in Jerusalem, the setting where the beggar finds himself is majestic. Medina was an Asiatic market which had made religion a material commodity. Jerusalem is a western theater that has made a performance out of religion. In Jerusalem, the hotels are half-churches; their servants are half-priests and the chambermaids are half-nuns. They all keep their habits, their crucifixes, their smoking jackets, their garters, their white headscarves, and smocks in the same closet. I always thought the priests of the The Church of the Holy Sepulchre to have fake beards. When they bend down slightly, you can see the lump in their robes made by the butt of their pistols.

The tomb of Jesus, who did not die comfortably in his bed, is completely surrounded by Muslim gendarmes who guard it. I had already mentioned that each part of the church is apportioned to a particular nation. Each nation sweeps and cleans its own section, and only the feet of that nation are allowed to tread on it. If the broom of one touches the stone of the other, murder is done and blood, rather than tears, spatters the grave of Christ. Like walking sticks which are really sword sticks, in Jerusalem there are crucifixes that double as daggers.[58]

Because there is no agreement on just who is entitled to clean the tomb of Christ, it is covered in dust and rubble. Nobody can put back the bell which fell down because its rope broke. The Church of the Nativity was in the same condition. When Enver Pasha asked why the windows of the church were broken he was told that the different communities could not agree on who was to acquire the merit of paying for the repairs. Each time the matter came up it led to fighting and bloodshed. The commander in chief had the place surrounded by a team of gendarmes and was thus able to secure the repair of the church windows.[59]

The greatest day of the St. Sepulchre church is the day of fire, the day that Christ is resurrected! All of us, the young officers at headquarters, had decided to see this great day. The door of the Church of the Holy Sepulchre is a work of art. On the arch of the doorway in deep alcoves resembling the firing holes of fortress battlements there were the pots of basil planted by the priests. First we saluted a portly *hodja effendi*, the keeper of the key.

---

58 Falih Rıfkı Atay, *Zeytindağı*, 53.
59 Ibid., 54. One of Enver Pasha's titles was commander in chief of the Ottoman military forces.

Then they showed us around the treasury; with gold silver and diamonds worthy of a bank's vault. Finally, after the priests had firmly secured the doors, we were shown to our *loges*. The *loges* even had numbers, and the *loges* reserved for important personages have their names on them.

The communities were stuffed into their places cheek by jowl. The gendarmes with drawn bayonets took up position behind them. Everyone wears his cross on his chest, holding clusters of candles. The candles, after they have been lit by the sacred fire rising from Christ's tomb, will be sold to the Christians.

First the Orthodox Patriarch, then the patriarchs of the other communities, all wearing robes rimmed with silver thread and golden crowns, walked around the crypt striking their staffs on the stones, then they lined up in front of the door. A few people searched the person of the Orthodox Patriarch. In order for the faithful to believe that the true flame emanated from the crypt they had to ensure that the person entering it was not bearing any matches.

The Patriarch entered the crypt, a deathly silence reigned. An enterprising merchant on the upper stories was attaching his rope to a basket in order to lower it down to his man waiting below.

Then all the bells of Jerusalem rent the air. The Patriarch emerged from the crypt, pale, anxious and delirious. It was required that he drop his crown in his haste. But because the crown was vastly expensive, and it was to fall into a prearranged place, a novice priest was waiting with the rim of his habit extended. The Patriarch made a small movement, dropping the crown, and was left bareheaded. Now the nearer candles are being lit from the candle of the Patriarch and those further away from those in front. The merchant's basket has descended and clusters of his candles are being lit.

The acrid smell of thousands of candles, and the cloying smoke covered the lower church and reached the upper *loges*. We threw ourselves out in a wave of nausea. [60]

If Christ could come back in spirit today and see the scene we had just witnessed who knows to which cross he would have nailed these patriarchs?

As we were getting in our carriage, the first market for the burned candles was already shaping up in front of the church and the Muslim *hodja* was readying his key to lock the door.

---

60 Ibid., 55.

The Israelites

The name of Jerusalem brings to mind Christianity. Yet neither in Jerusalem nor in Palestine is there an issue of Christianity. The Christianity of Jerusalem is the political issue of Orthodox Petersburg, Protestant Berlin, atheist Paris, Catholic Rome, and Anglican London.

The most important question of Jerusalem [is] the Jewish/Arab Question: a handful of Jews and six hundred thousand Arabs! I had occasion to tour Jewish Palestine from Jaffa to Jerusalem several times. All the new villages and towns in Palestine are the work of the Jews. This Palestine is not just new, it is brand-new. The *mukhtar* [headman] of the village is an English Jew who wears a smoking jacket for dinner. Red-cheeked German Jewish girls ride back to the village in their carts from the vineyards, singing. As to the Muslim Arabs, they are at the service of these masters: the grape is crushed by the Arab laborer but the wine is drunk by the well-fed Jew.

In old Palestine the Arab village is a mound of earth. The gardens are in ruins, the people naked, their eyes sickly.

In Jewish Palestine the towns are surrounded by the scent of oranges, orderly roads are bordered by prickly pear hedges. In the month of February women with uncovered necks and breasts sit in sumptuous hotel lobbies that they have decorated with orange blossom and roses, dreamily gazing at the horizon as they await the end of the war.[61]

If you want to see that tears are useless, visit the Wailing Wall where Jews have rested their heads and cried for hundreds of years. The tears of hundreds of generations have not caused one centimeter of wear in the wall.

If you want to see the great power of money, you should see the Zionist colonialism that is making Jewish the shores of Palestine and the interior, driving the much larger Arab population to the desert.

Hundreds of years of tears is not worth one lump of gold. One speech by Balfour is more effective than all the Psalms of David.[62]

---

61 Ibid., 56. Falih Rıfkı's views comparing Arabs and Jews comprise some shrewd observations combined with a bizarre mixture of anti-Semitism, grudging admiration for Jewish accomplishment, and anti-Arab prejudice.

62 Ibid., 57. This is a reference to the Balfour Declaration which was approved by the War Cabinet on October 31, 1917 when the British Foreign Secretary Lord Balfour declared that the British would "[view] with favour the establishment in Palestine of a national home for the Jewish people." The declaration was published on November 9, 1917 in the *Jewish Chronicle*, two days after the British forces entered Gaza. Rogan, *The Fall of the Ottomans*, 348.

The Jews did not balk from any extent of flattery in their efforts to avoid the wave of terror. In their villages they always offered us the most ripe of oranges and the oldest of their wines. One day, a village *mukhtar* clad in his smoking jacket, presented to me two pretty Jewish children, a boy and a girl, dressed in white and red, he was saying,

"We want them to read a poem this evening for the Commander Pasha, which one do you think is most likely to please him?"

In the new Palestine, German, French, all languages are spoken. Only the Jewish language of Hebrew, the language of the state, Turkish, and the language of the majority, Arabic, is not spoken. [Jewish] villages are full of couples that look like they have just come out of a middle-class dance hall. And the naked Arab hangs around in doorways, gnawing away at leftovers and half-eaten oranges.[63]

The money of the Jewish West has bent the arm of the Arab Orient and it has established a colony of bankers in this land where the sun shines most brightly and the land bears the sweetest of fruits.

But Palestine was not providing the wheat to nourish the army fighting in the desert. On the contrary, the wheat coming from Aleppo, Hama, and Homs was eaten by the army and the Jew. The Fourth Army asked:

"I wonder if it would not be good idea to send the Jews eating the wheat to where the wheat is grown?"

From the very next day, leave alone the newspapers of Paris and London, even the papers of Vienna and Berlin were clamouring:

"Never!"

As soon as the news got out about the exile of the Jews, all the states that were at war against each other united against us. The Jewish bankers who had managed to turn the Protestants, Catholics, Orthodox, all of the Christians against each other, who made their *pessah* bread with Christian blood during 1914–1918,[64] managed to unite all of the churches in favor of the synagogue against the mosque.

To abandon the villas of Jaffa, the orange groves, the Jewish land that had been established all these years and go forth into the mud brick towns of Hama and Homs among wheat fields?

"Never!"

---

63 Falih Rıfkı Atay, *Zeytindağı*, 57.
64 Falih Rıfkı is, no doubt, referring to the infamous "blood libel."

But Cemal Pasha was not a raw politician. He knew who the Zionist leaders were. He summoned them and told them,

"You have two choices. Either I exile you as it has been done to the Armenians. You will abandon your homes and gardens and walk towards where the wheat is, or I will set up delegations of your own people to guard your vineyards and gardens, and I will give them gendarmes and soldiers as guards. I will then send you by train. However, for the second choice, all the Vienna and Berlin press must be silenced."

It was certain that the Jews were not waiting for an opportunity to show themselves to be stupid. They went to the telegraph station at headquarters. With two lines they silenced the two big cities and then London and Paris. In fact, they evacuated Jaffa and went to Homs and Hama without even a nosebleed, and the Arabs who were left were not even able to eat any of their oranges in peace.

The reason for their exile was the fact that Palestine was an excellent center for espionage. No doubt, it would be more difficult to send intelligence on camel back from Homs across the desert to the [British] headquarters at Baghdad than to send information by rowboat to a British gunboat just offshore.[65]

(Portraits). [On Halide Edib and others]

Cemal Pasha, who had become obsessed with the idea of Ottomanizing Syria, wanted to start up modern Turkish schools similar to those in Beirut set up by the Americans and the French. These schools would attract the boys and girls of Beirut simply by the excellence of their education.

In those days I was in Istanbul. I received a cable from the Commander advising me that I was to work towards bringing to Damascus Halide Hanım and a few Turkish teachers she would choose. After some deliberation and asking a few people Halide Hanım agreed to leave Istanbul.[66]

---

65 Ibid., 58, 59. Cemal Pasha did indeed take measures to reduce the threat of Zionism in Palestine. Among the measures he took was the exile of prominent Zionist leaders, and the obliging of Jews to take Ottoman citizenship. Çiçek, *War and State Formation in Syria*, 82–86.

66 Ibid., 60. Halide Edib, *Memoirs of Halide Edib* (London: John Murray, 1926). Halide Edib Adıvar, variously known as "the first Turkish feminist," a "militant Turkish nationalist," a "traitor" who was "pro-American Mandate," one of the few who could dare to criticize Mustafa Kemal to his face, was asked by Cemal Pasha to become the general overseer of schools in the Fourth Army district. She made three trips to Syria,

So we set out on our travels with the women instructors filling two train coaches. For the ideal girls' school, a building had been set aside in Beirut which had been abandoned by the French. I was listening to the plans of the veiled Muslim nuns (*çarşaflı sörler*) who were going to Syria to give a new style of education to the girls of the country. [67]

At a station some way from Adana the late Bahaettin Şakir boarded the train. I introduced Halide Hanım. Although she knew Bahaettin Şakir by name and reputation, she apparently did not have any idea until then what his role was in the policy regarding Armenians. As to Bahaettin Şakir, until then he could not have even imagined any Turkish nationalist who did not think like him on the matter.

After a long argument Bahaettin Şakir got off. Halide Hanım took me aside and said:

"You have made me unwittingly shake hands with a murderer."

As to Bahaettin Şakir, on the platform he leaned close to my ear and whispered:

"We should forbid promising youths like you from having contact with this woman."[68]

Halide Hanım wanted to give up neither her womanhood nor her masculinity. In her soul the two sexes, female and male, the beautiful woman seeking to attract, and male ambition seeking to dominate, made endless

---

the first in 1916 when she and her sister Nigar established a primary school there, the second in the same year for a few weeks when she agreed to write a report for Cemal Pasha on educational reform in Syria, and the third when she accepted the post of Director of Cemal Pasha's educational establishments in January 1917. She arrived with an entourage of fifty female teachers. Edib was fully in agreement with Cemal Pasha on the role of education to counter foreign (primarily French) influence in Lebanon. Çiçek, *War and State Formation in Syria*, 184–185.

67 Falih RıfkıAtay, *Zeytindağı*, 61. This school was the Notre Dame de Nazareth, which is still active in Beirut today. The commemorative plaque referring to the Virgin Mary in the garden reads: "They have appointed me guardian of their home. I guarded them in the times of trial: 1914, 1915, 1916, 1917, 1918."

68 Ibid. Bahaettin Şakir was known to be one of the bloodiest perpetrators of the Armenian Genocide and had been one of the founders of the Special Organization (*Teşkilatı Mahsusa*) which organized and carried out the mass killings. Evidently he had no qualms about talking openly about what he was doing and felt he could discuss it with Edib whom he knew as a Turkish nationalist. Halide Edib was opposed to the CUP policies of deportation of Armenians, but she would later go on to become anti-Armenian and state in her memoirs that she had been opposed to the Armenian policies of the government but, "I did not know then what I know now." See Halide Edib, *The Memoirs of Halide Edib*, 387, 388. See also Raimond Kevorkian, *The Armenian Genocide: A Complete History* (London: I. B. Tauris, 2011), 218–219.

battle. Hanım was a figure you could meet everywhere in the West, but for the Orient she was a novelty.

While we were on the way to Aleppo Halide Hanım had already defended the view that we should give Syria autonomy. I was thinking what a contrast this was to Cemal Pasha who was bragging about how he was going to make Lebanon into another Konya. It seemed that Halide Hanım was to leave the education of the children of Beirut to her little helpers and occupy herself more with the education of the adults.

Halide Hanım bought all the *bric a brac* needed for the school in Beirut. Me, an officer in uniform, she a woman, we shopped in the souks of Beirut for cutlery in a horse drawn buggy. One evening I listened to how she had picked the lice off the Arab children, on another occasion how she had scolded the *Mutasarrıf* of Lebanon for not seeing a famine victim lying in the road. Despite Cemal Pasha, she managed to keep the chapel in the school intact.[69]

She saw Cemal Pasha as a sword she could draw at will. But Cemal Pasha's stubborn and stern head was not the sort of hilt that she could easily manipulate.

Because Cemal Pasha knew that she had considerable following among the new, young *avant-garde*, he put up with her whims. The Beirut school was in fact clean, orderly, and even better than the old French institution.[70] Cemal Pasha had the quality of leaving things he did not understand to the experts and giving all the support he could to people he trusted. But the Vali of Beirut, with whom Hanım was obliged to work, was a strange personage who constantly displayed how brainless he was.

After meeting Halide Hanım, he became enamoured with schools, science and playing the inspector. One day he was inspecting the American College in Beirut. He had no idea about any of the classes taught there. Yet it would not do to leave without criticizing and showing some sign of erudition. He had to have something to tell the Commander that evening.

---

69 Falih Rıfkı Atay, *Zeytindağı*, 62. See also *Nazareth 1842–1992* (commemorative pamphlet honoring the school), 36: "In 1917 Halide Edib Hanim was appointed director. She was intelligent and open and respectful to all beliefs. For two years there would be peace, the nuns would accept the role of domestic servants of Turkish mistresses in order to keep the convent and the church."

70 Falih Rıfkı Atay, *Zeytindağı*, 62.

It was the turn of a professor who had studied mathematics in America. He was a genuine scholar but he was a timid, shy soul who approached everyone bent double, muttering, "Your Excellency."

The Professor was trying to explain one of his latest inventions to the Vali while bent double, with a great smile of pride on his face. The Vali interpreted the timid and shy demeanour of the scholar as weakness and fallibility. Knowing that Beirut was under blockade and that the invention in question could not have been imported, he sniffed easy prey:

"No, no, I cannot possibly allow you and such an institution as this to use such outmoded equipment."

The cylinder that the old American professor was holding in his hand leapt up like a thing alive. The scholar went purple and swallowed his smile as if he had inadvertently choked on the seed of a tasty fruit that he had been eating.

The Turkish teachers were beside themselves with shame.[71]

The wrong address. [The executions of the murderers of Krikor Zohrab and Vartkes Seringuilian]

The Commander of the Fourth Army was declaring,

> Send me the deported Armenians, I will settle them in the interior of Syria.

He did not believe that the Armenians could do any harm in Syria. The policy of the Fourth Army was as follows: to turn harmful Armenian majorities into harmless Armenian minorities!

It was also possible that the Armenians dispersed into Syria would be a guarantee against militant Arabism. . . . Like the Circassians or the Kurds. There was even a committee formed to convert the Armenians [to Islam] and give them houses and land. This committee met once in my office. But it soon slacked off. Hanım was greatly in favour of the protective policy of Cemal Pasha. Bahaettin Şakir and his friends were accusing Cemal Pasha [of protecting the Armenians].[72]

---

71 Falih Rıfkı Atay, *Zeytindağı*, 63. The Vali in question was Azmi Bey, whom we have met in the Introduction. He had been Chief of Police in Istanbul before coming to Beirut. There is reference to the same episode in the memoirs of Münevver Ayaşlı, see below.

72 Ibid., 64. Cemal was in fact accused of being "too soft" on the Armenians. Kaiser, "Regional Resistance to Central Government Policies."

Wherever there had been uprisings such as Zeytun, Bahçe, and Urfa, they were brutally put down, but no attacks were allowed against the deportation caravans. Some elements who had attacked the caravans had even been hung.

Cemal Pasha also carried out a long correspondence with Talat Pasha to save two Armenian members of parliament, Zohrab and Vartkes, who had been sent to the military tribunal at Van. He was saying, "Release them, I will send them to Lebanon, they will do no harm."[73]

Talat Pasha assured him that Zohrab and Vartkes were not in danger, yet he was saying,

"Let them stand trial. We cannot prevent it."

The Commander showed them the latest order in the lobby of the Baron Hotel.

Zohrab started to cry, Vartkes embraced me at the entrance.

"I am ready to go but if they only did not send this man."

But then he looked at me straight in the face and said:

"Sometimes the old Vartkes in me, the *komitaji*, raises his head and says, what the hell man, let what is to happen, happen. Then I think of my young wife, and the present feeble Vartkes replaces Vartkes the old *komitaji*."

Both of them were taken away. Some days later we received news that the gang of Çerkez Ahmet and Nazım had killed Zohrab and Vartkes on the road. Cemal Pasha could not tolerate this.

We had gone back to Jerusalem. One day a cipher arrived from the Vali of Aleppo, I think it was Celal Bey. The Vali was saying:

> Çerkez Ahmet Bey and Nazım Bey came to see me. They said we hear that Armenians are being protected in Syria. It looks as if Cemal Pasha does not have anybody fit to do the job there. Let him leave it to us, we will finish them off.

This was a perfect opportunity. Cemal Pasha ordered the arrest of both of them. But Çerkez Ahmet and Nazım had figured out what was going on

---

73 Vartkes Seringuilian was a prominent member of the Dashnak (Armenian Revolutionary Federation). He was deputy for Van in the Ottoman parliament from 1908–1915. He was murdered in 1915. Krikor Zohrab was a prominent Armenian lawyer and intellectual who was also a deputy in the last Ottoman parliament. He was a leading figure in Armenian political and intellectual circles. He was murdered in 1915. Kevorkian, *The Armenian Genocide*, 55, 93, 164, 252.

and left for Istanbul on the first train. Cemal Pasha was beside himself with anger, he was raining telegrams on Adana and Afyon. The two friends had just managed to get to Istanbul and save their lives.

He ordered in a telegram to the Central Command: "Send these two men to me to Damascus with all of their baggage, I take full responsibility."

The Central Command [of the CUP *Merkez-i Umumi*] did not want to let them go. This began a whole series of cipher telegrams between Cemal Pasha and Talat Pasha. Talat Pasha finally decided that this would be a good opportunity to get rid of them.

The two friends came to Damascus. Yet there was no stopping the demands for special treatment and interventions on their behalf. When Çerkez Ahmet's and Nazım's belongings were searched, women's earrings, rings, and jewels were found.

The Court Martial had acquired a perfect weapon. It was clear that these two brigands had committed murders not for an ideal, but to become rich. Telegrams in their support continued to rain down from Istanbul. The Court Martial ruled in twenty-four hours that these two murderers were to be executed and the decision was sent to Jerusalem. I have already spoken of the fact that [according to wartime regulations] local commanders had the right to carry out executions and subsequently inform General Headquarters. The murderers of Zohrab and Vartkes were hanged the next day in Damascus.[74]

The tent

We are now fighting in Gaza on the Palestine front. The desert has fallen to the British. The wells, the canals, the transportable roads, Beer-i Sebi and Hofar, gardens planted in the sand, unknown amounts of gold and silver, all of this has evaporated like a mirage.[75]

Our troops are so few that Bedouin freely pass between two units stationed side by side and rob passers-by. An English tank, not finding

---

74 Falih Rıfkı Atay, *Zeytindağı*, 65–66.
75 On March 26, 1917, in the First Battle of Gaza the British failed to capture the city. Between April and October there was something of stalemate in southern Palestine. On October 31–November 7, at the Third Battle of Gaza, the British broke through Ottoman lines. See Rogan, *The Fall of the Ottomans*, 328–333.

anybody to kill on either side, has become a metal skeleton, baking in the Palestinian sun.[76]

Our front line lacks water, we are able to find bread and petrol only with great difficulty. As for the British, with the security of the empty desert behind them, in their trenches they drink Nile water from taps.

Cemal Pasha, who was not a good soldier, has excelled himself at logistics and supply. One day, during the most intense fighting in Gaza, he was unable to stay in his room so he went to the telegraph office just outside the perimeter. The Commander of the Fourth Army was tracking the progress of a petrol coach all the way from Adana by telegraph. He did not eat, he did not drink, he worked with the zeal of a front line supply officer. He was burning with anger. Finally, having received news that the coach had left Damascus, he was pleased. He left the telegraph station and turned to us, saying,

"They advise great commanders to be calm in battle, but it is not possible!"

Just at that time Enver Pasha and his entourage had arrived. We all went to the front. We pitched our tents under the desert sky. I do not know what happened towards evening. Nobody could approach the tent of either the commander in chief or of the Commander of the Fourth Army. Far from us, the two tents faced off, each angrily ignoring the other. Whenever a stray breeze caused one of the tents to flutter, we awaited some news, some event. An officer frequently went back and forth to the telegraph office from Enver's tent. The desert night, bright with moon-like starlight, settled on the tense profile of the two tents. At some point after one of the many to and fros of the officer there were signs of movement in Enver's tent. The canvas billowed, retreated, billowed again, like a wind creating a wave pattern, and reached Cemal Pasha's tent. We all breathed a sigh of relief. It was as if the outlines of the tents had somehow become less severe, as if they had thawed out. The Pashas Enver and Cemal emerged from their respective tents and walked towards each other with even steps. Enver Pasha opened the box he was holding and the gleam emanating from it lit up the desert night.

---

76 Falih Rıfkı Atay *Zeytindağı*, 67. Tanks actually proved to be of limited use in the Palestine campaign, being easily destroyed by Ottoman artillery. Rogan, *The Fall of the Ottomans*, 332: "Ottoman gunners destroyed three out of the eight tanks deployed."

Cemal Pasha was being decorated with one of the highest decorations in the land, the diamond-encrusted Mecidi (*murassa nişan*).[77] The commander of the Fourth Army had heard that this decoration had been given to the commander in chief and had been offended that he had been passed over. The commander in chief, having received approval from the Palace, was now pinning his own jewel on the chest of his friend the Minister of the Navy.

In all the tents, waves of glad tidings rose like a well-directed orchestra. They had made peace.

From Gaza we could hear the deep booming of artillery. British cannon were battering the Imperial Crown of the Ottoman Empire.

So this is the story of a fleck of diamond!

A little while later, Enver Pasha was promoted to Full General (*Birinci Ferik*). This was a heavy blow for the Commander of the Fourth Army. I do not know what passed between the Commander and the Governor of Beirut, but from the next day onwards a flood of telegrams began to arrive congratulating the Commander on having been promoted to Full General.

Cemal Pasha was put in a difficult position.

He wrote to Istanbul:

"What can I say? If I say I have not been made Full General I will lose face, nor can I acknowledge [the messages of congratulation] as I have not been promoted!"

Two days later Enver Pasha congratulated Cemal Pasha on becoming Full General.

So this is the story of two centimetres of silver thread![78]

Gold and wood

I had gone to Syria with paper money. Life, even in big cities like Damascus, was cheaper than small towns in Anatolia. One day an order was sent to all the Syrian telegraph offices: "You are to collect all the gold and silver coins."

---

77 Falih Rıfkı Atay, *Zeytindağı*, 68. The decoration here is probably one of the higher Mecidi orders known as "in diamonds." Edhem Eldem, *Pride and Privilege. A History of Ottoman Orders, Medals and Decorations* (Istanbul: Ottoman Bank Archive and Research Center, 2004).

78 Falih Rıfkı Atay, *Zeytindağı*, 67–69. The reference to "two centimeters of silver thread" refers to the silver thread insignia of full general. Falih Rıfkı is evidently satirizing on the futility of petty jealousies between Enver and Cemal as the Ottoman Empire is crumbling.

That very day this news was leaked by Arab officials of the postal service and Turkish paper lost value. I remember that a few of our people had been sent to buy wheat from the tribes of the Hauran, who had never rebelled against us. The officers and the sheikhs struck a bargain. But when they found out that the wheat was to be paid for with paper, they asked permission and retired to their tent for long discussions. This was their response:

> We love our state. We are loyal servants of the Sultan and Caliph. That is why we do not want to refuse the paper currency, we will accept it if you count a one lira note for one hundred piasters.

Wheat, horses, camels, all manner of services were paid for in gold in Syria for the duration of the Great War.[79]

. . . The army and officials we all received part of our salary in gold. Paper money was useful and profitable only in transactions to do with the state.

On another occasion we had gathered the Druze sheikhs of the Hauran in Damascus. The first-rate sheikhs were to receive a decoration, the second-rate a ceremonial robe (*hil'at*) and the third-rate five or ten gold pieces. As the *ağnam* tax had been lifted, the Druze had no reason to unite and rise up against us, but we wanted to make sure that they were firmly bound to the state by their chests, by their backs, and by their purses. Army commanders were authorized to award decorations up to the third rank. As Sheikh Es'ad said prayers, an elderly captain distributed decorations, a military aide gave the robes, and I handed out money. As one of the grand sheikhs was receiving the Mecidi Order Third Class, he pushed away the cordon of the decoration, and eyeing the gold muttered,

"I want some of that."

In the Great War a large part of the Ottoman treasury was eaten up by the desert and the tribes.[80] Yet every day we were running short. Among

---

79 Falih Rıfkı Atay, *Zeytindağı*, 70. This amounts to a devaluation of hundred to one. One of the major objections to Cemal Pasha's rule in Syria was his insistence on payments being accepted in Ottoman paper money. The reluctance to accept the currency was part of the reason for the famine in Lebanon as merchants demanded payment in gold. Fawaz, *The Land of Aching Hearts*, 135–137.

80 Falih Rıfkı Atay, *Zeytindağı*, 71. Eldem, *Pride and Privilege*, 432–433: "The war, especially in Arab provinces, brought the Ottoman army in contact with a local population that had until then been to a large extent excluded from the system of honors in the Empire. . . . In most cases, the lower classes of Mecidi and Osmani were used for this purpose, most of all by Cemal Pasha, the commander of the Fourth Army. Thus, in

Cemal Pasha's advisors there was an accountant. Perhaps on his advice one day we issued the following order: "Paper and silver are to be considered equal in value. Anyone not obeying this order will be punished severely by exile or hanging."

We were running our trains on wood. We even had to burn Palestinian olive trees as fuel for our engines. Even though the Syrians came to accept the parity of gold and paper, they withdrew their services as purveyors of any sort of wood. The railway was almost at a standstill. The Vali of Damascus, Tahsin Bey, who was in charge of the supply of wood, may recall better than me, but at one point we had to announce that wood would be paid for this much in paper or this much in gold coin, thus we had to admit officially, with our own signature, the difference between gold coin and paper money.[81]

Particularly the desert Bedouin had no religion but gold or precious stones. On the chests of sheikhs near the front you could see British and German decorations side by side. The sheikh would ask who you were, if you were English. [If so, he would declare],

"Long live the English!"

Or, if you said you were Turkish,

"Long live the Turks!"

You just needed to calculate the appropriate decoration or amount of gold. At that instant what you wanted done was done. The Bedouin, who stole horses from the British and sold them to us, on their way back would steal our horses and sell them to the British. There were also quite a few who would hide right in the middle of the battle fronts, putting their lives in danger, in order to steal the abandoned material from the losers before the victors arrived.

After the great rout, the last carriage that we had to abandon in the station in Damascus was full of decorations.[82]

August 1916 he distributed a total of ten decorations to the leaders of the El Fakir tribe. [T]his information rather calls to mind the treatment of the "natives" by some of the western powers in their colonies, in an effort to co-opt them into a system of relative loyalty and allegiance by the modern equivalents of trinkets and beads in the form of the very lowest insignia of the existing orders." Evidently, the sheikh Falih Rıfkı is referring to was not taken in by the "trinket" and demanded hard cash. On the use of decorations as a means of assuring loyalty see Deringil, *The Well-Protected Domains*, 35–37.

81 Falih Rıfkı Atay, *Zeytindağı*, 71.

82 Ibid., 72. After the fall of Damascus on October 3, 1918, and Aleppo on October 26 it was only a matter of days before the Ottomans signed the Mudros Armistice on

Yet another soirée [Falih Rıfkı meets the famine]

We have stayed too long in Jerusalem; now we are going to the mountains of Lebanon and Beirut. I yearn for the sea. I have never spent this long far from the blue sea. Jerusalem is a dry and frowning city, full of rabbis, priests, and *hodjas*. We are all looking forward to the much-vaunted freedom of Beiruti society and the Lebanese girls.

As soon as our train entered the border of Lebanon, alongside the green forests and the prosperous appearance of the villas of the rich, we saw the Syrian hunger. Children with distended bellies falling over each other to grab an orange peel, skeletal women gnawing a piece of leftover bread, here we saw for the first time the suffering of those behind the lines. On the one side a completely empty sea, on the other a completely empty desert, between them a long thin alleyway, on the top end of this alleyway there is the army which is eating up everything in Aleppo, Hama, Homs, Karak, and Hauran. Lebanon and Beirut, who grow no wheat, are starving and Jerusalem is in a state of semi-starvation.[83] The sea in front of Beirut is an endless watery desert. This dusky and attractive city has suffered the most from the dungeon of the blockade.

The word was out,

"This time, the Beirutis are preparing a brilliant suarée for us, and then," a whispering in your ear, "who knows what sultry women we shall meet?"

The Commander settled into his own house, we were accommodated at the Hotel Bassoul. On the broad wharfs of the port without ships, one could hear Arab tunes in the evening; a warm breeze lifts the slits of yellow-lined silk robes and an even warmer waft of pleasure, like the humid warmth of a *hamam*, works its way into our bones. Late in the day we went to the big mansion where the *soirée* was to be held. From all the gardens we can hear the soft tones of the Arab *yalelli*. On the roads, the thin and pale population stand to attention, saluting. The chief of staff told me one day,

October 30. Rogan, *The Fall of the Ottomans*, 378–381. One of the Ottoman officers defending Damascus, Lieutenant Muhittin Vecihi, described how the German officers forced the Turks to abandon a train carriage full of precious goods, commandeering the train, "having no concern but to save themselves." *Erkan-ı Harb Binbaşısı Vecihi Bey'in Anıları: Filistin Ricatı* [The Memoirs of Staff Officer Lieutenant Vecihi Bey: The Retreat from Palestine] (Istanbul: Arba Yayınları, 1993), 91–92.

83 Falih Rıfkı Atay, *Zeytindağı*, 73. See section in the Introduction relating to the famine in Lebanon.

"Do you want to see the best example of how little we belong in Syria?" I looked at him.

"The sight of that eight-year-old boy saluting me out of fear!"[84]

The heavy and spicy Syrian buffet, the best fruits, and a vast assortment of drinks ranging from the strong *araq* of Zahle to the wines of the Rhine. All those present are the smiling *beau monde* of Beiruti society, Muslim and Christian. They are levantines of a different sort, the Turkish, Armenian, and Greek women of Beyoğlu westernized in a different manner. The French of Galata issuing from the Arab throat, vaudeville jokes left over from Parisian artistes on tour! Pleasure and drink are flowing like water. The tense nerves of those who have come from the stone of Jerusalem and the sand of the Canal melt away. As dawn was breaking, worn out and listless, I left the mansion with a friend. In order to reach the hotel one has to take the side streets.

Suddenly I was frightened and I stopped. A deep wave of pitiful wailing sound was coming toward us like the haunting echoes from a deep well. The whole street is moaning. We were hearing the moans of those in their death throes from hunger, those walking skeletons who were crawling toward us on the street.

A refuse cart passed by us, I saw an arm dangling out. The municipality was collecting the dead and the nearly dead. It was necessary to silence the streets before dawn. The sweepers of ordure and death are completing the sad morning *toilette* of Beirut.

I wanted to vomit all I had drunk, women's laughter, electricity, the whole of Beirut and the war. Like the murderer of those about to die, I froze, expecting at any moment, from any quarter, the arm that would seize me. When I went to bed that night I tried to reduce my pain by pressing my fist into my stomach. That dawn in Beirut I saw the real face of the war.[85]

The Viceroy[86]

Because Cemal Pasha was something like the delegate of all the ministries of the government, there was almost nothing that he was not involved in. Because of this in his headquarters there was no shortage of local and

---

84 Ibid., 74. The chief of staff mentioned here is Ali Fuad Bey, whom we will meet below.
85 Ibid., 75.
86 Ibid., 76. Falih Rıfkı actually uses the term "Visrua," clearly meant ironically as there is no such rank in the Ottoman command structure.

foreign experts: there was even an expert in antiquities and town planning. One was the Director of Berlin museums Professor Wiegand and the other was a member of the Academy of Rome, the Swiss Professor Zürher.[87] Because the Germans wanted to colonize the [Ottoman] Empire after the war, they sent some of their best men among us as reserve officers. I believe that the best studies of Anatolia and Syria were done by these Germans. Cemal Pasha's strong point was knowing how to benefit from their expertise. I have rarely met another statesman who made such good and fruitful use of expertise. It is a great shame that all of his accomplishments are now lost in lands that no longer belong to us. After the rout in Palestine, as we were going back to Istanbul on special train, only then did he comment, while gazing upon the poor lands of Anatolia,

"I wish I had been sent to serve here."

But in 1914 Cemal Pasha had great faith in the Empire. He was sure that he would be able to Ottomanize Syria and Palestine. At the train station at Haydarpaşa [as he was leaving for Syria his] speech, which I do not want to remember, [began:]

"If I return without conquering Egypt. . . ."

It is still a painful memory. . . .

. . . Cemal Pasha also created model farms with the help of foreign experts. The Tana'ayel farm was one of these.[88]

---

87   Ibid. See also Çiçek, *War and State Formation in Syria*, 194: "Theodor Wiegand, a German officer and an expert on monuments [was appointed] as the head of the Command for Monument Protection (*Denkmalschutzkommando*) which was created to unearth, protect, and restore Syria's historical monuments. . . . Wiegand carried out a project with his team to inventory the monuments of Syria. They prepared two albums. The first was published in Berlin with the support of Cemal Pasha and funding from the army. In addition, in 1920, another publication was released, this one regarding the activities of this command, in Berlin and Leipzig with a foreword by Von Kress. These books not only include information about Syrian monuments, but also give details about the geography of the region, the structure of its valleys and mountains, etc. The first inventory book can be seen as an attempt by Cemal Pasha to increase the "legibility" of these lands that he was ruling, most likely to penetrate them in a more sophisticated way, and to prevent the illegal trafficking of such monuments to Europe. In addition to these inventory efforts, the Command for Monument Protection restored monuments from the Byzantine, Arabic, and Turkish periods. The intervention of [Maximilian] Zürcher and Wiegand's team saved the ruins from Byzantine times from total destruction."

88   Falih Rıfkı Atay, *Zeytindağı*, 77. The model farm in question at Tana'ayel in the Beqaa valley of Lebanon was actually confiscated from the Jesuit fathers. Tautel and Wittouck, *Le Peuple Libanais*, 9.

Because he was a businessman, he broke the back of bureaucracy and the bureaucratic mentality. At one point he ordered that all petitions had to be responded to in twenty-four hours. Any official who was not able to finish the task in twenty-four hours had to answer to his superior, and anyone whose was demand was delayed had the right to ask for an explanation from a superior officer.

On one occasion there was a question of a major road to be built. It had to be finished by a certain time. In those days we were resident in Lebanon. Cemal Pasha ordered Hulusi Bey, the Governor of Damascus [to finish the road in the given time]. Hulusi Bey answered:

"It is scientifically impossible."

To prove the impossibility he sent his chief engineer.

The chief engineer came to Ayn Sofar. He was loaded with bags and papers. All this paper and rulers were dedicated to one thing: to prove that this road needed by the army could not be finished in the time desired!

I had accompanied the chief engineer to his meeting with the Commander. He was very sure of himself. As soon as he entered the room, the Pasha's face took on a dark countenance.

"Now throw all those things that you are carrying on that table!"

The engineer was shocked.

"All of them, down to the last paper! Now come and stand in front of me."

The bespectacled engineer was left standing there empty-handed.

"This is what I am ordering you to do. You will tell the procurement people how many picks, shovels, money, and workers you need and you will go right back to Damascus. If the road is not finished on the given date, I will hang you where the last stone has been laid."

Of course you have guessed that the chief engineer was not hung and the road was finished exactly on time.

Today's readers will wonder at the easy use of words such as hanging. During the Great War words like killing, hanging, shooting had all become commonplace like a five-*lira* fine.[89]

I remember seeing a whole pile of telegrams thrown in front of a telegraph officer [who was told]:

I will hang the man who causes a moment of delay!"

Th man would have to be in a thousand places at once.[90]

---

89 Falih Rıfkı Atay, *Zeytindağı*, 78
90 Ibid.

[Cemal Pasha's concept of law]

"Your Excellency, I have brought [the text of] the law."

"What law?"

"You had ordered that a certain matter be dealt with in certain way, yet the law is clear, the matter cannot be settled in the way you ordered."

Turning to his aide:

"Bring me a blank sheet of paper."

Immediately [he dictated] a rush telegram to the Ministry of War:

"Change law such and such in the way I have indicated and send me the text by rushed telegram."[91]

A piece of cloth cannot be ordered so easily. I had complained about bureaucracy. All the complaints [against them] may be true, yet the mentality of lawlessness that was prevalent during the Great War was as harmful as the bureaucracy.

... There is no doubt that the best solution is to make good laws. Where there is no respect or trust in the law, the damage is so great that no bad law can do as much damage.

... In the last days at his seaside home in Boyacıköy, Cemal Pasha [said]:

"I want to do something, yet I am confronted by the law. What is the law? I made it, I can unmake it."[92]

In Beirut, it was possible to open up a large boulevard by legal means, but it would be expensive. Azmi Bey ploughed through the neighbourhoods and plots like a steamroller and opened up the road. The governor of Izmir Rahmi Bey and the governor of Konya Muammer Bey did the same. They were all broad, handsome roads. But who had the right to compensation? Is it not better to pass the most draconian socialist laws and solve the matter of compensation, rather than [pretend to] keep a strict record of compensation rights while summarily levelling whole neighborhoods?

In the Great War security of persons and property was reduced to nothing.[93]

---

91   Ibid., 80.

92   Ibid. The Young Turks were notorious for their disregard of laws. The saying, "No law? Make law!" (*Yok kanun? Yap kanun!*), attributed to Enver, says it all. The conversation Rıfkı describes probably took place days before Cemal, Enver, and Talat escaped on a German torpedo boat on November 1, 1918. Rogan, *The Fall of the Ottomans*, 387.

93   Falih Rıfkı Atay, *Zeytindağı*, 81. On the extremely heavy handed requisitions carried out during the war see Eddé, *Beyrouth: La Naissance d'une Capitale*, 147, 149: "One third of

The most vivid example of insecurity in Syria during the war years were [the cases of] exile. The Fourth Army used the law made for the Armenian deportations to "exile until the end of the war those people and their families who were harmful [to the war effort]." Every day we would receive telegrams from the provinces: "[S]uch and such family is harmful (*muzir*). We request that permission be granted for them to be exiled to an appropriate location."

The formula for the answer was very easy: "It is approved that they be exiled to X. . . ."

I am only leaving blank the place of exile. It was entirely up to the Commander to fill in the appropriate location from Erzincan to Bursa.[94] Do not think that this is unimportant. Those who were sent to Bursa or Konya managed to see the end of the war. In the Great War, it was somewhat more difficult to travel to Erzurum in winter and to wait out the end of the war.

The matter that Ali Fuad Bey objected to the most was this issue of exiles. One day I had written yet another such formula for exile. After Ali Fuad Bey would affix his initial *F*, I was going to take it to the Commander. Ali Fuad Bey read the paper, and then turned to me and said,

"Why do you insist on writing this way?"

Obviously I could only follow procedure. He said:

"Look, this reply can also be written like this and sent to the Commander."

He produced a draft along the lines of "this terror is enough" and said, "Please write this up in your hand and take it to the Pasha."

I did as he said. Cemal Pasha went bright red with anger,

"How can you write such a reply?"

I told him that it was the order of the chief of staff. Under the draft he penned a repost something to the effect of "I forbid anyone from interfering in political matters that are being decided under my authority," and said, "Take this to him." I did. That day we were to attend the inauguration ceremony of the *Al Sharq* newspaper. Ali Fuad Bey remained closed up in his room. Cemal Pasha waited for a short time and then, being apprised

---

Beirut *intra muros* was requisitioned." Yet the French felt that they were actually picking up where the Ottomans left off, "it was necessary to complete the salubrious work begun by Cemal Pasha."

94 Falih Rıfkı Atay, *Zeytindağı*, 81 Rogan, *The Fall of the Ottomans*, 290: "The Ottoman authorities had exiled an estimated 50,000 people by the end of the war." This number is probably an exaggeration. See the section on the "Red Book" in the Introduction.

of the situation, he left. When we returned they told me Ali Fuad Bey wanted me. He gave me a petition that I was to give to Cemal Pasha. As far as I remember, the sum of the text was something like, "As I find myself deprived of the moral and material attributes needed to serve you, I beg to be allowed to resign." I know well the anguish felt by the chief of staff in those days. Afterwards he never saw the political correspondence. I would communicate directly with the Commander. I think this had some effect on Cemal Pasha. We had gone to Lebanon, taking with us the file of a family whose exile had been demanded. The Commander had decided to give his answer in Lebanon. In the office of the *Mutasarrıf* he asked for the documents concerning the family in question. This family lived in a village. The *Mutasarrıf* had passed on the allegation [against the family] to the sub-prefect (*kaimakam*), the sub-prefect had passed it on the head man of the commune (*nahiye müdürü*), he in turn had passed it on to the local sergeant of the gendarmes. Whatever the sergeant had decided, it was that decision that, denunciation upon denunciation, had made its way to the desk of the Commander. Cemal Pasha said to the *Mutasarrıf*,

"I, the Commander in chief of Syria and Western Arabia, how can I decide a life and death matter for a family on the word of a sergeant of the gendarmes?"

Nonetheless, because of these denunciations, hundreds of victims of the settling of past scores, hatreds, and jealousies were rotting in the Anatolian heartlands for years.[95]

Our residences and our guests

In Anatolia there were the fronts of the war where tents and trenches were more comfortable than the houses in small towns and villages. In Germany, the best food was to be had at the front. I had already mentioned that we had a choice of headquarters where we would reside according to the season, or even the days of the season. In Jerusalem it was the German hospice, in Damascus the Hotel Victoria or the villas of the Salihiyya neighbourhood, in Aleppo the Baron Hotel, in Lebanon the Hotel of Sofar, and in Beirut the Hotel Bassoul. Because of this we actually spent very little time at the front.[96]

95 Falih Rıfkı Atay, *Zeytindağı*, 82, 83.
96 Ibid., 84. The Baron Hotel was owned by a prominent Armenian family, the Mazlumian brothers, who set up a secret network to aid Armenian deportees during the Genocide.

When it snows in Mount Lebanon, in Beirut, a half hour's drive by motorcar, you find the most pleasant spring weather. When Beirut burns in the summer, in Sofar, at two hours' distance, you find the cool spring mornings of Istanbul in April. Damascus is heavenly in spring. In winter Jerusalem does not get cold. . . . The mountain roads of Zahle, the Souk al Garb where the sunset is best, the beaches of Beirut, all these are scenes that are sorely missed by those who have spent time in Syria.

We had many important guests at our various residences. In Lebanon it was a big event when the Maronite Patriarch, whom the Maronites worship as a god, was obliged to come to the Hotel Bassoul. He had never left his monastery. Finally one day he had to appear in person before Cemal Pasha. Because he did not eat with anyone's spoon but his own, and because he would not touch anyone's towel but his own, he had brought his own towel and personal effects with him. Even if he was only a Maronite god, it was still interesting to see a god riding in a motorcar.[97]

The sheikhs of the desert tribes are clever. No matter how much you reassure them [as to their safety], no father and son will come together. If Nuri Sha'lan comes, his son Nawwaf will remain in the desert. A large section of the endless desert between Damascus and Baghdad is in the hands of the Ruwallah tribe. Nawwaf and his father are rulers there. This young and handsome man came together with his poets, jesters, and chamberlains and stayed a few days at the headquarters. One day I asked him whether it was difficult to cross overland across the desert to get to Baghdad. [He replied:]

"Let me show you a star and give you a paper with my seal. On a camel you can get there in ten days and ten nights."[98]

A star above you and a piece of paper in your hand, ten days and nights alone in the vast desert. What Nawwaf said was right. However, if the members of some other tribe see your sealed paper, there is no doubt that it will immediately lose its value. That paper, a guarantee of safe passage for a Bedouin of the Ruwallah, is a death sentence for the Bedouin of the Ibn Rashid.

Ronald Grigor Suny, "They Can Live in the Desert but Nowhere Else," in Ronald Grigor Suny, *A History of the Armenian Genocide* (Princeton: Princeton University Press, 2015), 325.

97 Falih Rıfkı Atay, *Zeytindağı*, 84.

98 Ibid., 85. Nuri Sha'lan and his tribe, the Ruwalla, initially remained nominally loyal to the Ottomans but went over to the Sharifian side later in the war.

In the desert of the tribes, apart from the guiding star indicated by Nawwaf there is another guarantee of safe passage: gold! When a gold coin is thrown onto the sand, it makes no sound but makes everything possible. Every day Nawwaf would stay in his room until noon, then with a healthy countenance, his beard trimmed, he would come down to the garden with his three slaves and seat himself in wicker chair next to a flower bed. I always wondered what jokes those black slaves, all in contortions of mirth, were telling to keep him amused until lunchtime. He always had a carnation in his hand, his demeanour dignified, his laugh measured, natural, and in good taste. Only twice a day did Nawwaf make himself ridiculous: at table, with fork in hand, when he would eye his neighbor at table and mimic his gestures![99]

There was only one thing wrong with the sheikhs of the Hauran who came to visit us: the acrid smell of their beards lingered for one week in any room they had been in. The color of the Druze beard is like henna and its smell is like vinegared cinnamon. On one occasion we had invited two sheikhs who were brothers, they were to be given decorations and gold. After we had made them welcome, the older one came to see me privately and whispered in my ear,

"You can actually give him less [gold] because his influence is without importance."

After he left, the younger brother came to see me, and leaning even further into my ear, said,

"You can actually give him nothing at all, because he has no influence."

The guests we feared at headquarters were not the visitors from the desert, from the *badiye*, from Salt or Amman. The ones we feared were those who came from Berlin. Von der Goltz managed to make his way to Baghdad without doing any damage. We had good reason to be suspicious of Falkenhayn when he came to Jerusalem. Nawwaf had been given a purse of gold by Cemal Pasha. Falkenhayn, although he had actually brought gold, took away Cemal Pasha's army and his command.[100]

---

99 Ibid.
100 Ibid., 86. Field Marshall Colmar Freiherr von der Goltz was the German commander of the Ottoman Sixth Army stationed in Iraq in 1916. General Erich von Falkenhayn was the German chief of general staff. In the summer of 1917 Cemal was relieved of his command and Falkenhayn was made commander on the Palestine front. Rogan, *The Fall of the Ottomans*, 245, 343.

I now think that Cemal Pasha was not justified in his initial dismay. Because the gift that Syria had in store for the ex-commander in chief of all the German armies was not something to be envied: total collapse!

The crack [The fall of Cemal Pasha]

. . . We all knew as well as the politicians in Berlin why the Germans accorded such importance to Syria and Palestine. There was never a short-age of German commanders and German experts who were sent among us as reserve officers. The German marching on the Canal was called Von Kress. This personage who resembled a skeleton made of nerves rather than bones was the leader in the desert war. The ex-commander in chief of the German army, von Falkenhayn, was, I think, planning to reconquer Baghdad with the forces collected at Aleppo. Because that was not possible, they gave him the Palestine front. Von Kress was under the orders of Cemal Pasha. Falkenhayn and after him Liman von Sanders took over the com-mand without Cemal Pasha. The British flood that none of them was able to stop, was stopped by a real commander, a Turk, Mustafa Kemal Pasha, just below Aleppo. The line of defense that Mustafa Kemal chose there was to become the Turkish frontier of the National Pact.[101]

. . . There is a difference in color between the old Ottoman gold coin and the German gold. What we saw most in Syria was the reddish colored gold of Berlin. Was it because they had spent a great deal of money, or that they no longer trusted the capabilities of Cemal Pasha, or was it because great results were expected from handing this front to our German allies? In any case, I remember that we went through a great crisis.

As von der Goltz Pasha was leaving for Baghdad from Aleppo, we had held a large feast [in his honor] at the Baron Hotel. The old general declared,

"I am going to drive the British into the sea where they belong."

Some time later we had saluted his dead body in a black coffin, again in Aleppo station.

One morning when I saw General Falkenhayn at headquarters at the Mount of Olives, I wondered what sort of destiny this ramrod-straight, arrogant commander would bring to Syria. The British were as excited as

---

101 Falih Rıfkı Atay, *Zeytindağı*, 97. The National Pact (*Milli Misak*), with considerable alterations, was to define the frontiers of the Turkish state as recognized by the Treaty of Lausanne in 1923.

we were about the this news, the *Times* commented, "Falkenhayn in Syria is like a beached whale."

For a long time Cemal Pasha was torn between anger, suspicion, and hesitation. It was impossible for Falkenhayn to serve under him like von Kress. It was not feasible for two great figures to be stationed in a single army command. Finally, after much agonizing, a compromise was reached. Von Falkenhayn was given the military command, and to Cemal Pasha, who did not want to give up dreams of Syria and wanted to return to Istanbul with the trophy of an intact Syria—maybe also playing on his weakness for pomp—was accorded a showy title: the Commander in chief of Syria and Western Arabia (*Suriye ve Garbi Arabistan Umum Kumandanı*)![102]

Something like a second commander in chief . . . Artillery, machine guns, rifles, and swords under the orders of the German, and all Cemal Pasha was to get were these four words above his signature.

In truth [what this meant was] that Falkenhayn who had become a Pasha would take care of military matters and Cemal Pasha would be something like a supply officer in charge of civilian matters and logistics for the army. The Minister of the Navy, who had become a Viceroy in that huge land with the simple title of Commander of the Fourth Army, had lost his crown in the hubris of becoming Commander in chief of Syria and Western Arabia. We all felt that this collapse weighed heavily on him. His title of commander in chief was something like the titles of honorary pasha bestowed on the Bedouin sheiks in the empty desert.

One day we heard that one of Falkenhayn's junior officers had commandeered a building that took his fancy in Damascus. Cemal Pasha, who could line up patriarchs, emirs, and sheikhs in front of him, who could order the hanging of senators and members of parliament, who had limitless power, was now having great difficulties explaining himself to a junior officer. That great monument of marble, pure power, and pride, which we had thought indestructible, cracked like clay with the twitch of a finger of a little German. Through this crack I glimpsed the bitter reality of the fall. When the elephant of power does not get fed its fodder of success, it turns its trunk against him who is mounted on its back and destroys him.

---

102 Ibid., 98–99. On September 26, 1917 Falkenhayn was officially appointed the supreme commander of Ottoman forces in Syria. Çiçek, *War and State Formation in Syria*, 262: "As a result, Cemal Pasha's Fourth Army was abolished and a new commandership was created to rehabilitate his tarnished honour, the general commandership of Syria and west Arabia."

Falkenhayn's Syrian reign was to be short, and he, like the German general after him, was gnashed by the teeth of the rout, and barely escaped the bayonets of the British.

It was not Cemal Pasha who was falling, it was Syria. But because it was a land enamoured with gold lace, obsessed by rank and decorations, it fell not like the Anatolian villages, silent and abandoned, but draped in the uniforms of field marshals, ministers, and commanders in chief. Its fall was altogether more resounding and pompous.[103]

Farewell

. . . Oh, three battalions. Oh, for three battalions . . .

We cannot even provide this little reinforcement to our Turkish soldiers shedding their blood to defend Jerusalem in the trenches of Nebi Samoil. Yet, in that year we had managed to find a surplus of twenty thousand Turks to send to Galicia.[104] We were sacrificing a whole mass of Anatolian lads to the desert and scurvy for Medina that was lost and gone. One day when I entered the Commander's room I found his eyes red from crying: Jerusalem had fallen to the British. In a cipher telegram in his office I read how the Turks there had fought heroically. We did not abandon Jerusalem like the Israelites, we abandoned it like Turks. Those descending from the heights of Nebi Samoil towards the Muslim and Christian temples will remember the last day of the Turks.

The words "Jerusalem has fallen!" spread like news of a death in the headquarters. Already we needed to save our tears for Beirut, Damascus, and Aleppo.

Now we were only thinking of Anatolia and Istanbul. To the Empire, its dreams, and imaginings, farewell! The Dead Sea, glimpsed through the pines of the Mount of Olives, as if its sun would never set, as if it would

---

103 Falih Rıfkı Atay, *Zeytindağı*, 98, 99. Liman von Sanders, who succeeded Falkenhayn, was almost captured by British forces in Nazareth on September 20. Rogan, *The Fall of the Ottomans*, 375–376.

104 Falih Rıfkı Atay, *Zeytindağı*, 100. In August–September 1914, the Austro-Hungarian army had suffered heavy defeats against the Russians and Serbs in Galicia where they suffered a loss of 350,000 men. In September 1916, at the request of the Germans an Army Group, some twenty thousand Ottoman troops were sent to reinforce the Galician front. *Birinci Dünya Harbinde Türk Harbi: Avrupa Cepheleri* [The Turkish War in World War I: The European Fronts] (Ankara: Genelkurmay Başkanlığı Harp Tarihi Dairesi, 1979); Rogan, *The Fall of the Ottomans*, 100.

never see dusk, was now spreading and deepening like a grave drawing the Empire into its maw.

I am gathering my things and my papers. We are now leaving Damascus. Cemal Pasha will resign in Istanbul. As the train moves forward, it seems as if we are jettisoning Syria and Lebanon like ballast. Tomorrow we will find ourselves among the villages of Anatolia without Damascus, without Lebanon, without Jerusalem, without Aleppo, without Beirut; destitute and thinking only of the survival of our lives, hearths, and homes.

My Commander, as he eyed the destitute land of Anatolia, said,

"I wish I had served here."

Indeed, if he had only served here . . . If only that beneficial flood of gold and energy had flowed over these still, empty, and abandoned parts of the fatherland. He said:

"If I stay, my greatest wish will be to serve in Anatolia."

If he stays, if they allow him to stay . . . Anatolia is looking at all of us with anger, suspicion, and distrust. To the mother from whose breast we have taken hundreds of thousands of her children we are now only bringing back ourselves and our desolation.

In the station, a woman is standing asking everyone she sees,

"Have you seen my Ahmet?"

Which Ahmet, which Ahmet out of one hundred thousand?

Extending her arm from under her torn garment, she points in the direction the train has come from:

"He went in that direction. . . ."

That direction? To Aden, to Medina, to the Canal, to Sarıkamış, to Baghdad? Was it ice, or sand, or scurvy, or water, or the typhus-bearing lice that chewed up your child? Even if he has escaped them all and you see your Ahmet, you will find him as much of a stranger as I am. The light has gone out of his eyes, his cheeks are shrunken, his shoulders droop, and you will ask him,

"Have you seen my Ahmet?"

None of us have seen your Ahmet. But your Ahmet has seen us all; he has seen the hell that even Allah could not describe to Mohammad.

Now all the winds from the west and east, from left and right are howling, shrieking collapse. Anatolia is sprawled on the railways, roads, inns, and fountains looking for her children. Trains, motorcars, trucks, all with their blinds drawn, with their lamps extinguished, secretly rush past towards Istanbul.

Anatolia is looking for her Ahmet. Ahmet who until yesterday was even more dispensable than a belt of cartridges. We now see his true worth in the eyes of the mother eagle with folded wings and withdrawn claws, who fixes us with her gaze.

If we could only tell her for what we spent her Ahmet, if we could only tell this mother what we gained in return, if we could only give her something she could be proud of.

But we gambled Ahmet away![105]

Foreword to the 1956 Edition of Zeytindağı

ÖLBERG

İstanbul, June 1, 1956

[*Falih Rıfkı visited his old haunts in the 1950s and wrote the following lines in the foreword to the 1956 edition of "Zeytindağı":*]

I wonder if we could call it the "Pilgrims' Inn"? It was on the Mount of Olives in the midst of a large pine grove. It resembled a German hotel if you looked at its rooms with their baths, if you looked at the part that was a church, it resembled a monastery, if you looked at the *shwesters* in their headscarves walking about as if bringing news of their patients, it looked like a hospital. During the First World War it was the Headquarters of the Fourth Army.

Now, from Jewish Jerusalem, from far away, I am looking at its white ghost on the hill that has become a veritable forest. It is in the Arab sector of the city. We are separated by the sentinels of two enemy states. It seems that if I could go over there now I could not avoid being immediately confronted by the pale-faced *shwester* who used to summon us to our noon and evening meals by beating a huge bronze cauldron. We used to call her the "drummer" (*davulcu*). Memories, memories of youth! It is as if they are merry schoolchildren who have been enclosed, and when I open the door they will spring out and put their arms about me!

Here is Cafer . . . I used to know him from the General Headquarters of the Committee of Union and Progress. Those at Headquarters at the

---

105 Falih Rıfkı, *Zeytindağı*, 101–102.

Mount of Olives are jealous of newcomers. He was a very well-behaved young man from Rumeli. When you first meet someone at [Mount of Olives] you feel as if they look you up and down as if saying, "Now where did he spring from?" Cafer, the young man so far from home, seeing that I could not meet the Commander until the next day, found me a bed, fed me, and asked me for the news from Istanbul. Although I knew he was close to Unionist leaders such as Talat, Nazım, and Bahaettin Şakir, I did not know what he was doing here. In effect, he was an entity without a rank. He must have been one of those who were in charge of the Commander's cipher correspondence. . . .

. . . My poor batman Mehmet! When my friends went on riding excursions I would go to the hills around the Mount of Olives to do some target shooting. I had a British rifle, spoils of war. Mehmet, whose facial expression never changed, as if he was the prisoner of an eternal secret of fate that could never be demanded or revealed, would, as he stood there, go to places years away from where he was and only slowly return when he was called. I cannot forget how he would smile slightly when I hit the target. If I could go there [now], if I called out, "Mehmet!," no doubt he would spring from the depths of forty years and come to my side.

The years had flowed down one upon the other, like a curtain whose rail had broken. Now it was as if we had quit the dream and had woken up.

Ölberg, German for Mount of Olives, *Jabal Zaytun* in Arabic, *Zeytindağı*, just the name of my book.

There was never a Turkish Jerusalem. Was there an Arab Jerusalem? No. Nor Catholic, nor Orthodox, nor Jewish. Jerusalem was the place exchanged by unseen armies under the banners of Crusaders' crosses and the stars of David. This time on this side of the city, I see a place as Jewish as it was under Solomon.

When I returned, I was so full of my memories that I wanted to read *Zeytindağı* again. It has become difficult to find in bookshops. That was the reason I wanted to issue a new edition.[106]

---

106 Falih Rıfkı, *Zeytindağı* (Istanbul: Pozitif Press, 2014), 5–7. There is now a new edited version combining *Ateş ve Güneş* and *Zeytindağı* (Istanbul: Pozitif Press, 2017).

Plate 1 Cemal Pasha and his staff on the front steps of the Augusta Victoria Hospice in Jerusalem (Notice the *bas reliefs* of angels in the background.) Ali Fuad is seen on Cemal Pasha's right. The fifth officer from the right in the front row is Küçük Cemal Pasha. The young officer inclining his head in the back row is Falih Rıfkı. Iclal and Tunca Örses Archive.

Plate 2 A delegation from the Ottoman parliament visiting the Gallipoli front. The officer who is pointing in the center is Mustafa Kemal. Courtesy of Ayhan Aktar.

Plate 3 Cemal Pasha with Bedouin Sheikhs. Take away the *kalpak* (military *fez*) replace it with a pith helmet and you have a classic pose by a member of the British *raj*. Library of Congress. American Colony of Jerusalem.

Photo album World War I Palestine and Sinai. http://hdl.loc.gov/loc.mss/mamcol.059.

Plate 4 Yemeni Sheikhs visit the front as guests of Cemal Pasha. **(Cover)** Library of Congress. American Colony of Jerusalem. Photo album World War I Palestine and Sinai. http://hdl.loc.gov/loc.mss/mamcol.059 Photo 78.

Plate 5 Cemal Pasha and entourage being hosted by German airmen. Cemal seems to be enjoying a cigar. The officer seated opposite him is Ali Fuad. Iclal and Tunca Örses Archive

Plate 6 The surrender of Jerusalem. December 9 1917. According to the diarist Wasif Jawharriyyeh the figures shown are

1. Police commissioner Ahmad Sharaf
2. unknown
3. Tawfiq Muhamad Saleh al-Husayni
4. mayor Husayn Salim al-Husayni
5. lawyer Rushdi al-Muhtadi
6. Hana al-Laham (with the surrender flag)
7. Salim elias al shamandi (the driver of Jamal Pasha's car, from Lebanon)
8. The Policeman Husayn al-Asali
9. Jawad Ismael al-Husayni
10. Daoud Muhammad al-Husayni
11. Amin al-Husayni (nephew of Muhammad Saleh al-Husayni)
12. Burhan Taher al-Husayni
13. Police commissioner Haj Abdel Qadir al-Alami.
14. The two British soldiers are Sergeants Sedgewick and Hurcomb.

Courtesy of Issam Nasr.

Plate 7 Turkish prisoners of war prepare a meal from scraps that they were given. Tunca and Iclal Örses archive.

Plate 8 Ottoman remains in the Jordanian desert. Uniform buttons, a horse bridle bit, coins, seals. Courtesy of John Winterburn. Photograph from the GARP archives.

Plate 9 Commander of Ottoman Camel Corps Arif Bey with his officers. Courtesy of Tunca Iclal Örses Archive.

Plate 10 The visit of Cemal Pasha to Syria Protestant College (Beirut) 1917. Five of the personages featured in this book appear on the same image. The young officer first from left on second row is Falih Rıfkı [Atay], the officer to the right of Cemal Pasha is Ali Fuad [Erden], next to him first from right on the bottom row is Fahreddin Pasha the defender of Medina. Howard Bliss appears to the left of Cemal Pasha. Courtesy of the AUB Archives.

Plate 11 The Mevlevi Batallion in the Mevlevi lodge (*tekke*) in Galata. The photo is possibly the ceremony of farewell before they leave for the front. Courtesy of Iclal and Tunca Örses.

Plate 12 One of Cemal Pasha's visits to Beirut. The crowd has assembled in the *Hamidiyya* gardens. The Building on the right if the Beirut Municipality. Courtesy of the Saint Joseph University Archives.

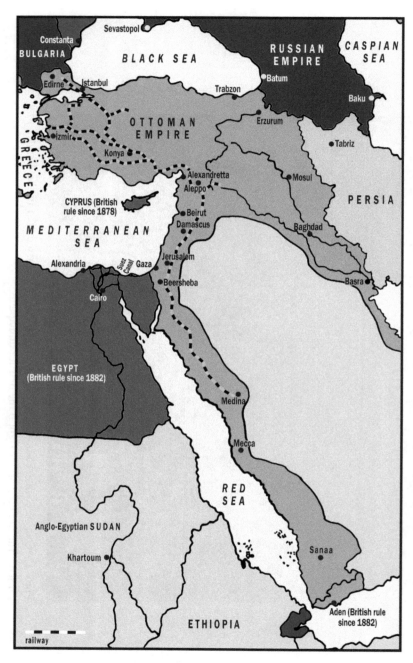

The Ottoman Empire, 1914

Map 1 The rail network of the Ottoman Empire in World War I.

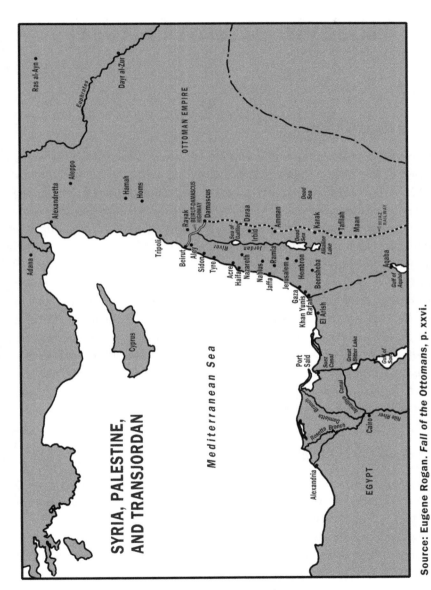

Source: Eugene Rogan. *Fall of the Ottomans,* **p. xxvi.**

Map 2 Syria, Palestine, and Transjordan.

Chapter 2

Hüseyin Kazım [Kadri]

Hüseyin Kazım [Kadri]

[*One of the founders of the Committee of Union and Progress, and one of the founders of the "Tanin" newspaper that later became the official organ of the CUP, Hüseyin Kazım was in many ways an exceptional character. After falling out with his erstwhile comrades, Kazım settled with his family in Beirut in mid-1914. His wife had been born there, her father, İsmet Pasha, had been military commandant in Beirut for thirteen years, and the family had many friends in the city. Kazım notes that he was disgusted with politics in general and the CUP in particular. As he was a man of independent means, he did not need a salary and was able to afford to rent a winter home in Beirut and a summer home in Sofar. He was a scholarly man who preferred a life of the mind over politics. He stated that he was happy to get away from Istanbul and the CUP and immerse himself in scholarly work in Beirut where he writes, "I was able to make extensive use of the very rich libraries of the great Jesuit fathers (aba-i yesuiyye)." He did not come into the orbit of Ankara as most of his generation did after the war. In fact, he developed a very critical attitude to the whole republican project.*][1]

[Serves as Vali of Aleppo]

From the first day . . . I felt a deep hatred for the people of this place, who could not have sunk lower in morals. It must be said that the adulation of these people, their cringing seeking to curry favour, was caused by the officials of the government!

From the very first day, I saw that the Turks who had ruled this land for four hundred years had done nothing for it. All the locals wanted from us was justice. All the Turks had done was to rob Syria. No one had thought

---

1   Hüseyin Kazım Kadri, *Meşrutiyetten Cumhuriyete Hatıralarım* [My Memoirs from the Constitutional Period to the Republic], ed. Ismail Kara (Istanbul: Dergah, 2000).

about meeting the needs of this land in education, agriculture, industry, trade, and finance. All the people wanted from the Turks was "justice"; unfortunately, there was no evidence whatsoever of it being provided.

In Syria, whatever sign one sees of civilization, the people owe this primarily to the French and, more recently, to the Americans. All the Syrians saw from the Turks was "bad faces and bad words." The policy the Turks had pursued in Syria was nothing more than creating some sort of balance by using the notables against the common people. On the other hand, as seen in all the other Arab lands, the fact that the oppressing notability was never free of factionalism and infighting served the interest of the Turks.

To tell the truth, the Turkish officials and the local notables had formed a "system of mutual interest" (*müşterek ül menfaa*). As a result of this, the people were greatly oppressed.[2] [*Hüseyin Kazım gives a few examples of this "system."*]

"The villages of such and such in the district of so and so which had been inhabited by such and such tribe have now been given to honorable . . . Pasha as his private property according to the decision of the Provincial Administrative Council." Thus the land which the poor peasants had cultivated for years was stolen from them. This scandal was condoned by the authority of the governor. . . .

. . . The well-known notable oppressor Müderriszade Fuad Bey makes it known that he wants to buy half a *dönüm* of land from a village in order to dig a well as an act of charity in the memory of his mother. The villagers, stating that as the land was destined for a work of charity say that they will donate the land free of charge. Fuad Bey, appearing to want everything to be legal and above board, insists on buying the land and being issued with a title deed. Later, with the collusion of the land registration officers, he lays claim to the whole village. . . .[3]

[Move to Beirut]

[*After his falling out with the CUP Kazım is offered several posts, among them that of Consul to Bombay, the Armenian Reform Commission due to be sent to the eastern vilayets (Hüseyin Kazım was asked by "some Armenians" to take part), and the governorships of Adana or Konya; he refused them all.*]

---

2   Ibid., 101.
3   Ibid., 105. See the section in the Introduction about the "Huseyin Kazım Affair."

He stated that he was planning to go to Rhodes, "where I wanted to spend a long time in contemplation," and had been assured that the Italian government would approve. He concludes this section of his memoir by stating, "But because of the wishes of my wife we preferred Beirut."][4]

My father in law, the late Ismet Pasha, had been the Military Commander of Beirut for fourteen consecutive years. Our family had many friends and acquaintances there. Our children would be able to receive a better education in the schools in Beirut. The climate was mild and pleasant.

Finally we decided to go to Beirut. In order to find a house I left two weeks before [the family]. On the way I crossed paths with a few personages from the group of Arab reformers who had come to Istanbul to form an alliance with the Ittihadists. My family joined me later. Eight months before the outbreak of the Great War we had been settled in Beirut. I was very happy to be away from Istanbul and the Ittihadists.

As soon as I came to Beirut I dedicated myself to writing *The Development of Turkish Languages and Literary Dictionaries (Türk Dillerinin Iştikakı ve Edebi Lugatleri)*. [For this] I was able to greatly profit from the sources I was able to find in the great and valuable libraries of the Jesuit fathers.[5]

After spending one summer in Beirut, the next summer we went up to Sofar. I was very pleased with the peace of mind that I had found in the mild winters of Beirut and the cool summers of Jabal Lubnan. However, after the declaration of war we became cut off from the world [and] we started having difficulties. No matter what, we were comforted and consoled that we were far from Istanbul. We spent this period with some anxiety, difficulties, and worries.

The Almighty allowed me to witness many things here. Cemal Pasha's excesses, his oppression; the malpractices of Turkish officials in Syria, their corruption, their stupidity, their lack of foresight, [all this] would fill many volumes.

After the publication of *The Memoirs of Cemal Pasha*, I wrote about the things I knew and the things that he [Cemal] hid or distorted. I gave this

---

4   Hüseyin Kazım Kadri, *Meşrutiyetten Cumhuriyete Hatıralarım*, 138. It is significant that he was asked by the Armenians to participate in the reform program for the Armenian vilayets. It seems his reputation for fairness and honesty preceded him. Rhodes had recently been taken over by Italy after the Ottoman-Italian war of 1912.

5   Ibid., 139. This would place Kazım's arrival in Beirut sometime in December 1913. He is referring here to the *Librarie Orientale* of the Jesuit St. Joseph University. Kazım Bey would go on to establish very friendly relations with the Jesuits.

[manuscript] to Ebuziyya Velid Bey for publication [in his newspaper] the *Tasvir-i Efkar*. But after the paper closed down they remained with him.[6]

I hope that these papers will be published one day so that the public can read all about what Cemal Pasha did in Syria and understand how and why that land was lost to us.

[The last days of the Ottomans in Syria]

Syria has characteristics that cannot be compared to Anatolia. I had already mentioned above that the Ottoman government took no notice of the administrative, economic, financial, agricultural, or scientific needs of this land, contenting themselves merely by drawing taxes from it. The foreigners, profiting from the vacuum that we left there, have insinuated themselves everywhere in Syria and Palestine, and, constituting important scientific and industrial institutions, have come to morally dominate this land. Lately, the political influence of the foreigners has become apparent. It is very significant that the Syrian reformers met in Paris and from there made suggestions and proposals to the Ittihadist government.[7] It is well known that for some time the French government has claimed some "rights" over Syria and Jabal Lubnan.

The most important condition in the debt agreement that Cavid Bey had signed in France just before outbreak of war was [the granting to France of the contracts] to build roads and railways in Syria as well as new privileges regarding the port of Junieh in Lebanon.[8]

At the time of my arrival in Beirut a French fleet that was cruising off the Syrian coast was in harbour. The visit of the French Admiral to the Maronite Patriarch in Bkerke and the Patriarch's return visit to the Admiral had been much noticed. Nobody had seen any sign of an Ottoman fleet![9]

While government officials refused to even accept a petition if it was written in Arabic, the Americans and French had established universities (*kulliye*) with excellent printing presses, which did a great service for

---

6   Ibid., 139. This manuscript has evidently been lost.

7   Ibid., 140. Kazım is referring here to the Arab Congress that met in Paris in 1913, with the knowledge of the Ottoman government which initially agreed with many of their demands but later whittled them down to almost nothing. Antonious, *The Arab Awakening*, 116–117.

8   Hüseyin Kazım Kadri, *Meşrutiyetten Cumhuriyete Hatıralarım*, 140. Cavid Bey was the Finance Minister of the Ittihadist clique.

9   Ibid.

the Arabic language. It is not difficult to imagine how the Syrian youth, especially the Christians, who saw that science, trade, industry, and power resided with the foreigners, educated in their schools, would look upon the corrupt and oppressive regime of the Ottoman government.

As to the Muslims, all that tied us together was religion. While it was possible to bind us all the closer through this religious affiliation, because of the ignorant and corrupt officials that were sent to Syria whose endless oppression and ignorance alienated [the people], even this religious attachment proved not to be enough and prepared the downfall of the Empire.

As to the so-called reforms of late, all that these meant was the handing out of decorations, official positions, and privileges, superficial things which played into the natural character of the Syrians, who are much given to intrigue.[10]

In earlier times Sharif Jafar Pasha, a descendant of the Prophet, was sent to Syria to win the hearts of the Syrians. The Muslims of Syria welcomed the Pasha and came to believe that with his intercession and efforts, some reforms could be carried out. However, the aim of the Ittihadists, as is their wont, was to [fool] the people, profiting from their ignorance and gullibility, with a conjurer's trick of distorting mirrors. Jafar Pasha, who made many promises in Syria, was unable to make the Ittihadists listen to him; thus, he returned to Istanbul forlorn and dejected. A short time after that, the Great War broke out. Because it was not possible to say anything against the state, which now had arms in its hands, all ambitions and projections were frozen and everyone was forced to wait on developments.

I told Cemal Pasha, who wanted to talk to me about the state of things in Syria, my thoughts and what I knew in detail. I told him that all the people wanted from us was "justice." He seemed to understand this need and he promised definitely to heed my advice. Then he proceeded to do the exact opposite.[11]

Cemal saw the sources of the [political] opposition in Syria in a different light. One day he had complained that the Syrians, particularly the Maronites, were favouring the French, and the Druze, the English. In order to explain the reason for this state of affairs I told him:

"In the first days that I was in Beirut a friend of mine invited me to a graduation ceremony in a French religious institution. Because I wanted

---

10   Ibid., 141.

11   Ibid. Sharif Jafar was the brother of Sharif Haidar who was sent to replace Hussein after the outbreak of the Arab Revolt. He was, therefore, the cousin of Hussein. He was also a member of the Ottoman Senate. My thanks to Talha Çiçek for this information.

to live the life of retreat in Beirut and did not want to mix with people, I refused to go. The next morning my friend came to see me and he said, it is just as well that you did not come. The French Consul gave a speech at the ceremony where he openly declared that France had a historic claim to Syria and that the land would pass into French rule sooner or later. The *Mutasarrıf* Bekir Sami Bey and all of his officials listened to these words without comment. I was sorry I went."[12]

Similarly, in the *Reveil* newspaper published in Beirut, [an article featured] the answer given by the French Foreign Minister to a question in parliament, where he said, "[Regarding] Syria which is to be French in the future, the British government has made it known that it has no claims on Syria and it is prepared to give guarantees."

[I asked Cemal Pasha:]

"Given that the Syrians saw that the Ottoman Ambassador in Paris made no response to this statement and given that the Syrians, more particularly the Maronites, who have since olden times been protected by France, is it not understandable or even reasonable that they should be inclined to be pro-French?"

I felt that Cemal Pasha had been hurt by these words. He had come to Syria as "a conqueror" but had to make do with being an "administrator." All he did in this country was to return defeated in the offensive against the Suez Canal, and then exile and kill some people with the meanest of excuses. He ruled in this way according to his own wishes. That is why we lost Syria.[13]

[After] Jerusalem had fallen and our armies were in a deplorable state because of hunger and all manner of deprivations, a personage who had been director of education in Beirut came to me and said,

"You know that Syria is about to be invaded. Jerusalem fell two days ago. In order to contemplate our future we gathered in the house of Sayyid Suheyl Pasha, who is from a Sharifian family from Yemen, where we had long discussions. We came up with the following measure to save our country from foreign occupation. If the reform program prepared at the time of Kamil Pasha was to be adopted by the government with a few alterations, giving administrative autonomy to Syria, we, together with the notables of Aleppo and Damascus, will go to Jerusalem. There we will tell General Allenby that we are willing to live under Ottoman rule for all eternity.

---

12 Ibid., 142. Bekir Sami Bey would later have a prominent place in the Kemalist movement as Minister for Foreign Affairs.

13 Ibid., 142. This is the only reference in Kazım's memoirs to the executions in Beirut and Damascus.

We will tell him that if he advances further he will find himself confronted by all the people of Syria. We firmly believe that the Allies who have entered this war to save Syria from the Turks and to constitute an Arab [!] government here will be forced to reconsider.

"[But in order to accomplish this] we must first reach an agreement with the government in Istanbul. We have prepared this petition. We would like you to join the delegation that will deliver it to Istanbul. You have been in Beirut for years. We consider you Syrian and one of us. We know that you will not shirk from rendering such a service."[14]

I replied:

"After things have reached such a pass, what good can come from such a proposal, this is a matter that requires contemplation and discussion. I am convinced as to your good intentions; your interest also lies in that direction. But you will not find the welcome that you expect from the Istanbul government. Well before this proposal of yours, the Vali of Syria, Tahsin Bey, told me, that seeing the danger for the future of this country, he applied to Istanbul with a proposition very similar to yours but received no reply. It is certain that they will refuse you. Whatever has been ordained by God will come to pass. Any intervention on my part would cause more harm than good. Since I have never been able to agree with the Ittihadists on anything, it is highly unlikely that they will take my advice."[15]

In fact, this attempt had come too late. It was very doubtful that the Druze and the Maronites or the young Arabs pursuing ideals of Arab independence would ever entertain such a proposal. If Cemal Pasha had been able to refrain from his oppressive policies in Syria, he would have found that the people were with him and he would have been able to defend the land against the foreigners. I had already mentioned that the Ottoman state had put in place a sytem of "mutual interest" between it and the notables of Syria, and that it was thanks to it that the state had survived. It was clear that the Syrian notability who were involved in, and benefited from, this "mutual interest" stood to lose from the collapse of the Ottoman administration.[16]

As part of the recent policies to pacify the Arab reformers, Youssef Sursock Bey had been offered a senatorship. He had refused because reasons of health made it impossible to leave Beirut.

---

14 Ibid., 24, 142–143.
15 Ibid., 143.
16 Ibid., 144. Kazım was right about this system of mutual interest. See Galvin, *Divided Loyalties*, 24: "Some merchants did grow rich from speculation, smuggling, and the sale of supplies to the Ottoman Fourth Army."

At a gathering where I was present, old Yousef Sursock Bey told an audience consisting mostly of Orthodox Christians,

"You want the French to come here. You poor, feeble-minded men! You do not stop to think how are you going to resist the French? With what organization and capital? Today you are in control, tomorrow you will become slaves. At best, Beirut will become nothing but a brothel!"[17]

It was clear that the Druze did not favour the French. The Muslims who made up the majority, despite the boundless oppression and insults of Cemal Pasha, did not want to separate from the Turks because of the bond of religion and in order to protect their national independence.

Shortly after the occupation of Beirut, in a gathering where I was present, there was a Tunisian officer, a captain in the French army, a certain Sayyid . . . of good family. When he found out I was Turkish, [he approached me and] he said,

"These Syrian Muslims have no idea! They do not know that in my country which is Tunisia, in Algeria and in Morocco, the French think of nothing but their own interests. I belong to a prominent family in Tunisia. I studied at the Saint-Cyr before I joined the army. Yet I am condemned to remain a captain until I die. This is the extent of the respect that the French accord us! You should have sent these men to the front so we could have killed them. Then the country would have been rid of them and their lies.[18]"

After the fall of Jerusalem our army had pulled back to a new defensive front. Cemal Pasha was due to return to Istanbul. He came to Beirut to bid farewell and attended a reception given by the municipality. In the speech he delivered that evening he spoke about the revolt of Sharif Hussein and put the responsibility [for this] on Enver Pasha's shoulders!

When Sheikh Es'ad Shuqayr translated the speech into Arabic there was no limit to the astonishment of the Beirut notables who were present.[19]

---

17 Hüseyin Kazım Kadri, *Meşrutiyetten Cumhuriyete Hatıralarım*, 144. The Sursocks were a prominent Greek Orthodox Beiruti family with seemingly boundless fortunes. See Fawaz, *The Land of Aching Hearts*, 124–125: "In the nineteenth and early twentieth centuries, one rhyme (in colloquial Arabic) was 'I would like to be a horse in the Sursock household so that I am fed pistachios and nuts." We will meet the Sursocks again in Münevver Ayaşlı's memoirs.

18 Hüseyin Kazım Kadri, *Meşrutiyetten Cumhuriyete Hatıralarım*, 144. Saint-Cyr is the elite military academy in Paris. Kazım refrains from giving the man's name to protect him.

19 Ibid., 144–145. It must be recalled that Cemal left Syria under a cloud. His removal was interpreted as a gesture to the Arabs who hated him. There was also intense jealousy

[Hüseyin Kazım witnesses the occupation of Beirut]

In those days we were living in Broumana. We had come down to Beirut for the treatment of my mother, who was a diabetic. After her death we went back to Aleppo. Soon after we heard of, and witnessed with our own eyes, the desertion of our soldiers and their officers. There was no doubt that the great catastrophe that awaited us was approaching.

One day the chief bishop of the Mar Isha'yya monastery, Pere Joseph, came to see me and told me that Doctor Dray, one of the teachers at the American university, was waiting for me at Beit Meri and that we should go together. I asked Pere Joseph what the Doctor wanted to see me about, he said, "You will see there. I am not authorized to tell you now."[20]

We found Doctor Dray walking back and forth in front of his house, obviously in a state of anxiety. As soon as he saw me, he said, "[W]e have firm information that the British army is going to mount a major offensive in one week. In such circumstances it is not safe for you to remain in an isolated place like Broumana. Dr. Bliss wants you to come to Beirut."

It was clear that these men were well informed about everything. We decided to stay a few more days [in Broumana].

It was certain that the situation was getting worse. I went down to Beirut and saw Ismail Hakkı Bey, whom I liked very much. He was in a state of extreme anxiety and restlessness. He had a map in front of him and pointed out to me the direction the British offensive. Because of a sudden raid to the rear of the army, our soldiers were deserting. The army command had just managed to escape with great difficulties. Mustafa Kemal

---

between Cemal and Enver. Çiçek, *War and State Formation in Syria*, 261: "[Any] reconciliation with the Arabs would require his dismissal."

20 Hüseyin Kazım Kadri, *Meşrutiyetten Cumhuriyete Hatıralarım*, 145. This is the Maronite monastery of Mar Isha'ya in Broumana in the Metn. Doctor Arthur Dray was the head of the the the dental department of Syrian Protestant College. In the summer of 1915 he was summoned by Cemal Pasha, who sent his personal car from Jerusalem, so that Dray might tend to a Turkish guest of the Pasha who had been shot in the face while in Cemal's car. The shot was probably intended for Cemal. Dray succeeded in saving the patient and promised Cemal that he would keep the matter confidential. Thus Dray, who was a British subject, was allowed to remain in Lebanon with a personal dispensation from Cemal Pasha. The house in Broumana that Kazım went to was given to Dray by Cemal. Among the locals it was an infamous place because Dray paid the locals for their work on the house in flour that he was able to get from Cemal even at the height of the famine. See Fawaz, *A Land of Aching Hearts*, 241–242. Howard Bliss was the President of Syria Protestant College, which later became known as the American University of Beirut (AUB).

Pasha was at that time commander of the Yıldırım Army Group in Syria. Ismail Hakki Bey said he [Mustafa Kemal] was the only one with whom he had managed to communicate.[21]

The next day we heard that Damascus had fallen. I cannot describe the chaos. Should one laugh or cry at the scene of the dispute between the Vali and the Chief Accountant for the payment of the camel drivers who had brought the archives of the Population Registry from Sayda to Beirut?

Ninety thousand liras belonging to the Ziraat Bank [the state bank] were waiting, stuffed into sacks. The Vali ordered that they be immediately sent to the station at Rayak. The commander of the local gendarmes, Hamdi Bey, said that the local gendarmes would almost certainly steal this money *en route* and that he could not take the responsibility.

It was a scene from hell, from the apocalypse. That night I was in the Vali's office. That night Colonel Refet Bey was there, he had just managed to escape the British. He was able to escape with a few riders towards Tripoli. The next morning the Vali also left with his entourage, giving me the letter that I was to hand over to the Chief of the Municipality. He also wrote a letter authorizing me to take over the seven thousand (*mecidiye*) of the Ottoman Bank. I took this money and gave it into the safe keeping of Yousef Sursock. Later I would return and take this money to the state treasury. That was all we were able to save from Syria.[22]

One week later I witnessed the occupation of Beirut. For days we were too frightened to leave our homes. At this point the Arab Government was declared, and Shukri Pasha Ayyubi, who had been tortured by Cemal Pasha, came to Beirut as the Vali.[23] The Arab flag with great ceremony was put up over the Serail and emotional speeches were made. Commemorations were held for those men whom Cemal Pasha had hung and the Place de Burc was renamed Place des Martyrs. The first order given by Shukri Pasha was that all Turks be exiled to Salt. My family and

---

21 Hüseyin Kazım Kadri, *Meşrutiyetten Cumhuriyete Hatıralarım*, 146. The "raid" that Hüseyin Kazım is referring to here must be the sudden appearance of British forces in Nazareth on September 21. Rogan, *The Fall of the Ottomans*, 376: "The German commander [Liman von Sanders] only just eluded capture. . . ."

22 Hüseyin Kazım Kadri, *Meşrutiyetten Cumhuriyete Hatıralarım*, 146–147. 7,000 *mecidiye* would have been paper currency and was the equivalent of 1,500 gold liras. 90,000 liras would be the Ottoman paper equivalent of 1,400 gold liras. My thanks to Edhem Eldem for this information.

23 Ibid., 147. "The aged and venerable Shukri Pasha al-Ayyubi was flogged day after day to within an inch of his life." Antonius, *The Arab Awakening*, 202.

I were to be exempt. My father-in-law İsmet Pasha refused stating, "We will not be separated from our compatriots. The Vali ordered our exile, so we will be the first to go." These words made them pause and they decided that because the Turks in Beirut had never done them any harm, we were allowed to stay.

The Arab State only lasted a week. After that the French and the British, despite their promises, lowered the Arab flag and put up their own! After this we had no news from Istanbul. We heard about the Armistice after the firing of cannon announcing it.

It was a few days after the occupation of Beirut. I was given a piece of paper when I came home. It said that the commander of the occupation army and his political officer Major Deedes (he was later to be promoted to general and assigned to Jerusalem as assistant governor. He had spent a long while in Ottoman service as a reformer of the gendarme forces. He spoke very good Turkish) were expecting me that evening at eight at the Deutcherhof Hotel. God knows I was very frightened.[24] It would be very difficult to make any sort of argument with an army commander. I immediately went to my friend Dr. Bliss at the American University and, showing him the paper [I had been sent] asked him what he thought. He replied:

"I do not think that they should have any ill intentions towards you. Still, go get your family and immediately come here. I will provide you with an appartment. You can live with me. The British cannot take you from me under any circumstances. Yet, I will go before you to see them on some pretext and in the course of the conversation I will ask them about you; I will thus find out their purpose. If there is any danger, I will try to neutralize it. In any case, I will immediately bring you here.[25]"

One hour later he came to my house [and told me]: "They have no bad thoughts about you. I can vouch for that. They only want to learn some things from you that have no direct bearing on your person. That is all."

---

24 Hüseyin Kazım Kadri, *Meşrutiyetten Cumhuriyete Hatıralarım*, 148. The Commander of the occupation forces in Beirut was General Bulfen. Whyndham Henry Deedes (1883–1956) was a British intelligence officer, also known as "Deedes Bey" for his excellent command of Turkish. Before the war he was involved in reforming the gendarme corps in the Ottoman Empire. After the war he went on to become the chief secretary of Sir Herbert Samuel, the first British High Commissioner in Palestine. John Presland, *Deedes Bey: A Study of Sir Wyndham Deedes 1883–1923* (London: Macmillan, 1942).

25 Hüseyin Kazım Kadri, *Meşrutiyetten Cumhuriyete Hatıralarım*, 148–149. Evidently, Dr. Bliss had very high regard for Kazım. It is interesting that there is no mention of this episode in the Howard Bliss papers at the AUB archives.

Therefore, relieved, I went to the hotel and met with them. The following conversation took place between us. The Commander said:

"You will now find out why we needed to inconvenience you. We would like your views on two matters. We thought that the locals would exaggerate and were of the opinion that the views of a neutral party such as yourself would be more useful.

"I would like to ask first, it is said that two hundred thousand people perished in Beirut and Mount Lebanon from hunger. Is this true? Was the death of this many people the result of government mismanagement, or was it done as a deliberate policy? . . . We also heard that more than eighty villages in the mountain [were emptied] and their people scattered. Is this true? We would like to know the reasons for all this."

After some hesitation I answered:

"I saw hundreds of people drop down dead from hunger. Some of these were locals and others were the crowds of people from the mountain who took refuge here. However, since I was not in an official position, I cannot tell whether this was because the government officials did not do their duty or if it was because of unavoidable conditions. Similarly, I was also an eye witness to the abandoning of villages and the scattering of populations in the Jabal. I cannot say whether the government is solely responsible for this disaster."[26]

I understood that these men would take my words as evidence and write their report accordingly. Naturally, I could in no way deny the disaster that had taken place, nor could I load all the responsibility on the government.

At this point the Commander asked:

"Are you not the person who tried to save the starving people of the Mountain by approaching Governor Ismail Hakkı Bey about transporting the grain in the depots of Latakia to Beirut by sea and have it distributed to the people? The Vali first agreed and then changed his mind! You were very upset by this and used strong language, is this not true?"

[I answered:]

"Yes, that is how it happened. Ismail Hakkı Bey initially agreed to help me but then he changed his mind, saying that he feared a general retreat of the army. He told me that if the hunger occurs as the army retreats towards

---

26 Ibid.

Latakia, the grain would be needed to feed the troops. . . . When he promised to help me he did not know that this would happen. I did not insist."

The Commander had not received the answer that he expected from me. I must also say that I had not divulged all the facts that I knew.

[Cemal declares that if the Christians die of hunger, it would be a good thing]

As to the real situation [it was as follows]. The *Mutasarrıf* Ali Münif Bey had been appointed to the Ministry of Public Works and had gone to Istanbul. Although quite a long time had elapsed, nobody had been appointed in his place. In any case, Ali Münif Bey was known to neglect his duties and spend time in seeking his pleasure. In fact, once he disappeared for seven days and no one knew where the *Mutasarrıf* was. It was later discovered that he was shut up in a house with Alfred Sursock Bey in Broumana!

At that time Cemal Pasha had come to Beirut. Together with Governor Azmi and the Vali of Syria, Tahsin Bey, they were sitting in a room on the second floor of Azmi Bey's residence. Mithat Şükrü Bey, the General Secretary of the Committee of Union and Progress, was also there. I had gone to visit the Pasha together with Veli Çelebi. They took us upstairs. The lower floor of the house was full of visitors who had come to pay their respects.

Tahsin Bey said,

"[T]hey still have not sent anyone to the Mountain [Mutasarrıfate], the people are dying from hunger. Nobody is thinking of feeding them. If you could write [to Istanbul] so that they could send someone soon."

In response to this warning the Pasha [Cemal] answered,

"That the people of the Jabal should be wiped out by hunger would be the greatest happiness for us. May the wretches perish, we will thus be rid of them!"

Yet when he [Cemal] came to Sofar, he would usually attach one or two carriages filled with grain to his train and he would distribute to the people as he saw fit. Needless to say, these people were not those who were starving.

[Here Kazım made a note as follows]:

At some point it was seen that Cemal Pasha distributed soup and bread to the poor and that he had appointed some men from Christian families to carry this out. I would later understand the reason for this. The newspaper

Le Temps, published in Paris, had run an article, which was sent to the Pasha personally, stating that "[t]he people of Syria are being destroyed by Cemal Pasha through hunger and he will have to answer for this in the future!" It appears that this was the reason why the Pasha suddenly changed his mind and started to pose as the affectionate protector of the poor! But by then what had happened had happened the dead were dead and the beaches of Beirut were full of the cadavers of the Lebanese peasants.[27]

[Hüseyin Kazım attempts to bring grain from Latakia]

. . . The story of the grain stocks in Latakia is worth recounting. It was very difficult and costly to transport this grain by land. Nor was it possible to transport it by sea because of the French ships stationed on the island of Arwad. These grains that were doomed to rot had officially been sold at auction to a man named Mustafa Izzettin, one of the corrupt notables of Tripoli. Vali Azmi Bey, who had been the friend and protector of this Mustafa Izzedin, had resigned and gone to Istanbul and Ismail Hakkı Bey, the *Mutasarrıf* of the Mountain, had been appointed in his place. I knew that this person was of noble character and totally honest and I loved him as a brother. In fact we were distant relatives. However, because he had spent all his life in the palace of Abdulhamid, he was timid, hesitant, and given to anxiety. Also, he was a bit too inclined to flatter Cemal Pasha. In the time that I was in Broumana, a charitable and humanitarian person by the name of Doctor Menasse had told me,

"At this rate the people of Beirut are also doomed to die of hunger. I have thought of a solution. The depots of Latakia are full of grain and there is no way the government will be able to use them. If you work with me in convincing the Vali, we can save these people. In Beirut we can find the capital necessary to buy this grain. Then we can transport this grain by sea and sell it at cost and distribute some of it free to the poor."

The good Doctor promised that he would be able to find capital for this venture. All he wanted from me was to intercede with the Vali. . . .[28]

---

27 Ibid., 150: "*Cebel halkının açlıktan geberip gitmeleri, bizim arayıp da bulamadığımız bir saadetdir. Varsın gebersinler, biz de onlardan kurtulmuş oluruz.*" See the section in the Introduction of this volume regarding articles in *Le Temps*.

28 Ibid., 151. I have not been able to identify Dr. Menasse.

In any event we decided to try it, and the Doctor and I walked from Broumana to Beirut.[29] The first thing we did was to gather in the municipality building to try to collect some money. Those speculators who were seeking to feed on the hunger of the people had filled their depots and were waiting for the price to rise even further. The price of wheat in those days, forty gold liras for two hundred *okka*, was not enough to satisfy their greed. Naturally, nothing came out of the meeting in the municipality, and despite the desperate pleas of the Doctor and the best efforts of the Chief of the Municipality, Omar Dauk Efendi, all we were able to raise amounted to ten thousand paper liras.

The Doctor was bitterly disappointed and ready to give up. We went together to the American College and saw Dr. Bliss, whom I asked to furnish us with a credit of one hundred thousand liras. He replied,

"If we had any money I would happily give it to you. But as you know, we are unable to communicate with the United States and I have been obliged to borrow money here and there at high interest."

[Hüseyin Kazım replied:]

"No, I am not asking you for money. I am asking your son-in-law. He can provide this money. In effect, we will be paying it back almost immediately. It would be sufficient to open an account in any bank."

Dr. Bliss's son-in-law was a young man who had millions. As I write these lines, my friend Dr. Bliss is long dead and his son-in-law has become the Director of the College.[30]

The following conversation came to pass between this person [Dodge] and us.

"First I have to know if you are personally going to be involved in this affair."

"Yes, I will be personally involved."

"But you cannot do this alone, you need at least two people to help you."

"Doctor Menasse will be with me, we will also include Davud Nahhul Efendi, the Master of the Beirut Freemasons' Lodge."

---

29 Ibid. The distance from Broumana to Beirut is 18 km. As neither was a young man, to walk this distance was quite a feat.

30 Ibid., 152. The person whom Kazım is referring to here is Bayard Dodge. Dodge succeeded Howard Bliss as President of Syria Protestant College after Bliss's death in 1924. There is no mention of this encounter in the Bayard Dodge papers in the AUB archives.

"Now it is done. These two people are the two most honest and respectable men in Beirut. I will assure you a line of credit worth one hundred and fifty thousand liras. I do not want ten *paras* as interest. I will also accept ten percent loss."

After speaking thus, he gave me a letter addressed to his bank. You should have seen the happiness of the good Doctor! The poor man was laughing and crying at the same time. From there we went to the Dutch Consulate. After explaining the matter to the Consul Monsieur Holch I said,

"This is what we want from you. You will give me a document stating that the grain transferred by sea from Latakia is being shipped entirely for distribution to the poor people, who are starving. None of it is going to be used to provision the army. You will write that you personally guarantee this."

Monsieur Holch accepted my offer and gave me the letter I wanted. We then went to the Papal Legate Monseigneur Cannini. He countersigned the letter I had obtained from the Dutch Consul. We were going to give this letter to the captain of the ship that we would send to Latakia to load the grain. We greatly hoped that the French blockade ships at Arwad island would not prevent the transfer of this grain. Otherwise they would cause of the death of thousands of people. Everything was ready. But then Ismail Hakkı Bey changed his language and told us he could not let us have the grain as the retreating army would pass that way and they would need it.

Doctor Menasse and I, greatly disappointed, returned to Broumana and gave the letter of credit back to its owner. Thus ended the matter that the British occupation commander would later question me about.[31]

[The evacuation of the last Turkish families from Beirut]

There were quite a few Turkish families in Beirut. During those days, a ship had been sent to evacuate the Damascus Red Crescent personnel. Some families used this vessel to be repatriated. In those same days we sent some fifty to sixty people with the cruiser *Waldeck Rousseau*, which was going to Istanbul. After that we were unable to find any conveyance and for some six months we had to find a way of providing for hundreds of families from all over Syria who had piled up in Beirut. A few of these people [came to see me and] told me that they had formed a committee to take charge of this matter and that they wanted me to be its president. Naturally, I accepted.

---

31 Ibid., 153.

The very next day, accompanied by the Chief of the Municipality Omar Dauk Efendi, I went to the British and French commanders and explained the issue to them. According to the agreement reached between us, provisions such as oil, sugar, rice, flour, potatoes, and soap were to be distributed to the Turkish families from the British army stores against my signature. Our committee was also approved officially. Thus we were able to provide for the livelihood of hundreds of families.

Yet the months were passing and our return to Istanbul did not seem to be in the offing. The British officer with whom I had contact, Major Thompson, was telling me, "We have many officers in Alexandria waiting for a ship to take them back to England. We are unable even to find shipping for them, leave alone provide for you, be a little patient."[32]

At that point I thought that I could use the good offices of the great Jesuit, Pere Chanteur, who had come back from France.

During the war I had often helped the Jesuits remaining in Beirut. Once when at the instigation of Azmi Bey, Cemal Pasha had decided to exile them to Diyarbakır, I had travelled to Damascus to intercede with Cemal Pasha, convincing him to allow them to go free. Also, I would occasionally intervene [to assure that] the government of the Jabal would send them grain to alleviate their suffering.

After their return to Beirut, Pere Chanteur, the Director of the French medical academy, Pere Marten, The Rector of the Yesuiyye [St. Joseph University], and Pere Katen, they all paid me a visit to thank me for all I had done to help the Jesuit order.[33]

---

32 Ibid., 154.

33 Ibid., 159. The Jesuits Hüseyin Kazım is referring to are the following. Pere Claudius Chanteur (1865–1949), *Provinciale* of Lyon, to which all Jesuit missions in Syria were attached. Chanteur returned to Beirut on Christmas day 1918. He was the *Superieure* of the Jesuit mission in Syria 1918–1921. "He was much respected by the High Commissioners Gouraud and Weygand who asked his advice." Lucien Cattin, Swiss Jesuit (1851–1929), was three times Rector of St. Joseph University (1897–1901, 1907–1910, 1919–1929). Cattin's life's work was the Medical Faculty, for which he was able to get recognition of its diplomas by a joint French–Ottoman jury. He was also the moving force behind the construction of the monument of Our Lady of Harissa in 1904. Cattin came back to Lebanon on Christmas day 1918. "Per Marten" is probably P. Paul Mattern (1869–1943). As he was from Alsace and hence technically a German stateless person (*apatride*), he was allowed to remain in Lebanon during the war years. He kept a meticulous diary of the trials and tribulations of the country, including the famine. See Henri Jalabert S. J., *Jesuites au Proche-Orient. Notices biographiques* (Beirut: Université de Saint Joseph, Faculte des Lettres et Sciences Humaines, 1987), 173–174, 218–219, 247–248. Another Lebanese Jesuit whom Kazım helped was Father Sheikho, a renowned

For once I decided to ask for their help and requested that Pere Chanteur intercede with General Allenby and the French authorities to find a ship to take the last Turkish families to Turkey. Pere Chanteur assured me that he would do his best to resolve the matter and immediately went to see the commander. Later, he came to my home and showed me a copy of the cable [the commander] had sent.

A week later, I was told that Major Thompson wanted to see me. When he saw me he said, "Your wish has been granted. In three days' time the ship *Ellenga* will be in Beirut to take you all to Istanbul. Make yourself ready and bring your belongings to the pier." We immediately sent word to our compatriots and started shifting our belongings to the pier. The ship arrived and docked, a huge ocean liner. Meanwhile, we were preparing the register required by the authorities. Every family had a document with photographs and a passport containing the information required, all our papers were in order. But the difficulty was finding porters to load all the accumulated belongings onto the ship; for this a great deal of money was required. Thompson insisted that the ship had to sail that very evening and that we should load our belongings forthwith. We were astonished. I thought for a moment then found a solution. I told him, "I will arrange to have these belongings loaded in two hours, but you must promise me that you will observe from afar and not interfere." Thompson laughed and replied, "I suppose you will show us a new miracle of your Prophet." I replied, "Yes! I do indeed wish to show you a new miracle of Mohammad." His rejoinder was, "Very well. I have no objection."

[In Beirut] there were hundreds of Egyptian porters used to carry the material of the British army. Their foreman, an Arab with a whip, was close by. I approached him, telling him we were Muslim refugees and requested that he order his porters to load our goods on the ship. The dear man immediately bellowed out, "Listen, lads! This uncle has asked us for something. These goods will immediately be loaded onto the ship and we will do our duty by our Muslim brothers!"

As soon as he had uttered these words, hundreds of Egyptian porters descended upon our belongings which they stored in the hold of the ship in less than two hours. Thompson was looking on, bewildered and enraged.

---

expert in Arabic linguistics. Tautel and Wittouck, *Le Peuple Libanais*, 158: "After the expulsion of the [French] Jesuits in 1914, thanks to his friendship with Hussein Qazim Bek, a leading member of the Young Turks, Father Sheikho was allowed to work every day at the Biblioteque Orientale. . . ."

I said, "Here is Muhammad's miracle." He did not answer but beat a hasty retreat. The *Ellenga* sailed at the appointed time. In the many years I had spent in Beirut I had had good relations with all classes of people. Headed by the Mufti, most of the notables and *ulama* of the city came to see us off.[34] We embraced in tears . . . Thus we left Syria forever. . . .

I had sold quite a lot of the provisions that I had taken from the British; thus I had accumulated quite a lot of money. Just before we left, I was given five hundred Egyptian pounds by the French military headquarters. In our time the municipality had made a collection and five thousand five hundred lira was left over. I asked for and was given this money, which I distributed to our compatriots on the ship. After bidding farewell to those who came to see us off, I boarded the ship. I was very tired. With great difficulty I managed to get the Ceylonese cabin attendants to prepare me a bath. As soon as I had entered the bath, the ship cast off. Just at that time, some people came to the door and asked me to come out. When I asked them what was happening, they could only tell me, "Come out, come out, you must see this!" Having somehow dressed and come out on deck, I saw the Egyptian porters who had carried our goods onto the ship plus thousands of Beirutis lined up along the pier. They had raised a flag and were shouting "*Allah yansuru'l Islam!*" (God Protect Islam). Our party were replying with the same words. I could not restrain my tears.

The English and French officers present were as if turned to stone, witnessing this demonstration of affection and emotion. Major Thompson had seen yet another miracle of Islam. This scene was a manifestation of the "brotherhood of Islam" that had taken shape and survived over the centuries. May God curse those who want to break this unity and destroy the *umma* of Islam!

[As the Turks were evacuating Beirut]

To the Ministry of the Interior.

This document has been prepared with a view to report on the activities of the committee that was formed to provide for the provisioning and repatriation of those Turkish families remaining in Beirut after the occupation

---

34 Hüseyin Kazım Kadri, *Meşrutiyetten Cumhuriyete Hatıralarım*, 155. The Mufti of Beirut at the time was Sheikh Mustafa Naja. He would later refuse to serve as Mufti of Lebanon despite being asked to by the French High Commissioner General Gouraud. Eddé, *Beyrouth*, 73.

of Syria. The total of the monies collected for this purpose was 274,811 *kuruş* and 10 *para*s. Of this 268,154 *kuruş* was spent and the remaining 6,657 *kuruş* and 10 *para*s were handed over to the Red Crescent.

> Head of the Commission:
>> The former Vali of Aleppo Hüseyin Kazım
>> 5 Nisan 335 (April 18, 1919)[35]

After the occupation of Syria, seeing the terrible conditions of the Turkish families who had accumulated in Beirut, a committee was formed consisting of men who were concerned to alleviate the conditions of their countrymen and facilitate their return to the fatherland. The first attempts to form this committee took place in November 1918. It was constituted with the aim of collecting funds from their compatriots for those families who had brought some modest belongings with them with great difficulties and were now seeking to sell them so as not to starve.[36] After the departure of the first convoy consisting of those who had left with the staff of the Red Crescent hospital of Damascus at the end of December, it became apparent that there was no further hope of a return to the fatherland. The situation of those families from various parts of Syria who had accumulated in Beirut had begun to draw attention.

In this situation it became necessary to broaden the membership of the first committee and to focus attention on the livelihood and lodgings of our countrymen.

The committee that was formed according to the conditions of the time made every effort to apply to the Municipality of Beirut to improve the conditions of the hundreds of families who found themselves stranded in Beirut, deprived of everything enabling them to survive. Thanks be to the Almighty, this effort was successful.

Our committee is proud to present this to the appreciation of our citizens and the judgment of history.

From the statement of accounts attached to this report it will be possible to get an idea of the sum total of the material and monetary aid obtained in the six months that elapsed from the first days to the departure of the first group of Turks on the ship *Ellenga*.

---

35 Hüseyin Kazım Kadri, *Meşrutiyetten Cumhuriyete Hatıralarım*, 323, appendix III. This document was found in a private collection and added to the memoirs by the editor, İsmail Kara.

36 Ibid., 324.

A large part of the efforts of the committee were directed towards the returning to their country of some four hundred and fifty families.[37] In order to achieve this aim we made constant applications to the French and British military authorities and the local government. In this way it was possible to make many convincing arguments regarding the necessity of the repatriation of these people. As a result, we were able to send sixty three men and women aboard the French cruiser *Waldeck Rousseau* that was going to Istanbul.

After this it became possible to send . . . families amounting to 829 souls to Istanbul on the ship *Ellenga*.[38] The committee undertook this duty to their fellow citizens by interceding with the government and the officials who were appointed to this task, loading their possessions on the ship, providing money and food such as bread, oranges, and cheese for the poor, and unloading the same possessions in Istanbul and handing them over to their owners.

In the six months that elapsed between the occupation and the return to Istanbul we consider it a duty to thank the following persons who showed kindness and humanity towards the Turks: the commander of the British 21 Cavalry Division General Bulfin and his second in command General Armstrong, the honourable Papal Legate Monseigneur Cannini, a member of the French military authorities, the Military Governor of Beirut Major Doezelet, and passport official Monsieur Bourgeois.

Another aspect of these events is that we are proud to acknowledge the help and humanity of Omar Bey Dauk, the Director of the Municipality [of Beirut]. This person, in all matters regarding us showed us the utmost support and kindness, making it possible to ease the conditions and provide for the livelihood of thousands of people.

As a last word, the Committee considers it a duty to thank the humanitarian and charitable Chief of the Municipality in the name of all the Turks.[39]

---

37 Ibid., 324. If we estimate that each family consisted of approximately four individuals, this makes for a population of 1,800 people as a conservative estimate.

38 Ibid., 325. Kazım leaves the number of families blank here.

39 Ibid., 323–326. Lieutenant General Edward Bulfin was one of the main commanders of the offensive against Jerusalem and other decisive battles on the Palestine front. Faulkner, *Lawrence of Arabia's War*, 358, 342.

Chapter 3

Ali Fuad Erden

Ali Fuad [Erden]

[*Ali Fuad Erden was very much the cynical, professional soldier. Major Ali Fuad was Cemal's number two man as the military chief of staff in the Fourth Army region. He greatly admired Cemal, but did not hesitate to speak his mind when he differed with him on key issues. He was also extremely cynical about the conduct of the war in the Syrian theater. He openly stated in his memoirs that the two Suez Canal campaigns, in 1915 and 1916, were hopeless operations, desired by the Germans and undertaken with the sole purpose of pinning down British forces that might otherwise be used in the Western Front. His memoir contains very interesting information on the execution of the Arab martyrs, which he was against. He is scathing in his criticism of the rich Beirutis and their indifference to the suffering of the poor during the famine. He was also extremely vain, likening himself to Saint-Just. He went on to serve in the army of the Republic, ultimately becoming the commander of the Military Academy.*

In his memoirs, Cemal Pasha stated, "Major Ali Fuad, who was my chief of staff, kept very detailed log books about the military operations in the Fourth Army zone which he later turned in to headquarters, I will request that he use these to write a military history."][1]

Introduction

This book is not intended to be a history of the Fourth Army. Nor is it a "memoir" that has nothing to do with what happened in the war. Nor does it consist only of anecdotes and stories related to the war. It is a

---

1   Cemal Pasha, *Hatıralar* (Istanbul: İş Bankası Yayınları, 2008), 173. Ali Fuad Erden, *Birinci Dünya Savaşında Suriye Hatıraları* [Memoirs of Syria during the First World War] (Istanbul: İş Bankası Yayınları, 2006).

collection of events, anecdotes, and stories; it is a few pages of our recent history. . . .

The Minister of the Navy Cemal Pasha became the Commander of the Fourth Army in November 1914. When the German Field Marshal Falkenhayn was appointed, the Fourth Army ceased to exist. That is to say that Cemal Pasha was the Commander of the Fourth Army for three years. During this time I served under Cemal Pasha as deputy chief of staff and, ultimately, chief of staff. The timeframe of this book is the period when Cemal Pasha was the Commander of the Fourth Army.

The [Suez] Canal Campaign occurred at the beginning of this period. That is why I mention it here, for some of the material I use is new. In any event, history is always new. New sources, new insights, new descriptions constantly renew it. I mentioned people, because history is made by people, and I mentioned particularly Cemal Pasha. Cemal Pasha left the stamp of his powerful personality on all events, and he made the history of the Fourth Army. Cemal Pasha was my commander and I still consider him my commander. I waited forty years to write my Syrian Memoirs. . . .

What is forty years?

Forty years is the time Moses spent in the Sinai desert raising new generations to reconquer the Promised Land.

Forty years means a time span of two generations.

Forty years means, excluding childhood, an entire life.

Forty years is the time elapsed since the Constitutional Revolution.

In this time much has changed in the world, which saw many wars, revolution, two world wars and the dawning of a new age.

In these forty years my recollections have been sifted, my emotions stilled, the regrets and agonies pacified. Memories have become history.

In my book I have striven to present "personalities" and "events" without any positive or negative exaggeration, without coming under the influence of my emotions, I have tried to write about them as objectively as I could. I present my "Syrian Memoirs" to my respected readers.[2]

---

2   Ali Fuad Erden, *Birinci Dünya Savaşında Suriye Hatıraları*, x. The memoirs were published for the first time in 1954 as a serial in the *Dünya* newspaper. The "Constitutional Revolution" that he refers to here is the Young Turk Revolution of 1908. Ali Fuad held the rank of Major while serving under Cemal Pasha.

An attempt at the Suez Canal

The aims of the "attempt on the Suez Canal" was not a precise order with a clear objective; it was more a general directive. The intention was to hold down the British forces in Egypt, to concentrate the forces that would be sent from Asia and Australia and prevent them from being sent to the Western Front. The conquest of Egypt was not mentioned in the directives of the German General Staff, nor mentioned in the orders of the Ottoman Deputy Chief of staff. The aim was simply a feint at the Suez Canal. The conquest of Egypt was imaginary propaganda. It was the face of the medallion to be presented to public opinion. . . .

[*After giving a detailed account of the military difficulties of such a campaign Ali Fuad Bey deemed it a hopeless venture.*]

Thus, the Canal Campaign, given the conditions of supply and logistics in 1914, was, essentially, an imaginary campaign.[3]

The center of attraction

Maybe we actually saw the Sinai desert as beautiful. The Sinai desert, one of the worst places on the globe, maybe we needed to see it as beautiful, convincing ourselves in our mind's eye. We were embellishing the terrifying emptiness of the desert with dreams of the land of Joseph and the Pyramids.

As we were marching on the Canal in the Sinai desert, full of such dreams, the center of attraction was Cemal Pasha. Cemal Pasha, the Minister of the Navy, one of the three great men determining the fate of

---

3   Ibid., 4. In fact, the Egyptian campaign was very much the desiderata of the Germans, particularly the Kaiser, who was convinced that it would lead to a general Muslim uprising in the colonized world. Enver was actually lukewarm on the idea, preferring a campaign against the Russians in the Caucasus. The German high command did not have much hope about the success of an Ottoman frontal attack on Egypt, given the strength of the British. The attack on the Canal was primarily intended to tie down forces that could otherwise be used on the European fronts. See Mustafa Aksakal, *The Ottoman Road to War in 1914: The Ottoman Empire and the First World War* (Cambridge and London: Cambridge University Press, 2008), 136, 137, 148, 150, 154. The Germans were planning an attack on Suez even before the Ottomans entered the war. Sean McMeekin states that the Germans actually thought that the British could be forced out of Egypt. Enver had led them to believe that an Ottoman action against Suez would lead to a mass rising of Muslims in Egypt. See McMeekin, *The Berlin-Baghdad Express: The Ottoman Empire and Germany's Bid for World Power* (Cambridge: Harvard University Press, 2010), 92, 94.

the state! He personified all our hopes and dreams. Cemal Pasha's style, his countenance, his presence, the determination and power that radiated from his person gave us faith and confidence. That beautiful, handsome white horse, and his magnificent rider, with his head slightly inclined to the right, plunged into deep thoughts and vision. . . . The two made up a magnificent image on the Egyptian horizon. This image was a symbol, a tableau that promised us victory. I was watching this tableau and drawing inspiration from it.[4]

[*At this point in the text Erden launches into a long tirade about how he admires Saint-Just and quotes numerous sayings attributed to him.*]

The real subject. [The Sinai desert]

I am sorry for the digression, respected readers. I now come back to my subject which is the Sinai desert. On January 20, 1915 we arrived at a point called Ibin. I say "point" because it really is a point, an artificial location. There was no such place on the map, nor was there such a place in the Sinai. It was more or less the center point in the desert where two faint caravan tracks, or, I should say, camel footprints, cross going from north to south and from east to west. That was why it was strategically an important point and because of this, it was a staging post for the army. Because it was a staging post for the army, it was also a telegraph station. Because it was a staging post and a telegraph station, it also had a flag. It had a red lantern for lighting at night, conical tents, and a name, Ibin. It was called Ibin because there was a mountain near it by that name. It was the last telegraph station. The telegraph line had been able to reach only this far. After this we were going to be plunged into the unknown and our communications with the motherland was to be only by mounted messenger.[5]

From Ibin, Cemal Pasha sent the following telegram to Enver Pasha:

January 18, 1915

Very soon I will be leaving for the Canal with a light load and a few staff officers. . . . If I die during our offensive on the Canal, I cannot think of anyone better than you to take over the command. Thus it would be my last

---

4   Ali Fuad Erden, *Birinci Dünya Savaşında Suriye Hatıraları*, 20.
5   Ibid., 24. This is as close as a stiff-upper-lip soldier like Ali Fuad can get to describing what we would today call "the middle of nowhere."

wish and testament that you come from Istanbul to Jerusalem to finish this great endeavour. May Allah grant victory to Islam, my brother. Commander of the Fourth Army and Minister of the Navy.

Ahmed Cemal

The following telegram arrived from Enver Pasha.

January 19, 1915.

I am sure that the Almighty will grant you victory in this great effort. *Inshallah* I will come there to salute you as the Second Conqueror of Egypt. Let me take the occasion to say that we are suffering very heavy casualties in the battles here. . . .

This telegram from Enver Pasha was not really a reply to Cemal Pasha. Yet it was an indirect reply. The Deputy Commander in chief had sensed a certain melancholy in Cemal Pasha's wording and wanted to boost his morale. Enver Pasha's telegram contained both a sweet dream and bitter reality: "the Conqueror of Egypt" was the dream and the "heavy casualties" were the reality![6]

The magic scene: the Suez Canal[7]

On the night of February 1–2 the army headquarters was established. Suddenly we found ourselves confronted by a magic scene: the Suez Canal!

This was the scene before us:

On the opposite shore several searchlights, positioned every two to three km. were crossing their beams, turning night into day. In this flood of light the canal was shimmering like a silver corridor. Sea traffic was continuing along the canal and ocean liners, brilliantly lit up, were slowly making their passages. On the other shore, the town of Ismailiya was flooded in light and the towns of Tussum and Sarapeum appeared to be peaceful and secluded. Here and there, the dark silhouette of warships could be seen, appearing black against the skyline.

---

6   Ibid., 25. Enver Pasha calls Cemal the "Second Conqueror of Egypt," referring to the previous conquest of Egypt in 1516 by Sultan Selim I. It is also an indication of the megalomania characteristic of Enver and Cemal. Enver was referred to as Deputy Commander in chief of all Ottoman armed forces because in theory the sultan was the Commander in chief.

7   Ibid., 27.

The beauty of the canal, this movement to and fro, this calm and carefree appearance, this peaceful and happy scene was infuriating. An expeditionary force had crossed the Sinai desert, had appeared before the canal, and passage along the canal had not even been interrupted. This meant that the expeditionary force was not being taken seriously, it was demeaning and insulting. In order to redeem this insult, we should have sunk these ships with artillery fire to show the passage makers and inhabitants of the canal that the expeditionary force was to be reckoned with.

The British had unhesitatingly decided that the canal was the best line of defense. But according to the British themselves,

> To use the Suez Canal which was the vital artery of the Empire as the front line of defence, was not without danger. The greatest danger was that the Turks might sink a liner in the canal. This success on the part of the Turks would mean that the canal might be closed for weeks. The troop ships coming from Asia, Australia, and New Zealand would be obliged to round the Cape of Good Hope and would not come in time to deliver their troops to the battle fronts in Europe.[8]

Indeed, we could have sunk a few of these ocean liners with our heavy mortars and thus closed the canal for a long time. This was well within our capabilities, and this course of action would perhaps have been the best, the easiest, and the most in keeping with our aims. Why was this not done? Was it out of consideration for the rules of war, out of humanitarian considerations? Or was it that we simply did not want to reveal that our aim was to cross the canal in a sudden raid, or did we not want to reveal that we had heavy artillery? Or did it simply not occur to us? Or had we not dared? I am not in a position to answer.[9]

---

8   Ibid., 28. Ali Fuad is evidently quoting from British sources on the Great War. He repeatedly refers to British sources without providing precise references.

9   Ibid. This is as close as Ali Fuad gets to criticizing the decisions of his superior, Cemal Pasha. The sinking of ships in the canal was indeed part of the operational order of the Expeditionary Force. See Rogan, *The Fall of the Ottomans*, 121–123: "Seizure of the canal was but one part of the operation. Sinking of ships to obstruct the canal was a far more realistic objective than the capture of well entrenched British positions on the canal." When it became clear that the crossing was a disaster, the Ottomans did switch tactics and bombarded the British warships, the *Hardinge* and the *Clio*, and the French cruiser *Requin*, inflicting heavy damage before the guns were silenced by British fire.

The offensive. [The decision to cease hostilities and the retreat]

[*For the next few pages Ali Fuad Bey gives a highly detailed and accurate account of the attempt to cross the canal and its failure using both Turkish and British sources.*][10]

The commander of the army Cemal Pasha, having cool-headedly considered the position, and at the suggestion and insistence of chief staff officer Von Frankenberg, decided to end the hostilities that were taking place under unequal conditions. The chief staff officer had told him: "The offensive cannot be maintained with any hope of success. We must cease hostilities. If hostilities are immediately stopped we may yet save the Fourth Army. But if we delay the decision, the army may face catastrophe." During the night of February 2–3 the expeditionary force began its retreat from the canal under the cover of darkness. The operation lasted until the morning. The infantry dragged the heavy guns back across the desert. All the forces made it back to our base of the previous night. . . . The British were completely unaware of the retreat and had thought that the offensive would be renewed on the morning of the February 3.[11]

[The belated telegram from Enver Pasha, dated February 5, 1915]

On February 5, a messenger riding a camel brought the following telegram.

> To the Command of the Fourth Army
>
> As the failure of an offensive against the canal will have a very negative effect on the whole of the Islamic world, such an offensive should be carried out only if success appears to be certain. Therefore, until the means for such a certain victory are assembled, you are to restrain your activities to holding down the British forces and preventing the passage of shipping in the canal.
>
> Enver

---

10 Ali Fuad Erden, *Birinci Dünya Savaşında Suriye Hatıraları*, 32–40. The accounts of the battle he gives are in keeping with recent sources. Rogan, *The Fall of the Ottomans*, 115–125.

11 Ibid., 41. This account also tallies with recent sources. Rogan, *The Fall of the Ottomans*, 123: "The British, expecting the attack to be renewed on 4 February, were surprised to see that the bulk of the Turkish force had disappeared overnight."

[Cemal Pasha's response to this was the following:]

Ibin. February 5, 1915.

1. I received your telegram as I was returning from the offensive against the canal.

2. The only way that the traffic of shipping in the canal can be stopped is by artillery fire, and for this it would be necessary to keep a considerable force in front of the canal. This is impossible given the difficulties of the supply of water, provisions, and ammunition. Experience has shown that the only way to close down the canal is by gaining control of both sides.

3. After we have established mobile raiding parties we will be able to harass the traffic in the canal.

Commander of the Fourth Army and Minister of the Navy, Ahmed Cemal[12]

On February 16 army headquarters were established once more in the Augusta Victoria hospice in Jerusalem. In comparison to the dream of conquering Egypt, the actual result of the Canal Offensive can be qualified as a disaster. Yet if the aim was indeed to make a feint against the canal, the Canal Offensive can be considered a success. A feint (or dummy attack, *gösteriş*) had been carried out and as a result 75,000 British troops have been pinned down. General Falkenhayn stated, "As a result the British attack on the Dardanelles has been postponed, and this had made it possible to use this time to somewhat improve the defences of the Dardanelles. The Canal Offensive has accomplished its strategic aims."[13]

The report sent by Von Frankenberg. [Cemal Pasha's general assessment of the Canal Offensive]

"The forces taking part in the First Canal Offensive were the 11,000 bayonets of the Eighth Army Corps and the 9,000 bayonets of the First Division. The human and material resources at hand had enabled me to form a judgement that a raid across the canal would be possible. Thus I gave the order to

---

12 Ali Fuad Erden, *Birinci Dünya Savaşında Suriye Hatıraları*, 47. These telegrams are significant documents as the archives of the Ottoman forces are kept by the current Chief of staff Military Archives (ATASE) in Ankara and access to them is notoriously difficult.

13 Ibid., 48.

attack the canal. I knew that the enemy had at least twice the number of my forces dedicated to the defence of the Canal alone. If I was able to cross the canal with 20,000 bayonets at a point to be determined at the last moment I would have the superiority in numbers and I would be able to destroy the enemy forces at that point. I would then be able to destroy the canal at points north and south of [my bridgehead]. I would thus have made it impossible for enemy warships to provide relief. I would thus be in control of the west bank of the Canal. These were my thoughts when [I ordered the first offensive].

The attempt was not a success. Yet, the forced marches in the desert and the offensive against the canal have given us valuable experience for a second attack of greater proportions."[14]

The Augusta Victoria Hospice[15]

This building, the hospice of Augusta Victoria, named after the Empress of Germany, on the Mount of Olives just to the east of Jerusalem, is a magnificent structure. It was a fine example of German architecture in its simplicity, solidity, and beauty. Yet, the architect had not allowed for the strength of the winds on the Mount of Olives and this had meant that another exterior wall had been built around it, with a sort of corridor created between the two walls. The hospice was surrounded by a pine grove and rose gardens. In the rose gardens there were also strawberry and vanilla patches. The park looked out onto the Dead Sea and the Transjordan valley. The Dead Sea, 390 metres below sea level, had very dense grey water (in olden times they would throw condemned men into it, who would float). This sea was some one thousand meters below us. The mountain top from which Moses was able to glimpse his "Promised Land" was a long way away. On the other side of the Dead Sea, the mountains of Moab (Eastern Jordan) formed a dark purple line on the horizon. Beyond the horizon stood the deserts of Arabia.

In three years, the Moab would be a battlefield. The revolt in the Hijaz was to spread to southern Syria and the Hijaz front was to unite with the British front in the Sinai somewhere to the east of the Dead Sea. After serving for three years as the Army chief of staff I would be transferred to the

---

14 Ibid., 49. Nowhere does Cemal make any mention of Kres von Kressenstein, the brains behind the Canal Offensive. The force taking part in the Canal offensive was closer to 25,000 men.

15 Ibid., 59.

Eighth Army Corps and then I would serve on the Transjordan front. From the Transjordan the mountains of Jerusalem would appear far distant and we would gaze upon them sadly just as Moses had gazed upon the land of Canaan. These mountains would be the headquarters of the Eighth Army Corps during the battles of the Transjordan. We would gaze with great sadness and melancholy at the hills of Jerusalem crowned by the hospice of Augusta Victoria.[16]

Everywhere, the building was spotlessly clean. Palm trees and phoenixes adorned its rooms and corridors. The cleanliness and maintenance of the building was the duty of an elderly and authoritarian Sister Superior called Sister Theodora. Cemal Pasha had sent out a circular order that even he was under the authority of the sister when it came to matters of cleanliness and order in the building. This had greatly increased the authority of the sister. . . .[17] Von Kress stated in his memoirs,

> On June 29, 1915 I had returned from the desert to Jerusalem. Cemal Pasha had temporarily removed his headquarters to Ayn Sofar in Lebanon. Thus we were lodged in the hospice of Augusta Victoria. The building was so clean that nobody would believe that a large general staff had been there for months.

A little anecdote

In the room used by three reserve officers Falih Rıfkı (Atay), Süleyman Saib (Kıran) and Nuri Sabit (Akça), a cotton sheet had been sliced by a knife. The Sister Superior wanted to know how the sheet came to be cut. The residents of the room did not know. Every day the sisters would come and ask. The officers were so wearied of these continuous inquiries that they offered to pay for the sheet. But the Sister Superior's aim was not to gain compensation for the loss of the sheet, but to know what had happened so she could put it in her report. One morning, a sister entering the room early saw that an officer was shaving and wiping his razor on a sheet. It became clear how the sheet had been cut. The Sister Superior added the following line to the directives that hung in each room: "It is forbidden to shave in bed."[18]

---

16 Ibid., 60. Jerusalem would fall to the British on December 9, 1917.
17 Ibid. Sister Theodora may well be the sister that Falih Rıfkı mentions as "the drummer" in the foreword to the 1956 edition of *Zeytindağı*. See above.
18 Ibid., 61. This boarding-school-like atmosphere is also reflected in Falih Rıfkı's memoirs.

The Augusta Victoria Hospice was a temple of peace and industry. The Fourth Army directed five fronts for three years from here; the Sinai front, the Hijaz front, the Coastal front, the Syrian front, and the internal front.[19]

The Arab revolt

. . . In 1915 most of the forces of the Fourth Army had been sent elsewhere. All that remained in Syria were the 23rd and 27th divisions, the coast guard, the gendarmerie, and the staff (officers) of the Eighth and Ninth Armies. All these forces were native and most of the officers were Arabs.

We were receiving the following intelligence:

The Arab officers likened the Ottoman state to a sinking ship and they carried out propaganda to the effect that they should save themselves from going down with it. There were [secret] oath ceremonies taking place among the Arab officers in the units. Turkish officers were to be killed one by one in their sleep, revolutionary committees were to be formed, Syria's withdrawal from the war would be announced and a separate peace would be made with France. The information we were getting from various sources supported this. . . .[20]

[*At this point Ali Fuad cites T. E. Lawrence on the possibility of an Allied landing in Iskenderun (Alexandretta). It should be noted that Lawrence was in favour of such a landing, which was seriously considered as an option. The idea was scrapped because of French resistance to a landing in a zone they considered to be in their sphere of influence.*][21]

The Fourth Army Headquarters: an isolated island in a sea of revolt

In Syria, apart from infantry and cavalry units quartered at headquarters, our forces consisted of a Mevlevi batallion, and a company of refugee

---

19 It is unclear what Ali Fuad Bey means by the "interior front" (*iç cephe*). It could be a reference to police measures against various targets like Arab nationalism or Zionism.

20 Ibid., 65. All this is not far from the truth. From the earliest days of the war two secret societies, *Al-Ahd* for military and *Al-Fattat* for civilians had been formed. *Al-Fattat* was active in Syria as an underground organization from the earliest days of the war although it is extremely unlikely that there were plans to murder Turkish officers in their sleep. See Rogan, *The Fall of the Ottomans*, 278. See also section on the execution of the Arab patriots in the Introduction.

21 Faulkner, *Lawrence of Arabia's War*, 170–171.

volunteers from the Deliorman region of Bulgaria, these two were the only Turkish troops in Syria. The Augusta Victoria hospice was as like an isolated island in a sea of revolt.

The situation was delicate and dangerous. One needed to act with caution and tact yet with determination and despatch to take the necessary measures. Cemal Pasha established contact with Enver Pasha. He arranged an order by the Ministry of War for the transfer of some two hundred officers from the Fourth Army to the Dardanelles to replace the officers who had fallen there. After these officers had left, the same number would be sent to the Fourth Army from various units and from Istanbul.

A list of some one hundred and fifty officers of known nationalist leanings was drawn up, and in order to cover up the real aim, some fifty Turkish officers were added to the list. The two hundred names were sent to the Ministry of War. The Ministry gave them new appointments, in groups of fifty. In the space of two to three weeks two hundred officers were sent to Istanbul.[22]

A revolution can be made only by "intelligence." The probable leader of the revolution

The revolt had to be led by someone of intelligence. The most intelligent of the Arab officers was Major Yasin Hilmi, the chief of staff of the Twelfth Army Corps. He would be the probable leader of such a revolt. The potential leader had to be removed from Syria. Fahri Pasha did not trust his own chief of staff and was suspicious of his actions.[23]

There was also [a potential leader in] Captain Mohammed Bey, the Damascene who was the chief of intelligence at Army Headquarters. But both these staff officers were valuable; service was expected of them in

---

22 Ali Fuad Erden, *Birinci Dünya Savaşında Suriye Hatıraları*, 66.

23 Ibid., 67. This is Yasin al Hashimi, the future Prime Minister of Iraq. As it turned out, Yasin al-Hashimi remained loyal to the Ottomans to the very end, refusing command of the Arab army during the war. He was "distrustful of the British and the Hashemites, and disdainful of the Arab Revolt, he had reportedly believed that Arab officers in the Damascus Army should spearhead any uprising against the Turks." After the war "he did receive his commission from the Arab government and . . . did everything possible to consolidate the Arab military under his sole command. . . ." A British intelligence report summed him up as follows: "His Turkish training has stamped him Turkish, the military Teutonized Turk, not the Effendi. . . ." Galvin, *Divided Loyalties*, 89.

the Ottoman army. In order to send them away tactfully, they were both given three years' wartime promotion pay. Yasin Hilmi Bey was sent to an important post in Istanbul and Captain Mohammed Bey was sent to another post in Syria. They had not yet gained entitlement of wartime promotion pay, and for the first time in the Fourth Army they were the ones to receive the highest amount.

Later in the war, Yasin Hilmi would be division commander in the army corps that was sent to Galicia. After that, he and his division would be transferred to Palestine, and—while I was on furlough—he would temporarily replace me as the Commander of the Eighth Army Corps in the battles on the Transjordan front. His younger brother, Lieutenant Taha, was the chief of staff of the Seventh Army in Yemen and he did his duty well until the end of the war. After the collapse of the Ottoman State he went to Baghdad and became army chief of staff. Captain Mehmed Bey was appointed chief of staff on an army corps in Ma'an and carried out his duties loyally and with success to the very end.[24]

Politicians who poisoned minds

It had been reported that some Arab politicians (the ex-MP for Beirut, Rıda Bey al-Sulh, and Abd al Qarim al Khalil) had been preparing an uprising in the regions of Sayda and Sur. This area was the least watched stretch of the coast. There was not even one company of troops there. There were only weak patrols of gendarmes. From there revolutionaries could easily establish contact with the enemy warships in the offing, and having poisoned the minds of the people of the area to create an uprising, help a landing at night from the enemy ships. They could then hold the mountainous ground to the north and would thus be able to defend themselves from attack from the north, east, and south.

After investigations showed that these men had poisoned the minds of the population and made preparations for a rising they were sent up before a court martial. By the end of August their trial was over. They were hanged.

The owner of the *Al Mufid* newspaper, Abdelghani al Uraysi and his two friends, fearing that the trial would reveal their complicity, fled to the

---

24 Ali Fuad Erden, *Birinci Dünya Savaşında Suriye Hatıraları*, 68.

desert. After three or four months they were captured by the sheikh of the Ruwale tribe and handed over to Cemal Pasha.[25]

The revolt in the Hijaz was not an Arab revolt

The attempt at an Arab revolt [in Syria] was nipped in the bud. After this attempt at revolution in 1915 there were to be no other events that would disrupt order in Syria and Palestine. The revolt in the Hijaz was not an Arab revolt. It was the revolt of the Sharif of Mecca, Sharif Husayn, and the Bedouin who had been bought by British spies, British gold, British wheat and rice. There were but a few officers from Baghdad and Damascus (such as the Prime Minister of Iraq, Nuri al-Said) at the headquarters of the rebels, they were the ones who tried to make it appear as a [general] Arab Revolt. [26]

Mining the Canal

The best way to harass shipping in the Canal was to mine it. Cemal Pasha had mines brought from the Ministry of the Navy. Each mine weighed 250 kilograms. A camel could carry only 150 kilograms. A special sling was made to carry a mine slung between two camels and this was how the mines were carried in the desert.

We had learned from the Bedouin that it was possible to reach the shore in the zone of overflow between Port Said and Al-Kantara, by paths that only they knew. It was thought that the British vigilance in the overflow zone would be relatively lax, accordingly the attempt was made to place a mine there. The commander for this task was to be accompanied by a German first lieutenant who had been a pilot on ships transiting the canal in peacetime. A unit made up of picked troops managed to lay the mine, unseen by enemy troops, on the night of April 8–9, 1915. Although the mine had been carried as far as the swampland on camels, crossing the swamp proved extremely difficult. Three days after the mine was laid the

25 Ibid., 68. Ali Fuad makes a mistake here, Rıda Bey al-Sulh because of his young age was not hanged but exiled. It seems there were indeed some badly organized plans along these lines. See the section on the execution of the Arab patriots in the Introduction.
26 Ibid., 69. In actual fact, there were many more Arab defectors among Faisal's ranks. Yet, Ali Fuad's point that the majority of the Arab officers remained loyal is valid.

British saw the footprints and discovered the mine. It seemed that the fuse had malfunctioned as three ships had gone over the mine.

But at least the knowledge that we were capable of mining the canal worried the canal authorities who stopped all transit at night and in daytime they only allowed passage after they had inspected the shore for footprints. . . .[27]

The defenceless mines were easily found by the enemy. It was impossible to defend the mines. It was clear that the British would inspect the canal daily before allowing passage. Yet, because the aim was simply to harass the enemy we continued to deploy mines.

In April, Gondos with 50 troops moved from Nahil to Shaluf and on the night of April 26 managed to lay two mines on the 125th km of the canal.[28]

On June 27, 1915, a reconnaissance unit commanded by first lieutenant Sırrı deployed a mine on the 133th km of the canal and a British ship struck it and sank, closing the canal. The officer in charge reported:

> . . . The land was smooth as far as the coast. I hid the camels behind sand dunes eight km from the shore. I loaded the mine on two quiet camels and proceeded on foot. Meanwhile we had to wait two hours for a ship with a searchlight to pass. It was full moon. At 23:00 we reached the shore of the canal. I sent the camels back. It took two hours to arm the mine. . . . At exactly midnight I gave the order to walk into the water to two soldiers and four Bedouin. I led in my uniform in water up to my throat. In order to prevent the enemy from spotting the mine from our footprints we proceeded north for one hour in the water for approximately one km. Then the soldiers and the Bedouin dragged the mine for twenty five minutes to the transit channel marked by buoys. Meanwhile, a motorboat with a machine gun was passing within twenty meters of the coast. Because everyone was extremely quiet it did not see anything and disappeared southward. At 1:20 hours the unit in the water returned. I remained on the coast with 15 soldiers.

---

27 Ibid., 77.
28 Ibid., 73. Ali Fuad identifies Gondos as, "[A]n enterprising and brave young Hungarian volunteer who had been an engineer on the oil rigs in the area before the war." One of the most remarkable silences in Ali Fuad's account is that he makes no mention of Kuşcubaşı Eşref Bey, who, according to his own account, was the mastermind behind the Canal Offensive. See Fortna, *The Circassian*, 140–165. Even if he was prone to exaggerate, there is little doubt that Eşref was in the thick of the action. See his sketch map on p. 164.

A mid-size mail ship crossed directly over the mine and half an hour later another ship passed, the mine did not explode. I left a small reconnaissance detachment and returned to the camels. On the morning of June 27, two powerful explosions were heard. The reconnaissance unit reported that they had seen a funnel and two masts sticking out of the water. As the mine was 3.5–4 meters from the sea bed, the ships with shallow draught had missed the mine.

The ship that sank was the *Teiroisas*.[29]

Cemal Pasha Boulevard

. . . The method employed by Cemal Pasha for road construction was quite simple. The required distance would be measured, the amount of time necessary for completion, taking into account the nature of the terrain, would be calculated, and to this some twenty percent more would be added. For each stretch of road, a certain individual or someone holding a certain post would be appointed and given the responsibility of completion by a certain date. They would be given all they needed in terms of tools, materials, etc. To the official order written by the chief of staff of the Fourth Army, Cemal Pasha would add the following sentence: "On that day I will inspect the road by motorcar. Where the car is obliged to stop [short of the required target] the engineer who is responsible will be buried." All the roads were completed before the target time and no engineers were buried. . . .[30]

I had heard it said that "the roads in in the Sinai were made of the bones of Syrian workers." This is a calumnious lie. During the First World War, the labor battalions in the Sinai were better fed and cared for than the labor battalions of Istanbul. . . .[31]

. . . Together with the roads that were needed for the war, Cemal Pasha also constructed roads that could be considered a luxury. In Jaffa he had built a boulevard 35 meters wide and 800 meters long lined with dates and orange trees. In Damascus a boulevard 45 meters wide and 650 meters long called Cemal Pasha Boulevard. In Beirut he built a perfectly appointed

---

29 Ibid., 80–81. The extreme difficulty and danger of walking in water up to one's chest dragging a primed mine indicates how seriously officers like Lieutenant Sırrı were about fulfilling their orders to harass the British.

30 Ibid., 88, 89. These tallies with the account given by Falih Rıfkı above.

31 Ibid. This is clearly a disingenius assessment of the conditions of the labor battalion, most of whom were simply worked to death.

park, a club, and a casino. The roads that were to be constructed would be marked with red on the city map and the next morning construction would begin.

These boulevards and parks were, in times of peace, decorative symbols of civilization, but in times of war they were useless. It would have been better to use the engineers, architects, and the hundreds of workers who were employed at these works for national defence.[32]

Waterworks. [Logistical preparations in the desert.]

[Ali Fuad Bey gives detailed descriptions of how wells were constructed in the desert]

. . . An Austrian expert together with two artesian teams were brought in. And an expert called Von Grieve was brought in from Germany, who was capable of finding water by means of a "divining stick" called a "*baguette divinatoire.*" I would imagine that Moses's staff which he used to find water in the Sinai must have been something like this. . . . Von Grieve was paid seven gold liras a day for his work. He was somewhat elderly, naïve, and capricious. To make sure that he did not fall ill in the desert we did our best to make him comfortable and fed him on delicacies (*kuş sütüyle beslerdik*) such as artichokes, pineapple, and asparagus. But he was not really useful. We made better use of the local water diviners. . . .[33]

[*Commenting on the railway, water supply, and sophisticated infrastructure that was prepared in the desert, İsmet İnönü wrote in a letter to Ali Fuad Bey:*]

". . . From camels to *dekovils* to the railway, all the primitive and advanced tools are in your magical hands; it is as if Noah and Edison are dancing arm in arm."[34]

The important staging posts in the Sinai desert had become little settlements with gardens, reservoirs, buildings, white and khaki tents. These settlements were connected by good roads that motorcars could use.

---

32 Ibid., 90. Ali Fuad Bey was obviously impervious to the symbolic nature of this construction work. Zeynep Çelik, *Empire, Architecture and the City. French Ottoman Encounters 1830–1914* (Seattle: University of Washington Press, 2008).

33 Ali Fuad Erden, *Birinci Dünya Savaşında Suriye Hatıraları*, 91.

34 Ibid., 95. Ismet İnönü was to become the second president of the Turkish republic after the death of Mustafa Kemal in 1938. A *dekovil* is a man-powered form of transport used in railway construction.

All of this was the result of one-and-a-half year's labor. All of these things are examples of what human will and intelligence can do in the dry and merciless desert. The *Le Temps* newspaper had run a leading story where it was stated: "The Turks whose habitual indolence was whipped by the Germans have achieved gigantic accomplishments in the Sinai desert."[35] The first half of this sentence is a total lie and the second half is entirely correct. The Turks were not whipped by the Germans. To do all this work they used Turkish engineers, German engineers, Austrian engineers, and Jewish agricultural experts from Palestine. The fact that the enemy qualified what was done as gigantic accomplishments shows that it was really just that.

The Turk in question was Cemal Pasha. It was Cemal Pasha's determination and creative will that overcame all difficulties, removed all obstacles, and created the "gigantic accomplishments" that seemed to be a dream. In the spring of 1916 Enver Pasha, who was inspecting the desert, said, "I did not believe that the desert could change this much." Enver Pasha was very stingy with praise and thanks. Coming from him, these words were more valuable than coming from the enemy. But the greatest praise would come from Ismet Bey, the Chief of Logistics of General Headquarters who declared, "I learned determination and persistence from the Fourth Army." Cemal Pasha was greatly touched by these words.[36]

Cemal Pasha: a man of action, an administrator, a planner, and organizer

. . . Everyone feared Cemal Pasha. No one mentioned him as "Cemal Pasha" or simply by his name. He was "His Excellency the Commanding Pasha" (*Kumandan Paşa Hazretleri*) or "The Great Cemal Pasha" (*Büyük Cemal Paşa*). This was not just to distinguish him from Mersinli Cemal Pasha who was called "Little Cemal Pasha" (*Küçük Cemal Paşa*), but because people genuinely believed he was great. The German officers in Syria when speaking amongst themselves, would refer to him as "Seiner Exzellenz Marschal."

. . . Cemal Pasha knew how to punish, reward, terrify, and forgive.

---

35 Ibid., 99: "*Les Turcs dont l'indolence coutumière a été fouetté par les Allemands ont réalisé dans le désert de Sinai un oeuvre gigantesque.*" French in the original.
36 Ibid., 100. At this point in the text Ali Fuad Bey gives an extremely detailed account of the preparations for the second campaign against the canal.

He was, not officially but in fact, the General Governor of Syria and Palestine and the absolute ruler (*Suriye ve Filistin'in Umumi Valisi ve hakim-i mutlak*).

The authority he had achieved in Syria was fantastic. On his visits to Beirut and Damascus, the cities and towns would be festooned with flags. A flag was hung not just from every house and shop, but on each floor of each building. Cities and towns were covered in red for Cemal Pasha. I heard it from Sheikh Es'ad Shuqayr that someone once told him, "I would much rather hang out a flag than hang myself."[37]

. . . Cemal Pasha liked being popular, being loved by the people. In Jerusalem he had issued the following order, "[A]fter Friday prayers I will be receiving the petitions of the people at the Mosque of Omar. Anybody having a wish should come to the mosque." After prayers Cemal Pasha would kneel in front of the pulpit (*minber*), accompanied by his chief aide, surrounded by the *Mutasarrıf* of Jerusalem, the Chief of Police, the Commander of the Gendarmes, the Chief of the Conscription Bureau, and the Military Commander, who would all kneel around him. Opposite him, kneeling, petition in hand, the people! Cemal Pasha would read the petitions, indicate on each one the action to be taken, would hand it to the official concerned; everyone's affairs would be settled on the spot. This was a very practical way of conducting business. The Second Caliph Omar had used the same method.[38]

Cemal Pasha tried to project himself as cruel, and in appearances he was not wrong. In a letter to me dated March 27, 1916 he said, "*Inshallah* soon you will become Army Commander and you will replace our cruel and merciless administration by a charming administration that will distribute roses and jasmin." On another occasion he told me, "[N]ext to a cruel man like me one needs a man like you." By "a man like you" he meant, "soothing, attenuating, softening." He himself had asked for such "a man" and he himself continued to keep this man by his side. . . .[39]

---

37 Ibid., 105.
38 Ibid. This was precisely the practice that drew the suspicion of Istanbul, where some circles insinuated that Cemal was setting himself up as an independent ruler in Syria. This is referred to above in the memoirs of Falih Rıfkı.
39 Ibid., 106. There was in fact considerable tension between Cemal and his second in command. This was referred to in the memoirs of Falih Rıfkı above. The irony is palpable in the quote.

. . . In Morocco, Marshal Lyautey had applied his own principle which was, "to show force in order not to need to use it."[40] Cemal Pasha had no such formula. He would threaten, but there would be no need to fulfil the threat, his orders were obeyed in time, even before the allotted time. Cemal Pasha practiced favouritism, in fact, he liked favouritism. Talat Pasha had once said to me about him, "he works day and night . . . but he is too prone to make exceptions." What Talat Pasha meant by "exceptions" was favouritism. Once, during the war, I had complained to Cemal Pasha [the lesser] about the favouritism of Cemal Pasha. He had replied, "What to do? That is Cemal Pasha. He cannot change."

Cemal Pasha was the uncrowned emperor of Syria and Western Arabia (half a dozen countries emerged from the zone he ruled). But this uncrowned emperor was not rich and did not become rich. If he had wanted to he could become Croesus. The sources of wealth of Syria and Palestine (oil, silk, lemons, oranges, coffee) could have been sent to Istanbul by the wagonload on trains that went empty to the north.

In Istanbul during the Great War there were no lemons, oranges, or tangerines. . . . There were hundreds of thousands of gold coins in the safe of the army, and the commander of the Fourth Army had access to hundreds of thousands of liras in secret funds. These were all funds that were at his complete discretion. Cemal Pasha received his salary in gold; and maybe he paid for his household provisions in paper. He awarded gold to many. He paid them from secret funds. He allocated them coaches in trains. But he never allocated himself anything. He only gave, never took. . . .[41]

Cemal Pasha was not killed by the Armenians

. . . Cemal Pasha was killed in Tbilisi in 1920 while returning from Europe to Afghanistan. In appearance he was killed by "the Armenians." But in my

---

40 Ibid. "Il faut montrer sa force pour ne pas avoir à s'en servir." "Lyautey was feted as a great innovator, whose concern for preserving indigenous customs and traditions was seen by his contemporaries as compassionate colonialism." Eugene Rogan, *The Arabs: A History* (New York: Basic Books, 2009), 220.

41 Ali Fuad Erden, *Birinci Dünya Savaşında Suriye Hatıraları*, 107. The reference here is to the widespread corruption of the black market. During the war a whole class of disreputable entrepreneurs came into being called the "coach barons" (*vagon zengini*) who used privileged access to rolling stock to enrich themselves. See Zafer Toprak, *Türkiye'de Milli Iktisat 1908–1918* [The National Economy in Turkey] (Istanbul: Yurt Yayınları, 1982).

opinion it was not the Armenians who killed Cemal Pasha. Someone made the Armenians kill Cemal Pasha. Those who killed him were in turn killed by those who made them do it. They were killed because the dead do not speak.

May Cemal Pasha rest in peace! In our national history he is Cemal Pasha whom Allah has taken into his grace (*Rahmetli*). After his death he has deserved the honour of being remembered with prayers of thanks. He is buried in the honoured soil of Erzurum, that land of heroes, the border fortress.[42]

The defense of the coast

The coast [that was in the Fourth Army zone] stretched from Silifke to Gazze and was 900 kilometers long. The most likely spots for an enemy landing were the Gulf of Iskendurun, the coast of Beirut, the gulf of Acre and Haifa, and Jaffa. Any landing that would take place in the Gulf of Iskenderun would aim at cutting off the communications between Istanbul and the Third, Fourth, and Sixth Armies.

A major landing was not expected between Tripoli and Iskenderun. It was possible that Tripoli could be used as a support base for a landing that would take place on the Lebanese coast. Any enemy landing on the Lebanese coast would most likely seek to conquer Lebanon and cut railway communications. Any landing in Palestine would aim at preventing the campaign against Egypt by controlling the railway and conquering Jerusalem. . . .

. . . In 1915, the total effective strength of the Fourth Army was five weak divisions made up of native troops. There was hardly any heavy artillery. We could not directly oppose a strong enemy landing. Therefore, the coast could not be our first line of defence. It was bound to be a security zone.

These were the duties of the units in the security zone:

To prevent the landing of relatively weak forces.

To delay and hinder the landing of more substantial forces.

---

42 Ali Fuad Erden, *Birinci Dünya Savaşında Suriye Hatıraları*, 108. Cemal Pasha was assassinated on July 25, 1922 in Tbilisi by an Armenian hit team organized by the revolutionary Dashnaks. Eric Bogosian, *Operation Nemesis: The Assasination Plot that Avenged the Armenian Genocide* (New York, Boston and London: Little Brown and Co., 2015), 257–258.

Our main forces were to use all resources at their disposal to defend previously prepared defensive positions. These defensive positions were to be as close to the coast as was strategically possible. These positions were to be defended as strongly as possible and when in danger of being outflanked or pierced they would be abandoned following orders from the army corps. Behind these first lines of defence, second and third lines were to be prepared and defended as strongly as possible. The last positions of defence would be defended by divisions who would be ordered to fight to the last man. . . .[43]

Zeytun and Urfa [Armenian uprisings]

In the spring of 1915 there occurred an Armenian revolt parallel to the Arab revolt. But the Armenian revolt did not remain in the domain of thought and theory. The Armenians did not wait for the British to land in the Gulf or Iskenderun, or for the Russians to march on the same area. They revolted.[44]

The first acts of rebellion occurred at Zeytun in the northern end of our army zone. Zeytun has an important place in the history of the Armenian revolt. In Zeytun the Armenians attacked the gendarmes, rescued the Armenian deserters, took the weapons of the gendarmes and cut the telegraph wires. On March 11, 1915 they ambushed a unit of gendarmes who were escorting a shipment of ammunition from Marash. They then took over the government buildings and fortified the houses and monasteries in the Teke quarter.

On March 17, the Commander of the Fourth Army issued an order forbidding the Turkish population from taking part in any way [in the putting down of the revolt]. The order also specified that the Armenian population not taking part in the revolt was not to be harmed in any way. The order specified: "Let the people be in peace. The population is forbidden to take part even by helping the troops. Those Muslims who harm Armenians will be treated as outlaws." The revolt at Zeytun was suppressed.

On March 26, Cemal Pasha wrote to the Ministry of the Interior; "The rebels have been suppressed, let us resettle two-thirds of the Armenians of

---

43 Ali Fuad Erden, *Birinci Dünya Savaşında Suriye Hatıraları*, 109–110.
44 Ibid., 113. It is entirely disingenuous on the part of Ali Fuad to draw parallels between the so-called "Armenian revolt" and the Arab Revolt. He greatly exaggerates the former and artificially minimizes the latter.

Zeytun in flat plains heavily populated with Muslims and give them land."
The first convoy was sent to Konya. The Ministry of the Interior did not
approve of the deportations of the Armenians to Konya and for them to
be settled together there. It ordered that those Armenians deported from
Iskenderun, Dörtyol, Adana, Hacin, Zeytun, and Sis were to be sent to
south east Aleppo, Urfa, and Der Zor. . . .[45]

In Urfa, during the night of March 29–30 [1915], the Armenians
began to fire into the air. The next morning they fired on the gendarmes
who were conducting searches for arms. Bells were rung in the great
church. The Armenian population gathered in the church yard. The
hidden weapons were brought out. The *fedais* from Zeytun, Samsun,
Bitlis, Antep, and Marash together with deserters and locals formed an
armed force. The streets were closed off. Everybody was given a task
and rebellion was declared. . . . The rebels had calculated that because
the state was engaged in war, it would not be able to send a large force
against them. They had likewise calculated that against the weak local
forces they could hold out for seven or eight months until the arrival of
Russian forces.

When it became clear that the local forces were not enough to put
down the stubborn resistance of the Armenians, on September 27 it was
decided to send a force of regular army against them. This was to consist
of one regiment of infantry, one company of cavalry and one team of field
artillery with a 12-centimeter mortar. The force was to be commanded by
Fahreddin Pasha, the commander of the Twelfth Army corps.

The government forces asked the Armenians to surrender. When they
made insulting replies, the process of bringing them into line started. . . .
The Armenians fought tenaciously in Urfa. The uprising came to an end on
October 18.[46]

---

45   Ibid., 114. The "uprising" in Zeytun was one of the excuses for the infamous "temporary
     law" of May 27, 1915 which was to be the basis for the Armenian Genocide. In fact,
     the so-called uprising was a self-defense measure undertaken by radical Armenians,
     often at loggerheads with more moderate community leaders. The repressive measures
     taken did not in any way distinguish between active and passive Armenians, as Ali Fuad
     claims. Suny, *They Can Live in the Desert but Nowhere Else*, 252–253
46   Ali Fuad Erden, *Birinci Dünya Savaşında Suriye Hatıraları*, 117, 118. The resistance and
     courage of the Armenians of Urfa was to impress Fahreddin Pasha to such an extent that
     he was to use them as a role model for his own besieged troops in Medina in 1917. See
     below Naci Kıcıman's memoirs.

Armenian deportations

[*The general order for the deportation of Armenians was given by the "temporary law" (kanun-u muvvakat) of May 27, 1915.*]

These were the views of the Fourth Army Command on the deportations.

(1) Every Armenian as an individual is our citizen. The aim of the deportation is solely to reduce their concentration in areas where they can constitute a danger and render them harmless minorities.
(2) The procedure is to start from the coast and proceed upcountry.
(3) The convoys will proceed in an orderly manner and will be settled in security. All loss of personal rights will be avoided, any interference driven by hatred and vengeance will be prevented.
(4) The immigrants will only be settled in areas where they will the able to sustain themselves.
(5) The wounded, weak, seriously ill, and those who care for them will be exempted from deportation.

The Fourth Army determined that the immigrants would be settled in the districts of Hama, Hauran, Karak, and the south of Aleppo. The immigrants would be settled in the cities, towns, and villages in these areas. The order sent to the provinces on June 20, 1916 read: "Do not leave the Armenian people without bread, shelter, or graves. Lodge them in houses in groups of not more than ten. The sick will be left where they are until they recover. . . ."[47]

. . . In Adana some Circassians who attacked a convoy were shot in front of them. On June 19 Cemal Pasha issued the following order to the governors and military commanders: "It is being heard that the convoys are being treated cruelly. Acts such as these wound our national honor. For now I am issuing a warning. In the event of continuation or repetition I will send you before a court martial."

Bahaettin Şakir Bey sent Cemal Pasha a telegram: "We are sending ninety five percent of the immigrants from Trabzon, Erzurum, Sivas, Bitlis, Mamuretulaziz and Diyarbekir to the south of Mosul. We hear that you are

---

47 Ibid., 119–120. "Graves" here presumably refers to the instructions to respect the dead. This is an extremely sanitized version of what actually happened during the Armenian Genocide. It is interesting that Erden uses the word "immigrant" (göçmen) to refer to the Armenian deportees of the genocide, implying that their displacement was voluntary.

sending them to Aleppo." In reply Cemal Pasha scolded Bahaettin Şakir and warned him not to send any further telegrams. He also sent a telegram to the chief of staff to the effect of "I do not know any governor or army commander of that name. On what authority is this person meddling in my affairs?"[48]

. . . To send hundred thousands of people to far-off destinations, without proper preparation or organization resembles the migration of the tribes of ancient times. The staging posts on the roads, which were the supply lines of three armies, those of the Caucasus, Syria, and Iraq fronts, became infested with contagious diseases. The miserable conditions of the immigrant convoys made them the perfect conduit for the spread of yellow fever and typhoid. The convoys spread these diseases all along the supply lines and from there they spread to the armies. What happened? Among the armies and the population there were as many deaths if not more than the dead immigrants.[49]

. . . In order to improve the conditions of the immigrants (göçmen) who were to be settled in the area of the Fourth Army, a commission was created consisting of Hüseyin Kazım, [and others]. This commission did its job very well. The immigrants were settled in the towns and villages in the Fourth Army zone. Nobody was sent to the desert and nobody suffered even a nosebleed. A colony was formed in Damascus. These people came to control local commerce. Trained artisans were employed in the military factories together with their families. . . .

Cemal Pasha started an orphanage at Antoura monastery for one thousand immigrant children under the direction of eye doctor Captain Lütfi Bey. This was a perfect orphanage. Orphans and homeless children were well taken care of fed and cured. They were educated and very well cared for. Another orphanage was opened in Damascus and in Aleppo under the direction of the daughter of Altunyan and a German nurse.

The two hundred thousand Armenians currently living in Syria are these immigrants. The late Dr. Nazım told Emir Shakib Arslan about me saying, "he is the person who made a gift of two hundred thousand

---

48 Ibid. 121. By "south of Mosul" Şakir is referring to the infamous killing fields of Der Zor in the Syrian desert. Kevorkian, *The History of the Armenian Genocide*, 244.

49 Ali Fuad Erden, *Birinci Dünya Savaşında Suriye Hatıraları*, 121 This is a close as Ali Fuad Bey gets to criticizing the genocide, and even here, the Armenians are seen more of a health hazard than a suffering mass of humans.

Armenians to Syria." No, I made no such gift. I was merely following the orders of my superior officer. . . .[50]

"For Reasons of State" (*Raison d'Etat. Hikmet-i Idare*)[51]

An Armenian travelling in Aleppo was robbed on the road and his gold watch was taken. Cemal Pasha ordered the police chief to find the culprit immediately. One hour later, a resident of Aleppo who had taken the watch was arrested. Cemal Pasha sent an order to the legal advisor of the Fourth Army: "This man will be hung immediately! Write the order."[52] The legal advisor Vassaf Bey had just arrived that very day at headquarters. He was stunned by this order as soon as he arrived. Terrified, he muttered something about a trial, due process . . . Cemal Pasha cut him off: "He will be hung by administrative fiat (*hikmet-i idare*)." Did the term "administrative fiat" serve to assuage the conscience of the worthy jurist? A little later, the man was hung in front of the Baron Hotel where the jurist was staying. On the placard pinned to his chest it said, "[H]as been executed for violating the security of the communication lines behind the front."

I knew the French term, "Reasons of State" (*Raison d'Etat*). Captain Dreyfus had been brought before a court martial for reasons of state. After years in prison, Dreyfus had been tried again and acquitted. With this [acquittal], French law was acting on the principle of "there can be no Reason of State that is above the law" (*Il n'y a pas Raison d'Etat qui prime le droit*). But I had never heard the term "administrative fiat." They had

---

50 Ibid., 122. Hüseyin Kazım was alienated from this commission because he was seen as "too soft" on the Armenians. He makes no mention of his role in the memoirs cited above. Dr. Nazım was another leading perpetrator of the genocide. The picture painted here by Ali Fuad is in fact a far rosier image than the actual fate of the Armenians in the Fourth Army district. It has to be said that Cemal Pasha was considered the more moderate of the Enver, Talat, Cemal triumvirate when it came to the Armenians. It is also interesting that Ali Fuad makes no mention of Halide Edib and her role in the Antoura orphanage. Lutfi Kırdar also served as Director of the Antoura orphanage with Edib. He later became Vali and Head of Municipality of Istanbul in 1938–1949.

51 Ibid., 124–125. In French in the original. The "note of the editor" by Alpay Kabacali states: "in terms like "*hikmet-i hukumet, hikmet-i idare*, the word '*hikmet*' is used to mean "unknown or secret." It is used in the sense of "matters beyond the understanding of the government, the administration, or other parties." As is well known this has no place in a modern state with the rule of law."

52 It is highly unlikely that the man who was hung was actually the culprit. This is as close as Ali Fuad gets to criticizing Cemal Pasha.

not taught us this at the Military Academy. I do not know when or where Cemal Pasha got this term or what its legal foundations were.[53]

The coastal offensive. [The Allied blockade of the Syrian coast]

All throughout the war British, French and Russian warships (battle cruisers, torpedo boats and gunships) patrolled the coast of Syria. According to the order of the army command, the units of coastal watchers or security forces were not to fire on these ships, no matter how close they came to the shore. If the enemy attempted to send light craft, steamboats, or any craft bearing troops, (except for boats bearing a white flag carrying personnel charged with parley) they were to be fired upon immediately. Along the whole coast from Mersin to Gaza, enemy warships fired upon shore defences, police stations, barracks, tents, railway stations, rail and road bridges, gas depots, flour mills and oil distilleries, electric plants, windmills, small boats in shelters, sailboats plying the coast, any transport vehicles along the coast (carts, camels, horses), and the German consulates in coastal towns. Ships carrying aircraft accompanied these patrols, and airplanes from these ships bombarded rail bridges, stations, and other targets that were out of the range of the warships.

In the first months of the war the enemy would land troops at night and attempt to destroy railway bridges and cut telegraph lines. . . .

On August 24, 1915, a letter bearing the signature of Rear Admiral Dario from the warship *Jean d'Arc* in Port Said sent to the authorities in Jaffa stated, "As of noon August 24, 1915 all the Ottoman coasts from 36'50 degrees north, 38'18 east, and 31'20 north, 33'13 east are officially declared under blockade. All neutral shipping in this zone are to leave it in three days. Any ship attempting to break the blockade will be fired upon."

Thus the whole Mediterranean coast from Marmaris to Gaza was placed under blockade.[54]

---

53 Ali Fuad is referring here to the famous *Affaire Dreyfus* in 1894 when a Jewish officer in the French army was accused of spying for the Germans. The trial became a *cause celebre* in France dividing the country into *Dreyfusards* and *anti-Dreyfusards*.

54 Ibid., 126–127. The French controlled the island of Arwad just off the Syrian port of Tartus throughout the war and the island became a center for espionage. The leading figure in French espionage based on the island was the Lebanese businessman Bechara Buwari. The blockade was one of the main reasons for the devastating famine in Lebanon during the war. Fawaz, *A Land of Aching Hearts*, 88–93, 150–151.

Falih Rıfkı [Atay]

At headquarters we had a writer. The writer was Falih Rıfkı. Falih Rıfkı was not a linguist; yet his writings were pure prose itself, and most beautiful prose. It would have been possible to use his writing as a lesson in prose writing.

Just as Cemal Pasha admired my writing, unaware that he was actually admiring the style of Saint Just, I liked, and continue to like Falih's writing. For forty years I read him every day.[55]

After we had returned from the Canal Campaign and settled in the Augusta Victoria Hospice that had become headquarters, Cemal Pasha's aide presented a young reserve officer and stated, "This is Falih Rıfkı Efendi. His Excellency the Commanding Pasha ordered that he be appointed to the cipher service." At that moment I experienced a revolt in my soul. It was not appropriate to mix intelligence and literature with the cipher service, that is to say, with the inner circle of staff officers. Unable to restrain myself, I told the aide, "No!"

If the aid had gone to the Commander Pasha and told him, "The chief of staff did not accept your order, he said no," the Commander would have been extremely angry; I needed to go myself to explain. I told the Army Commander, "If you approve, let us put Falih Rıfkı Efendi in the Second Service. Let him be the director of the section of the service that deals with administrative and political affairs. At the same time he can carry out the personal correspondence of Your Excellency. Thus he will be two people, one attached to the army chief of staff, the other your personal secretary directly seconded to Your Excellency." The Pasha liked this solution and said, "Yes!" Falih Rıfkı was not appointed to the cipher service. He became the chief of the Third Section of the Second Service. He was given an office. In that room there was one officer but two personages. Every one of these personages had his own filing cabinet, his table, his chair, and separate files and file containers. Falih Rıfkı carried out the duties of these two person-ages with intelligence and ability.

Cemal Pasha had a great liking for him and he trusted him. He would send some of the confidential documents coming from the Grand Vizier

---

55 Ali Fuad Erden, *Birinci Dünya Savaşında Suriye Hatıralarıı*, 136. Falih Rıfkı became a prominent journalist in the republican period and was the founder of the *Dünya* newspaper where Ali Fuad Erden's memoirs were published for the first time. See Chapter 1.

or the Ministry of Interior directly to him, with the note "question to Falih Rıfkı Efendi" without letting me know. The reserve officer Falih Rıfkı never misused the trust and sympathy of the Commander of the Fourth Army, Minister of the Navy, Viceroy, and dictator of Syria. He was never spoiled. He did his duty to the end with honor and a clear conscience.[56]

Sheikh Es'ad Shuqayr

Sheikh Es'ad Shuqayr was the member of parliament for Acre in the Ottoman parliament. His official title at headquarters was "Army Mufti." He was a close companion of Cemal Pasha, his secretary for Arabic correspondence and interpreter. He was very intelligent and an excellent speaker. He spoke well and told entertaining stories. I would listen to him with great pleasure.

[At this point Ali Fuad gives a few quotes from Falih Rıfkı's "Zeytindağı" regarding Sheikh Es'ad Shuqayr.][57]

[On Enver and Cemal's visit to Medina][58]

... On the express train to Medina, Enver Pasha was shooting birds from the window. As soon as the deputy commander in chief alighted at the station at Medina, with his entourage and the notables of Medina who had come to welcome him, he went on foot to the holy tomb of the Prophet under its green dome. The people of Medina were lined up on either side of the road. Prayers were said and odes recited as blood gushed from the throats of the sacrificed camels. Enver's procession went by slowly under the burning sun, through this flood of blood, through the chanting of prayers and odes. The lightning inspection that he had carried out in Syria, Palestine, and the Sinai was transformed in Medina into a slow and respectful progress. It was as if the Deputy Commander in chief was not hearing or seeing the

---

56 Ibid., 136–137.
57 Ibid., 138–140.
58 Ibid., 184. Enver and Cemal were in Medina in February 19–20, four months before the actual outbreak of the Arab Revolt on June 6, 1916. Cemal was already plotting to overthrow the Sharif early in the war. Çiçek, "Erken Cumhuriyet Dönemi Ders Kitapları," 176: "[The Sharif] knew that it would be his turn after Cemal Pasha had dealt with the Arab movement in Syria."

ceremony in his honor. He had joined his hands on his chest in respect and piety, he was in a trance, his head bowed, crying silently.

The deputy commander in chief, Enver Pasha was going to have the honor of being received into the presence of the Supreme Commander of the Holy Jihad, The Holy Prophet. He was going to give his account of how he had carried out his duty, that is to say, the duty he was charged with as the Deputy by the Supreme Commander.[59]

I occasionally left the procession and observed Enver Pasha from the side lines. Enver Pasha was overcome by emotion and holy feelings. He was crying; tears were streaming down from his eyes. Nobody else was crying. Faisal Bey was not crying. His cold and aloof bearing as he was going to the grave of his great ancestor was in stark contrast to Enver Pasha. Who knows what he was thinking? Cemal Pasha was not crying. He had a stern and frozen expression. But having seen that Enver Pasha was crying incessantly, he shed a few tears, perhaps so as not to be outdone.[60]

[*At this point Ali Fuad diverges into a long aside on T. E. Lawrence and quotes extensively from Lawrence's "Seven Pillars of Wisdom," particularly the episode where the Arab Sheikhs approach Faisal and ask him whether they should kill Enver and Cemal. It is also interesting that neither Ali Fuad nor Naci Kıcıman, who was actually fighting Lawrence's bedouin troops, make any mention at all of Lawrence being present on the scene at the time.*][61]

On this occasion, Sharif Husayn, acting through his son Faisal, awarded a golden sword to Enver and Cemal Pasha each, and a golden

---

59 Ali Fuad Erden, *Birinci Dünya Savaşında Suriye Hatıraları*, 184.

60 Ibid., 185.

61 Ibid. T. E. Lawrence, *Seven Pillars of Wisdom* (Blacksburg, VA: Wilder Publications, 2011), 27–28: "In the end matters passed off well, though the irony was terrible. They watched the troops wheeling and turning in the dusty plain outside the city gate, rushing up and down in mimic camel battle, or spurring their horses in the javelin game in the immemorial Arab fashion. "And are all these volunteers for the Holy War?" Asked Enver at last, turning to Feisal. "Yes," said Feisal. "And they will fight to the death against the enemies of the faithful?" "Yes," said Feisal once again, and then the Arab chiefs came up to be presented, and Ali ibn el Hussein of Modhig drew him aside whispering, "My Lord shall we kill them now?" And Feisal said, "No, they are our guests." The Sheikhs protested for they believed they could finish the war in two blows. They were determined to force Feisal's hand and he had to go among them, just out of earshot but still in full view or the Turks, and beg for the lives of Enver and Jemal, who had murdered his best friends on the scaffold." On the same episode see, Martin Strohmeier, "Fakhri (Fahreddin) Pasa and the End of Ottoman Rule in Medina (1916–1919)," *Turkish Historical Review* 4 (2013): 192–223.

dagger to the Army chief of staff. On his part Enver Pasha presented Sharif Husayn with two War Distinction Medals in gold and silver.

[Telegram from Cemal Pasha to Sharif Husayn thanking him for the gifts:]

Medina. March 5, 1916.

To the Honourable Emir of Mecca the Holy.

I have the honor to inform Your Excellency that, together with his Honor the Deputy Commander in chief and Minister of War Enver Pasha, I have come to Medina to have the honor of paying my respects to the exalted resting place [of the Prophet].

I thank you for the sword that Your Excellency had the goodness to present me via his son Faisal.

I would like to express my most sincere congratulations for the War Distinction medals that were awarded to Your Excellency by the Exalted Personage of the Caliph of Islam. The Gold Medal of Distiction is the highest honor that can be bestowed by the Caliphate to those who served with sacrifices during the Holy Jihad. It has been awarded to Your Excellency as a token of esteem for the distinguished service you have rendered to the Holy Jihad. I would like to take this opportunity to inform you that Faisal Bey has also been rewarded the War Medal, and I had the personal honor of attaching it to his noble chest.

I await the camel regiment that is to be sent to join the Egyptian Campaign. Because the railway is very busy just now, a special train shall be sent for the transport of the holy warriors. These trains will come from the north loaded with grain and they will return bearing the holy warriors. Therefore, in order to avoid delay it is necessary to start assembling the holy warriors in the desert. Until their provisioning is completed, the holy warriors will be the guests of the Ottoman army in Medina. Weapons and ammunition will be provided in Jerusalem.

As a final comment, I would like to express that we have all been much impressed by the noble bearing and honorable comportment of Faisal Bey.

Commander of the Fourth Army and Minister of the Navy

Ahmed Cemal

Mecca the Holy. March 17, 1916

To the Fourth Army Command

It is my honor to acknowledge the great goodness of the Exalted Personage of the Caliph which has been compounded by the awarding of the war medals and to thank Your Excellency for your kind words of congratulation. I must also express my deeply felt thanks for the kindly disposition of Your Excellency regarding the holy warriors, may your hands be blessed. Our hearts are gladdened.[62]

Emir of Mecca

Husayn bin Ali

Odes of praise for Cemal Pasha

. . . In Syria everywhere and on all occasions odes of praise (*kaside*) would be composed honoring Cemal Pasha. At first they called him "The Second Saladin." Later, this was not enough, they raised him even higher that the "First Saladin." Poets and composers of odes used to compete with each other in flattering Cemal Pasha. At feasts Cemal Pasha would hear these odes with the stony silence of a god, he never thanked them and never made any gesture of modesty. Thanks reduce sanctity, objects of adoration do not stoop to express thanks!

On another occasion, again at some feast, Cemal Pasha made a speech. Everyone was listening in awe and submission with heads bowed. In his speech, in whatever context, Cemal Pasha spoke of the blessings of water and, citing the famous *sura* from the Qur'an, he said, "*wa min al-ma' kulli shay'en hayy.*"

Suddenly there was an outburst of murmuring. The correct version of the *sura* was "We made from water every living thing," "*wa [ja'alna] min al-ma' kulli shay'en hayy.*" Cemal Pasha had forgotten the words *ja'alna*. Syria was not able to stand that even one word should be omitted from the *sura,* but because no one dared to correct him, the assemblage had murmured all together the correct version. The combined murmuring of a hundred people had caused the outburst. These murmurs were to be the only opposition Syria ever showed to Cemal Pasha in three years.[63]

On the occasion of another feast, at which together with Syria's notables and intellectuals, the representatives of the Arab youth and the proponents of Arab independence were also present, a Druze sheikh, sword

---

62 Ali Fuad Erden, *Birinci Dünya Savaşında Suriye Hatıraları*, 186, 187.

63 Ibid., 195. The *sura* in question is *al-Anbiya'* [The Prophets] 21:30: "Do the unbelievers not realize that the heavens and earth were sewn together, but We ripped them apart, and from water created every living thing?" *The Qur'an: A New Translation*, trans. Tarif Khalidi (London: Penguin Classics, 2009), 259.

in hand, declaimed an ode praising Cemal Pasha to the skies. This ode, as much as it was an ode praising Cemal Pasha, was also meant to be a threat to the youth who wanted freedom and reform. The speaker paced the room swinging his sword in the air, everyone was listening with bowed heads. No doubt the ode accompanied with the sword had been pre-arranged. . . .

One day in Aleppo, after another ode composer had finished, the audience applauded enthusiastically. Ali Münif Bey, the Mutasarrıf of Lebanon, and myself were conversing in a corner of the room. Cemal Pasha, addressing Münif, called out to him, "Ali Münif, was it because of what they said about me that you did not clap?" Ali Münif said to me, "How did he see?" Ali Münif Bey had been seated behind a cabinet. There was no way Cemal Pasha could have seen him. His words were addressed not to him but to his companion.[64]

I had become sickened by odes. I did not want to listen and most of the time I did not. Yet I do remember two lines from one of them:

Before the countenance of Cemal princes and kings quail.
And before the beauty of Cemal the sun and moon are pale.

On another occasion the deputy for Latakia, Kamil al-As'ad, told Cemal Pasha, "I intend to collect all the odes said for His Excellency in a gilded volume." I was revolted. Inadvertently, I blurted out, "For God's, sake do not do it!" Kamil al-As'ad, much put out, said, "Why? Why?" Cemal Pasha interjected, "Why are you interfering? If they want to, let them go ahead." I was silent. But the gilded book was never written.[65]

The Red Book

. . . After the hangings Cemal Pasha ordered the publication of a Red Book.[66] The book was published simultaneously with its translations into other lan-

---

64 Ali Fuad Erden, *Birinci Dünya Savaşında Suriye Hatıraları*, 196. Together with the *sura* episode, this anecdote is one of the few occasions when we get a sense of Ali Fuad's dry sense of humor.

65 Ibid., 197. Kamil al-As'ad was "a member of the six large *muqata'ji* families of south Lebanon and leader of up to forty thousand Mutawallis (Shia)." He was later to distinguish himself fighting the French during Faisal's short-lived Arab Kingdom. Gelvin, *Divided Loyalties*, 123–124. This race in base flattery hoping to curry favour with Cemal was also remarked upon by Falih Rıfkı, see above.

66 Ali Fuad Erden, *Birinci Dünya Savaşında Suriye Hatıraları*, 211. This was a red-covered official publication justifying the actions of the Aley Tribunal and the executions. *Aliye*

guages.[67] He had dictated the book to Falih Rıfkı Efendi, who had edited it. The Army Commander sent Falih Efendi to General Headquarters in Istanbul with the manuscript to be published. I had not read the book. But I did read the draft of the letter introducing it which stated: "I am sending it by hand with Falih Rıfkı Bey, my personal secretary." I changed this phrasing to read, "reserve officer Falih Rıfkı Efendi, Second Lieutenant attached to the Army Chief of Staff." Cemal Pasha had struck this out and written [again], "My personal secretary Falih Rıfkı Bey." I went to my commander and submitted to him respectfully that, "There is no such post as a personal secretary in the table of ranks of the army, Falih Rıfkı Efendi is an officer attached to the Army Chief of Staff. As is known to Your Excellency, according to regulations, ranks from lieutenant colonel and above are referred to as *Bey*. All lower ranks are referred to as *Efendi*." We had an argument. It seemed that Cemal Pasha was angered by the mention of things like law and regulations. Because he was not just Army Commander, but also Minister of the Navy and in fact the Viceroy of Syria, he could have a personal secretary called Bey.

In the course of our argument, the Pasha said to me, "It is said that you are dominating me. So they say." This "they" was, no doubt, his personal entourage. I replied, "God forbid, Your Excellency! God forbid! It can never be a question of dominating, all my suggestions are only in keeping with my loyalty and attachment to your person!"

This argument could not go on indefinitely, I cut it short and left.

Half an hour later Falih Rıfkı brought the letter that he had written out in fair and submitted for the signature of the Army Commander. There was a small correction. Cemal Pasha had struck out "my personal secretary Falih Rıfkı Bey" and inserted, "Falih Rıfkı Efendi, Second Lieutenant reserve officer attached to the Chief of Staff."[68]

Divanı Harbı Örfisinde Tedkik Olunan Mesele-i Siyasiye Hakkında Izahat 4 (Istanbul: 4. Ordu Yayını Tanin Matbaası 1332/1916), 127 pages with 72 pages of documents. See section on the Red Book in the Introduction.

67   Ali Fuad Erden, *Birinci Dünya Savaşında Suriye Hatıraları*, 211. It was also published in Arabic.

68   Ibid., 212. There is something puzzling about this petty triumph on the part of Ali Fuad. It is the only time that he speaks of an open confrontation with his superior and it is highly unlikely that he would have dared to walk out of his presence. It is also curious that there is no mention of the incident in Falih Rıfkı's memoirs. It is also unlikely that something as important as the official account of the executions of the Arab patriots should have been formulated *in camera* between Cemal and his "personal secretary,"

The brigands

We received the following telegram from the governor of Aleppo.

> Today I was visited by the brigands Halil Bey and Ahmed Bey. They said that the work of killing (*taktil*) in the region of Diyarbekir had been completed, that they had come to Syria to continue their work and that they awaited orders. I had them arrested. I await the orders of Your Excellency.

In his reply Cemal Pasha had stated, "set them free."

After the answering telegram had been sent, Cemal Pasha sent copies of both telegrams to me via Falih Rıfkı for my information.

Halil and Ahmed were well known brigands (*komitaji*), steeped in blood. I begged the Army Commander to have them arrested and tried in a court martial. [I said]: "Your Excellency had a senator executed without asking anybody. To have these brigands executed is more difficult and demands more courage and power. Your Excellency is capable of this courage and power, and you should use it."

Cemal Pasha did not agree. We were in the wing of the Augusta Victoria Hospice that looks out on the horizon of eastern Jordan. It was early evening. A dramatic conversation was taking place between the Army Commander and his chief of staff. Ali Fuad's voice was becoming increasingly stronger and Cemal Pasha's voice was softening. Cemal Pasha was hesitant and faltering. He kept saying, "Fuad Bey, I cannot! I cannot!"

I was unable to convince the Army Commander. Half an hour later, Falih brought a telegram that had been sent from headquarters. It ordered the governor of Aleppo to have Halil Bey and Ahmed Bey arrested and sent to Damascus. Soon after that the governor informed us that they had left for Istanbul. The brigands had suspected that the situation was evolving against them and escaped. Cemal Pasha wrote to the governor of Adana ordering the arrest of these men, but the telegram was too late.

The brigands had left the Fourth Army zone. Cemal Pasha wrote to the governors of Konya and Eskişehir. Again, the telegrams were too late. The race between the brigands and Cemal Pasha had been won by the brigands who had made it to Istanbul. Once Cemal Pasha had made

---

Falih Rıfkı. On the *Red Book* and its contents see Tauber, *The Arab Movements in World War I*.

his mind up about them, and once the brigands realized this, he could not let them go. He wrote to Istanbul. Perhaps the Committee of Union and Progress Central Command wanted to get rid of these men [because they replied]:

"The debt of gratitude towards executioners and murderers is onerous. They seek to dominate those who have used them and needed them. Instruments used to do dirty work are useful for the duration of that work; but after the completion of that work they must be disposed of (like toilet paper)."[69]

Halil and Ahmed were finally placed under arrest by the General Headquarters in Istanbul and sent to Damascus where they were tried by court martial. The court martial was almost afraid to judge these men, the most vicious executioners of the CUP. The [members of] the court martial did not take this matter seriously, thinking they were made party to some sort of elaborate ploy.

Blood-stained gold pieces had been found among the personal effects of the brigands. The court martial finally came to a judgement. On the day that the report of their decision was due to Fourth Army headquarters, Cemal Pasha had to travel to Istanbul. On the day that he was to travel he signed and sealed an empty sheet of paper. When the official report arrived it was to be copied on this sheet and the decision acted upon. This is what happened. The executioners were hung in broad daylight.[70]

---

69 Ali Fuad Erden, *Birinci Dünya Savaşında Suriye Hatıraları*, 225–226. This account varies considerably from the account provided by Falih Rıfkı above. There is no mention in Falih Rıfkı's memoirs of any intervention by Ali Fuad. Falih Rıfkı actually states that Cemal was in hot pursuit of the two brigands for their murder of Krikor Zohrab and Vartkes Seringuilian, prominent Armenians who had been sent to the Fourth Army district and whom Cemal Pasha had tried to save. Halil and Ahmed were leaders of the notorious death squads of the Special Organization (*Teşkilatı Mahsusa*) which had turned Diyarbekir into a veritable killing field for Armenians. Çiçek, *War and State Formation in Syria*, 118–119. The senator mentioned by Ali Fuad was Abdul Hamid al Zahrawi who was hung in Damascus by the order of Cemal Pasha.

70 Ali Fuad Erden, *Birinci Dünya Savaşında Suriye Hatıraları*, 226–227. Alpay Kabacalı, the editor of Ali Fuad Erden's memoirs, provides the text of two telegrams related to the issue: "Telegram from Cemal Pasha to Talat Pasha, September 15, 1915: "Ahmet the Circassian and his friend Halil have arrived. Although more than one thousand five hundred liras was found among Halil's effects, Ahmed had no more than eight liras. From this I understand that Ahmed did not steal or loot. Accordingly, although I firmly believe that Ahmed committed these murders under the orders of the governor of Diyarbekir Dr. Reshid Bey, do you believe that Ahmet should be done away with?

Ismail Canbulat

Cemal Pasha wanted to make Ismail Canbulat the *Mutasarrıf* of Lebanon. I had opposed this saying, "He has blood on his hands!" (He had shot the police officer who came to arrest him.) Cemal Pasha was silent for a moment, then he said, "We all have blood on our hands!" This time I pretended not to hear and remained silent. Canbulat Bey did not become *Mutasarrıf* of Lebanon, but two months later he did become Minister of the Interior.

I was there at Canbulat's hanging. He died well. He kept his dignity to the moment of death. As he was mounting the gallows, his gold-framed spectacles fell to the ground. He said "Please put my spectacles on." He did not want to die without his spectacles that completed his identity. They brought his spectacles and put them on. . . . During his trial, Canbulat had given combative and arrogant answers before the Independence Tribunals.[71]

Lebanon. [The end of the *Mutasarrıfıyya*]

. . . Before the First World war, Lebanon was an autonomous *Mutasarrıfıyya*. The *Mutasarrıf* was chosen from among the Christians by the government and his appointment was approved by the Great Powers. Conscription was not enforced in Lebanon. It had a privileged status in relation to taxation. There were no Ottoman soldiers there. The population of Lebanon was some four hundred thousand. Most of them were Christian. It was said that there were many weapons in Lebanon. The population was pro-French. The most likely spot for a French landing was Lebanon.

Or should I confine myself to Halil? I request an answer by tomorrow evening." The answering cipher from Talat Pasha to Cemal was marked "to be decoded personally" and stated: "In any case he should be done away with. He can be very harmful in the future." Answer from Cemal to Talat, "It has been decided that Ahmet will be executed. Tomorrow morning the deed will be done in Damascus."

71 Ibid., 233. Ismail Canbolat (1880–1926) Born in Kosovo, of Circassian origin, graduate from the Harbiye military academy, Deputy from Constantinople. Canbolat was a member of the Ittihadist Central Committee and was general director of the Department of State Security; he was responsible for deporting Armenians living in Constantinople and the murder of those imprisoned in Çankırı who had been part of the first round up of Armenian intellectuals on April 24 1915. Kevorkian, *The Armenian Genocide*, 542. He was later to be hanged by the so-called Independence Tribunals that were set up by the Kemalist regime to root out Ittihadist opponents to Kemal.

The first administrative and political move that Cemal Pasha made when he arrived in Syria was the military occupation of Lebanon. He sent in an infantry brigade and a mountain artillery unit. This is the official declaration he made to the Lebanese people:

> Greetings to the people of Lebanon which is a part of the Ottoman fatherland (*vatan*)! Today martial law as declared in all of the Ottoman domains has been extended to Lebanon. Martial law means the temporary postponement of civil laws. Despite martial law, Lebanon will continue to be exempt from military service and taxation. I have sent a military force to protect the honor, property and lives of the Lebanese people. There will be no conscription. There will be no search for weapons. There will not be the slightest transgression against the lives property and honor of the people. Any acts to the contrary will be immediately and severely punished without exception. Institutions belonging to the enemy states will be evacuated, the priests and missionaries will be sent to Urfa and the nuns and nurses to Damascus.[72]

The government appointed a Muslim *Mutasarrıf* to Lebanon. In this way its status as an autonomous province came to an end. Colonel Rıza Bey was appointed the [military] commander of Lebanon. Colonel Rıza Bey was the hero of Yemen. In Ottoman times, the governors of Hungary would be chosen from the commanders of Yemen. The two extremities of the Ottoman state, Hungary and Yemen, were in a constant state of uprising. Yemen is mountainous, whereas Hungary is a plain. The Yemenis were tough warriors fighting for freedom. The Hungarians were fierce patriots! For commanders tempered in Yemen, the governorship of Buda would seem very easy (like Turkish *lokoum*). Rıza Pasha did very well as the commander of Lebanon. The Lebanese people liked the hero of Yemen. At feasts, the top-hatted, French-educated Lebanese notables were honored to carry his water pipe. Throughout the war, peace and order were perfect in Lebanon.[73]

---

72 Ali Fuad Erden, *Birinci Dünya Savaşında Suriye Hatıraları*, 256–257.
73 Ibid. The last real (Christian) *Mutasarrıf* of Lebanon, Ohannes Pasha Kouyoumdjian, had a very different take on Rıza Bey, "Colonel Rıza Bey was a tall, gangling, awkward man with a heavy and *gauche* manner. There was nothing about him of the Germanic military correctness that some Turkish officers affected. His face of a mastiff with protruding teeth, giving him an air of bestiality, did nothing to improve his appearance." Ohannes Pasha, *Le Liban*, 115. See the section "The end of Lebanese autonomy" in the Introduction.

In one of its memoranda, the *Mutasarrıf* of Lebanon made it known that the Lebanese wanted to volunteer for military service and train with weapons and ammunition. The Army Command replied that there was no need for volunteers as there were sufficient Ottoman troops to defend the country."[74]

The Blockade. [The famine in Lebanon][75]

Lebanon is not a country that produces much. In times of peace it was provisioned from the outside [neighbouring provinces] or by sea. All Lebanon grows is mulberry trees for silk production and fruit. Lebanon's income was dependent on tourism and silk. Lebanon suffered the most from the Allied blockade. It was very difficult to supply a population that amounted to half a million, including Beirut, from Hawran and Jabal Druz. Yet it was done. The Lebanese cog railway was used exclusively for the transport of provisions. But it was not enough.

It was suggested that some of the population be sent to areas closer to the sources of provisioning, where they would volunteer to work in the labor battalions (*amele taburları*). The Lebanese did not want this. No coercion was applied. The Lebanese preferred to die of hunger in their own country rather than emigrate and work in the labor battalions. The poor suffered greatly from the lack of provisions. Some people ate orange peels in the street.[76]

The King of Spain, Alfonso XIII, asked Cemal Pasha's permission to send a shipload of wheat as a gift to the people of Beirut and Mount

---

74 Ali Fuad Erden, *Birinci Dünya Savaşında Suriye Hatıraları*, 258. It is highly unlikely that any Lebanese would have volunteered for military service. One of the most hated aspects of the "days of the Turks," the *eyyam-atrak*, was actually conscription. Fawaz, *The Land of Aching Hearts*, 84: "[F]rom the start to the end of the war, the call for general mobilization met with considerable opposition in many localities, such as Hawran, Kurdistan, Arabia and Mount Lebanon." Only the die-hard Ottoman loyalist, the Druze Emir Shakib Arslan, raised a small force of Druze warriors at his own expense. They were never deployed. See Cleveland, *Islam Against the West: Shakib Arslan and the Campaign for Islamic Nationalism*. 66.

75 Ali Fuad Erden, *Birinci Dünya Savaşında Suriye Hatıraları*, 259. See the section on the famine in the Introduction.

76 Ibid. There is no mention in any of the sources of any such suggestion put to the Lebanese population. Even if it had, it would not have been surprising that they should have refused, given the fact that most of the workers in the labor batallions were worked to death.

Lebanon. Cemal Pasha immediately agreed and to provide security he suggested that the distribution of the grain be supervised by representatives of the Red Cross, the Papal nuncio in Beirut, and two American missionaries. King Alfonso, thinking that it would be the difficult to obtain the approval of Cemal Pasha, had applied to him first. When Cemal Pasha approved, he applied to the British government.

He was hoping that he would easily get the approval of the British government. But the British did not approve. Britain was waging total war. The British thought that the amount of wheat sent by the King of Spain would be withheld by the Turks from the amount they would otherwise have sent to Lebanon. That is to say that in a roundabout way the wheat sent by the King would be given to their troops who were fighting the British in the Sinai.[77]

The enemy press claimed that Cemal Pasha was deliberately starving the people of Beirut and Mount Lebanon; this was a lie, a total calumny. Cemal Pasha did his best to provision the people of Beirut and Mount Lebanon, Christian and Muslim alike. If he had deliberately starved them, after three years of war none of the half-million Christians would have been left. Quite a lot of people died in Mount Lebanon and Beirut from hunger. But the reason for this is not Cemal Pasha but geography. It is the blockade, the fact that Lebanon does not grow grain, it is the difficulty of bringing provisions by land from far away. It is also the fact that the Lebanese did not want to emigrate to locations closer to sources of food, and that they refused to join the labor battalions. [The reasons for the famine] are a combination of many negative factors, but most of all it is the strategy of Britain.

Britain exempted from the blockade the coasts of the Hijaz whose population it had encouraged to revolt, and it sold grain to them at the cheapest

---

77 Ibid., 259. The only other mention of such a ship occurs in the diary of Conde de Ballobar, the Spanish Consul in Jerusalem. It runs as follows: "I have taken steps so that an extraordinary journey of the 'Villanueva' will take place, whose arrival was already announced by the Transatlantic Company, but the leader of the military staff, Sadullah Bey, cut me off, announcing that, as of noon yesterday, the Allies had established a blockade of the whole coast. So, we can't even think of such a trip now that, henceforth no neutral ship would be able to approach Turkish waters. The news discouraged me completely since it was an excellent occasion for our commercial interests." Ballobar makes no mention that the ship was carrying wheat as a "gift" from King Alfonso of Spain, nor does he mention any elaborate arrangements for its distribution. Eduardo Manzano & Roberto Mazza, eds., *Jerusalem in World War I: The Palestine Diary of a European Diplomat: Conde de Ballobar* (London: I. B Tauris, 2011), 75.

prices, yet it did not allow the passage of a shipload of wheat sent by the King of Spain to the Christian population of Lebanon.

> Telegram from the Military Command of Medina to Fourth Army Headquarters
>> June 2, 1915
>>> On May 18 sailing ships bearing provisions arrived at Jeddah from Suwakin. The captains of the ships declared that the British had lifted the blockade on provisions to the Hijaz coast.

In contrast to this, the British intensified the blockade on the coast of Lebanon, and did not hesitate to sink ships carrying grain from other parts of the Syrian coast to provision the people of Lebanon and Beirut.

They attacked Cemal Pasha—very unfairly—and accused him. Yet no one accused Britain of preventing King Alfonso from sending grain to the hungry Christians, an accusation that would have been very justified.[78]

The executions

The official documents seized at the French Consulate at Damascus at the beginning of the war proved that that some of the leading Syrians had been in contact with the French with a view to securing Arab independence under French protection. Among these documents were some that concerned the members of the Arab Decentralization Party.[79]

In September 1915, Cemal Pasha decided that legal procedures would be commenced regarding some of the names mentioned in the documents. He had them tried by the Court Martial of Aley.

They were tried, convicted, and executed. For the second part of the trials of the revolutionaries, the president and one member of the Aley

---

78 Ali Fuad Erden, *Birinci Dünya Savaşında Suriye Hatıraları*, 259. The Allied blockade was a major factor in increasing the severity of the famine. The British sources show that they used the blockade as a weapon of war: "British correspondence in May 1916 makes explicit reference to, 'the blockade of the Yemen Coasts and the prevention of the exportation of grain and other necessities to Jeddah in particular and other Hijaz ports in general." As quoted in Fawaz, *The Land of Aching Hearts*, 89.

79 Ali Fuad Erden, *Birinci Dünya Savaşında Suriye Hatıraları*, 273. This is a reference to the Ottoman Administrative Decentralization Party (*Hizb al-Lamarkaziyyah al-Idariyyah al-Uthmani*) which had been established as legal party with the knowledge of the Turkish government. Zeine N. Zein, *The Emergence of Arab Nationalism* (New York: Caravan Books, 1973), 85. Other documents were discovered in the French Consulate in Beirut.

Court Martial were changed. The president of the Court Martial of Istanbul, Major of Cavalry Şükrü Bey, was appointed president, and the former aide to Crown Prince Yusuf Izzeddin Efendi, Major Hasan Bey, was appointed a member. Şükrü Bey and Hasan Bey came to see me the day they arrived at headquarters and asked for instructions regarding their duties. I told them, "One cannot give instructions to judges. The only instruction is the law and your conscience." My interlocutors were gladdened by my answer and said, "So our task will be easy."

But their task was not to be so easy.

. . . It was in the April of 1916. The president of the Court Martial in Damascus Major Şükrü Bey came to my office. The trials of the accused had been concluded and sentence was about to be passed. The accused were twenty men. There were senators, members of parliament, high-ranking officials and prominent journalists among them. The members of the Court Martial had decided that three or four should receive the death penalty, others should receive sentences of imprisonment for life or a definite period of incarceration. The court had hesitated to deliver the sentences and the president had come to ask the Commander's permission.

I said, "Go, put the matter to him, plead with him, if he does not accept fall to his feet and say, 'Your Excellency, think of the judgment of history.'"

Şükrü Bey left and came back five minutes later. He was totally pale. When he had entered the room, Cemal Pasha, who no doubt was forewarned why the president was there, received him with a very cold "What do you want?" Şükrü Bey presented the list of names with the sentences as decided by the court, declaring, "These are the decisions, I have come to present them to Your Excellency." Cemal Pasha, without even looking at the notes prepared by the court, wrote his own judgment beside each one. The judgement was always the same one word. Şükrü Bey [followed the advice of Erden, pleading with Cemal to evoke the judgement of history]. Cemal Pasha pushed Şükrü Bey's head, and said "May history fall upon your head. . . ."[80]

. . . Silence descended upon the president of the Court Martial and the chief of staff. But we communicated through our silence. This communication, that is to say, this silence, lasted a quarter of an hour. After a quarter of an hour Şükrü Bey rose. He was going to Aley, to deliver the death verdicts. A few days later Cemal Pasha would approve these convictions in the

---

80 Ali Fuad Erden, *Birinci Dünya Savaşında Suriye Hatıraları*, 274.

name of the Turkish nation and he would order their carrying out, again in the name of the Turkish nation. The Court Martial sent the documents [pertaining to the executions] and Cemal Pasha ordered his legal advisor Vassaf Bey to immediately put together an order for the executions. Vassaf Bey asked me, "How can I write an order immediately regarding trials that took months without studying the paperwork that amounts to hundreds of pages. I need at least a week." I told him, "You will write it as ordered by His Excellency. Under the draft you will not sign but simply inscribe, "by the official order of the Commander." And so he did. He brought me the draft. I did not sign it either. Later His Excellency asked him, "Why did you not sign it?" His reply was, "Your Excellency, I had no time to study the file." [The Pasha asked,] "Has Fuad Bey seen this?" [Vassaf Bey replied,] "He has." [Cemal Pasha asked,] "Why did he not sign it?" [Vassaf Bey replied,] "I do not know, sir." Cemal Pasha thought for a moment [and said], "As if I need your signatures" and signed the document.

Indeed, Cemal Pasha did not in any way need the signatures of his legal councillor or his chief of staff. During the Great War, a special law had been passed whereby army commanders could approve the decisions of courts martial which would subsequently be sent to Istanbul for approval by the Sultan. Cemal Pasha relied on this law when he approved and applied the verdict of the court martial. After the executions, the file on the verdicts was sent to Istanbul where it was presented by the Chamber of Ministers to the Sultan and duly approved.[81]

Cemal Pasha states in his memoirs:

> "There are some also who say that the crimes of those who were condemned and executed in Syria were covered by the general amnesty of 1913, so their subsequent conviction for the same offences was illegal. As I have shown in the Red Book, ""The Truth About the Syrian Question"" these people used the general amnesty to start their criminal activities afresh, and their conviction related solely to their crimes *after* that time."[82]

---

81 Ibid., 275–276. It seems fairly clear from Ali Fuad's account that both he and Vassaf Bey did not want to be party to the executions because of their highly dubious legality. There was in fact such a wartime measure that allowed summary justice to be handed out by commanders on the spot, but it was designed mainly for deserters.

82 Ibid. Jamal Pasha, *Memoirs of a Turkish Statesman*, 219. See the discussion of the "Red Book" in the Introduction.

The documents seized at the French Consulate concerned the period before the amnesty. Yet the Decentralization Party continued its activities from Egypt. The court martial did not believe that the accused had cut off all relations with the party after the amnesty. They [the accused] were not able to prove that they had. It fell to the court martial to prove that these men had continued to commit these crimes after the declaration of war.

I have not read the Red Book, nor the trial files, nor the order for the verdict. My impressions on this affair are entirely confined to the words of Şükrü Bey that I have cited above.

Half of the condemned men were to be hung in Damascus and the other half in Beirut. In order to appreciate the strength of the Arab uprising, and to see how the revolutionaries would die, I wanted to be present at the hangings in Damascus. It was necessary to know this for the defense of Syria. The verdicts were to be carried out in the Government Square at night towards dawn. For the elite and distinguished condemned men, sturdy imposing gallows were set up all around the square. In order to increase the light of the electric bulbs, gas lamps had been set up. The convicts came one by one in carriages. They quietly listened to the verdict read out by a gendarme officer. And, they died as quietly.

Apparently, those in Beirut died singing hymns of liberty. The people of Beirut would later proudly claim [on the basis of this difference] that they were more courageous than the Damascenes.

The last person to be brought to the execution ground in Damascus was Rafiq Sallum, a young Christian reserve officer. He saluted the gallows from which white ghosts hung by saying "*Assalaamun Aleiqum ya meshnaka* [Greetings, o gallows]!" He then marched quickly to the only gallows that was empty, the gallows that was meant for him, hands tied behind his back, almost as if he wanted to reach it as soon as possible. The executioner who was putting the noose around his neck threw his fez on the ground. Rafiq Sallum said, "You have no right to throw my fez on the ground." They brought his fez and placed it on his head. But they placed it askew and it was dusty. He was not aware of this. If he had been he would have said, "Dust my fez and put it on straight."

There were only a few seconds before the death of Rafiq Sallum. I was placed just opposite him, under the raw light of a gas lamp, I was examining this astonishingly calm young man. In the instance between life and death his face changed rapidly. First he became pale, then he went as white as lime. . . . At the end he became deep yellow. After he too was hung, a deadly silence descended on the place; the silence of the gallows and the hanged, the silence of those watching and the silence surrounding us.

Dawn was breaking behind the gallows. This dawn frightened me.[83]

. . . I returned to headquarters. It was by now daylight. The people had begun to fill the Government Square. Soldiers had formed a protective cordon around the gallows.

I looked out from the balcony: a great crowd, an obedient, well-behaved, quiet and unmoving crowd had begun to fill the square. In amongst this crowd, a space. In this space, all around, white objects hanging down from gallows. All of them surrounded by soldiers with long conical caps and armed with old rifles. These soldiers were the Mevlevi battalion who made up the Damascus garrison. These soldiers in their long caps with old guns, these people wearing turbans of all colours, *kaffiyas*, fezes, a veritable jumble of outfits, all this was like a scene from hundreds of years ago. A scene had emerged harkening back to bygone ages. A scene belonging to the last days of the Abbasid Caliphate![84]

The next day, all the Damacus newspapers ran special editions. In the leading articles the Army Commander's actions were being lauded as a great act in the name of defending the fatherland; praise and thanks was being heaped on the great saviour who had saved the fatherland from traitors, and seditious schemers. The most important newspaper in Damascus, the *al Muktabas,* whose editor was the old revolutionary Kurd Ali, ran a banner headline that consisted of the Quranic *sura,* "The punishment for those who spread sedition on earth is death by hanging or having their hands and feet cut off. . . ."

---

83 Ali Fuad Erden, *Birinci Dünya Savaşında Suriye Hatıraları* 278. Rafiq Razzik Sallum had been a member of the *al-Fatat* secret society who had made an extensive confession: "The information given by al-Uraysi, Sallum and al-Khatib was very valuable to the authorities, no less valuable than that drawn from the French consular documents. . . ." Tauber, *The Arab Movements in World War I*, 48.

84 Ali Fuad Erden, *Birinci Dünya Savaşında Suriye Hatıraları*, 279. The Mevlevi Batallion was largely used "to raise troop morale on the battlefield." They were also used for more mundane tasks such as guard duty. This seems to be their function in the scene that Ali Fuad is describing. On the Mevlevi Brigade see Mehmet Beşikçi, *The Ottoman Mobilization of Manpower in the First World War: Between Voluntarism and Resistance* (Leiden: Brill, 2012), 190–191. See also Plate 11.

These articles and *suras* were prepared before the hangings and this morning's papers were printed yesterday.[85]

Apricot blossoms

Today was the spring equinox. It turned out that it was also Cemal Pasha's wedding anniversary. Those who were close to him in the headquarters planned to present their congratulations and good wishes by offering a bouquet of flowers. I was told this by an honorable person who was not a member of the "close entourage" but had family links to Cemal Pasha [the agricultural advisor of the army command, Cemil Bey]. He felt that it would be appropriate for the entire staff to join in the congratulation ceremony.

From the gardens of Damascus smelling like paradise that evening we gathered yellow buds [from apricot trees]. The room next to the Commander's office was filled with thousands of apricot buds. The buds blossomed overnight and all the officers at headquarters met in the room at nine o'clock.

Outside, barely a hundred paces away, the yellowed faces of men dangling from the gallows, and inside a rose garden drowning in the heady aroma of apricot blossom! The hanged and the roses! This was the ultimate contradiction and irony. The Army Chief of Staff presented His Excellency the Army Commander with a big bouquet of yellow apricot blossom together with his best wishes in the name of the entire headquarters staff. Cemal Pasha, smiling, happy and full of good cheer, accepted the bouquet, and the congratulations of the chief of staff, thanking him.

At the end of the ceremony I heard a voice from the depths of my conscience. It was a terrible voice. I shuddered.

The Syrian government declared May 6, 1916 to be "Martyrs' Day" (*Yowm Shuheda*). Martyrs' Day is a moral crevasse. The Lebanese government named the square of the executions "Place des Martyrs."

---

85 Ali Fuad Erden, *Birinci Dünya Savaşında Suriye Hatıraları*, 280. Erden's knowledge of the Qur'an appears to be somewhat imprecise. The *sura* in question was probably *Al-Maida* [The Table] 5:33: "*Inama jadha ul-ladhin . . . yas'una fil-ard fasadan an yuqtalu aw yuslabu aw tuqta' aydihim wa arjulihim min khalf aw yunfu min al-ard*" ["In truth, the punishment for those who make war against God and His Messanger, and roam the earth corrupting it, is that they be killed, or crucified, or have their hands and feet amputated, alternately, or be exiled from the land"]. *The Qur'an: A New Translation*, trans. Tarif Khalidi, 87.

Two and half years later, on September 30, 1918, Damascus was about to fall. When the Ottoman army under the command of Liman von Sanders had evacuated Damascus and was falling back on Aleppo, the families of the military and civilian officials and the students of the military academy had also left with them. Sharif Faisal's Bedouin held the Rabuva Pass that the Damascus-Rayak railway passed through and set up machine guns on both sides. As the train carrying the families of the officials and the military cadets was going through the pass, the Bedouin commenced a crossfire. Children and mothers died. The massacre at Rabuva is "the day of the innocent martyrs." The "day of the innocent martyrs" deepened and widened the crevasse of "Martyr's Day."[86]

Judicial matters

According to Cemal Pasha, all the courts in the army zone were executive instruments of the army command. Their responsibility and obligation was to ensure that the orders of the Commander could be suited to the law. In practice, this idea and its application led to misunderstandings. Sometimes we would receive orders such as this: "After a short trial [he] will be executed." Sometimes officers in the field would be ordered to execute by firing squad. Sometimes death sentences would be passed according to "administrative fiat" (*hikmet-i idare*). It had been known that a convicted man would be "executed first and tried later." (Such was the case of a sheikh named Turki who had been accused of disturbing the peace in Damascus in 1917).

The commander of the Sinai Front, General von Kress, was the legal superior of all of the German units in the desert. On one occasion, Cemal Pasha had demanded that a German officer be tried in a German court martial. The general answered: "German judges do not act according to the orders of their superiors but according to the law. I am, therefore, absolved from carrying out your order." Cemal Pasha had to put up with this warning

---

86 Ali Fuad Erden, *Birinci Dünya Savaşında Suriye Hatıraları*, 280–281. It is very unlikely that such an event could have occurred. Given the fact that Faisal's forces entered Damascus on October 1, 1918, it is difficult to conceive how such a raid could have been planned by Faisal the day before his troops entered Damascus. My thanks to Talha Çiçek for his views on this issue. Email communication, October 14, 2016. Nor is the event mentioned by T. E. Lawrence. It does not appear in Faulkner's *Lawrence of Arabia's War* or in Rogan's *Fall of the Ottomans*.

from General von Kress and he did not insist. No Ottoman legal officer in the Fourth Army ever made such a pronouncement.

The Mufti of Gaza and his son were caught, suitcase in hand, while trying to escape from Gaza to the desert in order to flee to Egypt. They were brought before a court martial. The court martial declared that it "considered the opinion of the Army Commander the strongest testimony and evidence." Both father and son were sentenced to death and hung at the gates of Gaza. . . . The Army Corps Commander Fahreddin Pasha told me one day, "If His Excellency the Pasha ordered me to hang my own father, I would not hesitate."[87]

Beirut is the pearl of Syria

Beirut is the pearl of Syria. As the blockade led to the famine that destroyed the weak and the poor, the rich of Beirut (the old and the new rich) lived a life of peaceful ease and luxury in their magnificent villas surrounded by the aroma of jasmine and shaded by banana trees and orange groves. . . .

For the rich of Beirut, this was a dream life, and the peaceful blue Mediterranean that their homes overlooked was the symbol of this dream. Every two or three days the silhouette of a warship of the blockade would appear, but these ships would harm noone except the sailboats which were smuggling ammunition to the Sinai front. They would silently disappear on the day after they were seen, like ghosts, quietly and peacefully. Occasionally, the metallic sound of an aircraft would be heard. This was the only military excitement the Beirutis experienced. For the duration of the war, the glittering heights of Beiruti society were not disturbed by the sound of artillery or machine-gun fire.

The only thing daring to disturb the peace of Beirut was the moaning of the starving during the night. But this moaning would not last long, the poor wretches would soon die and be silent. Towards dawn, before the city woke up, the official refuse collectors of the municipality would remove the bodies, load them onto carts, and transport them to a common ditch. By the time the sun rose magnificently and gloriously over the

---

87 Ali Fuad Erden, *Birinci Dünya Savaşında Suriye Hatıraları*, 290–291. It is clear that Ali Fuad disagreed with such summary justice but could not do much about it. This is the same mindset that caused Cemal to push for the execution of the Arab patriots. As will be seen below, Fahreddin Pasha was quite ruthless when it came to deserters and captured Bedouin in Medina.

often snow-capped peaks of Mount Lebanon, the street would be long since cleansed.

The beauty of nature, the shimmering sea, the snowy mountains, the constant blooming of roses of all colors, orange trees, tangerines, banana groves and pines; [all this] belied the tragic fate of the city.

Some nights the moaning of the streets would be silenced by the dance music from the brilliantly lit villas.

In the *salons* of those villas, the rich who had enriched themselves from the grain put aside for the Sinai front, or destined for the [army in] Medina, uncaring and happy, would vie with each other to flaunt their happiness like the diamonds of their wives.

For the Beirutis living this life, the Turkish armies fighting on the Sinai or Hijaz fronts were nothing but a force engaged in a hopeless struggle that was criminally delaying the much anticipated peace and liberation.

When Enver Pasha came to Beirut, one very hot summer evening, a feast was held in his honor in the Municipality Gardens in the open air. The feasting lasted an hour. During this feast, the cries of the hungry *"Juan! Juan!"* were not heard and the scrawny trembling hands stretched through the metal bars of the garden, begging for a morsel of bread, were not seen.[88] Peace and order were perfect in Beirut during the First World War.

---

88 Ali Fuad Erden, *Birinci Dünya Savaşında Suriye Hatıraları*, 294–295. Fawaz, *Land of Aching Hearts*, 122–123: "In wartime, Beirut notables entertained top Ottoman officials in their homes in extravagant style, hoping to curry favor and perhaps land . . . [in] exclusive arrangements."

Chapter 4

Münevver Ayaşlı

Münevver Ayaşlı

[*Münevver Ayaşlı was the daughter of the Director of the Tobacco Regie, Caferi Tayyar Bey. Tayyar Bey had risen to the rank of major during the Balkan Wars (1910–1913) but had been forced to resign from the army. Cemal Pasha, who had been his close friend during his army years, was instrumental in his appointment as Director of the Regie in Aleppo in 1913 and his transfer to Beirut in 1915. The former Director had been a French citizen by the name of Monsieur Dekouza. When the war broke out, as an enemy alien, he was exiled to Urfa and appealed to Tayyar Bey to use his influence to have his place of exile changed to Istanbul. This Tayyar Bey did and by way of thanks, Dekouza offered the Tayyar Bey family his house in Beirut. Tayyar Bey accepted and the family moved to the new house. Although Münevver was only eight years old at this time, it seems she was quite a precocious child. Much of what she recounts in her memoirs can be verified by cross-checking other sources, such as her account of the last days of Ottoman presence in Beirut. Her account largely matches the events described by Hüseyin Kazım cited above. She went on to become a prolific writer in the Turkish Republic and made a name for herself as an intellectual of the Islamic right.*][1]

Aleppo

. . . We are on the train going to Aleppo. My mother is sad and anxious, fearful, [thinking], "What if my children become afflicted by the Aleppo

---

1 Münevver Ayaşlı, *Geniş Ufuklara ve Yabancı İklimlere Doğru* [*Towards Distant Horizons and Foreign Climes*] (Istanbul: Timaş, 2003). The Tobacco Regie was the tobacco monopoly of the Ottoman empire. It was a major French interest. Münevver Ayaşlı, *İşittiklerim Gördüklerim Bildiklerim* [What I Heard, I saw and I Know] (Istanbul: Boğaziçi Yayınları, 1990). Hatice Yıldız, *Münevver Ayaşlı. Hayatı, Eserleri ve Sanatı* [Münevver Ayaşlı. Her Life, Works and Art], unpublished MA thesis, Konya Selçuk University, 2009. My thanks to Halim Kara for this reference.

boil?" It is widely believed that whatever part of the body, hands or face, is exposed when the person first sights the fortress of Aleppo, that is the part of the body where the boil appears. Because of this one needed to take off one's shoes and expose one's naked soles to the fortress. Accordingly, we took our socks and shoes off, and stuck our naked feet out of the window, thinking that if we must be afflicted with the boil, it would at least be on our soles. The whole group, all the Turks, stuck their feet out of the train windows as we approached Aleppo. That is how they greeted the fortress of Aleppo.[2]

[*The Cafer Bey household rented a large house situated very close to the official residence of the governor of Aleppo.*]

Whenever we were to go out, Süleyman Efendi [Cafer Bey's orderly] would find us a clean carriage; he would sit beside the driver and help out with my mother's shopping. My mother would never leave the carriage. Süleyman Efendi or the tradesmen would bring our purchases to the carriage. . . .

It was at Aleppo that I witnessed for the first time the pomp and circumstance of the state. The Vali of Aleppo, Celal Bey, on his way to the government building, would pass beneath my window between eight and ten o'clock. Later, in the afternnon, between five and six, he would pass again on his way home. I would never miss the passing of the Vali. What a procession it was. . . . He would sit alone in an open-topped *phaeton*, a policeman opposite him, another policeman alongside, two lance-bearing cavalry in front and two behind. I loved to watch these processions. It was the state that was passing. I loved and respected my state. I wanted it to be powerful, I wanted it to be very powerful. The Arabs also wanted to see [this procession] which was a manifestation of the power of the state.[3]

War is declared

One day a great noise broke out. A great commotion, cries of joy, the beating of drums. The Arabs have mounted each others' shoulders making

---

2   Münevver Ayaşlı, *Geniş Ufuklara ve Yabancı Iklimlere Doğru*, 12. The disease in question is the *cutaneous leishmaniasis*, the "flesh-eating boil." It is a skin infection caused by a single-celled parasite that, in this case, is transmitted by the bite of a phelomine sandfly. Centers for Disease Control and Prevention, *Resources for Health Professionals*, accessed October 13, 2017, www.cdc.gov/parasites/leishmaniasis/health_professionals/index.html.

3   Münevver Ayaşlı, *Geniş Ufuklara ve Yabancı Iklimlere Doğru*, 14–15.

pyramids, walking down the road like that. It apperared that this joy was because we had entered the war, World War I, in 1914.

These Arabs who would later betray us had entered the war with such manifestations of joy, ready to fight shoulder to shoulder with us.[4]

Suddenly, Aleppo was enlivened, it came alive. The Canal front was opened. The Fourth Army had been charged with a difficult task. Its commander was Cemal Pasha, who was also the Minister of the Navy.

. . . Aleppo was full of Turks. We decorated our houses with red and green flags. My dear father also liked the green flags. I liked them very much as well. In our house, we always had a green flag alongside the red one. How could we know that one day the green flag would be seen badly?[5]

Falih Rıfkı Bey

A house had been rented for the staff officers. Who was staying at the house? The chief of staff of the Fourth Army, Colonel Ali Fuad Bey, my brother's friends from the Galatasaray *lycée*, Fikret Şefik Bey, Nuri Sabit Bey, and Ohrili Kemal Bey.

Falih Rıfkı Bey had also been appointed to the Fourth Army. He wanted to become friends with my brother and his crowd. He wanted to go riding with them. But the four friends would shun him. They would mount their horses and be gone before he came around. It fell to me to answer the poor Falih Rıfkı Bey. He would arrive at our house on his horse and ask where they were. I would answer from the balcony.

"They are not here, *Effendim.*"

"Where did they go?"

"We do not know, *Effendim.*"

The poor Falih Rıfkı Bey would go away disappointed.

[The truth was that] Falih Rıfkı Bey did not know French. The four friends would speak French among themselves. The four friends were good riders, whereas Falih Rıfkı Bey sat on his horse like a sack. The four were from Galatasaray, Falih Rıfkı was not.[6] All four were from Beyoğlu, Falih

---

4   Ibid., 18.
5   Ibid. The "green flag" referred to here is the flag of the Islamic Caliphate. The Ottoman sultan was also the Caliph of Islam. Ayaşlı is referring to the outlawing of the green flag after the abolition of the Caliphate by the Kemalist republic in 1924.
6   Ibid., 21. Galatasaray was the elite imperial *lycée*.

Rıfkı was from Cibali.[7] Falih Rıfkı was not *chic*; in fact, he never even wore his uniform properly, his *kalpak* was like a lemon peel on his head. [8] In sum, they did not like Falih Rıfkı Bey, found him very *alaturca* [conservatively Turkish] and slouchy, they shunned him.

Who would say that this man, unwanted and shunned, would go on to become a star who would outshine them all?[9]

[Münevver Ayaşlı on the Armenians]

. . . In the the First World War the Mehmetcik [the Turkish equivalent of the "Tommie" nickname given to British soldiers—SD] was fighting on so many fronts: the Caucasus front, the Canal front, the Galician front. The war was a matter of life or death (*can pazarı*). A matter of life or death for the Ottoman state and the Turkish nation . . . In Erzurum Mehmetcik was facing the Moscovite (*Moskof*) in front and the Armenian [was attacking] from behind. There were many Armenians in Erzurum and they were all a "fifth column" for the Russians. The Armenians had Russian gold and Russian weapons. The Turkish army, fighting for the country, for honor, was being stabbed in the back. Mehmetcik was caught in a crossfire. The government had to find a solution. The solution had to be found quickly, otherwise the Erzurum front would collapse. . . . In this regard the policy of the government was in no way a massacre [genocide] but a deportation, that is to say, pull the Armenians back from the war zones and exile them to inner Anatolia, possibly Urfa. No massacre, only deportation. . . .[10]

This was difficult, very difficult, but it was done, it had to be done. There were no roads, no tracks, they were to leave their homes and set out from Erzurum, leaving behind their homes, [and] their work. They were to travel by oxcart. Where to? The distances were long, and even longer if you had to go by oxcart. The country was at war, there was no security. The roads were full of deserters, brigands, and Kurds who were enemies of the Armenians. The Armenian convoys had to pass through

---

7 Beyoğlu was the Europeanized quarter of Istanbul. Cibali was a modest neigbourhood in the Golden Horn area.

8 The *kalpak* was the military version of the fez and had become the uniform headgear of the Turkish army officer corps after the Young Turk Revolution of 1908. See the illustrations in this volume.

9 Münevver Ayaşlı, *Geniş Ufuklara ve Yabancı İklimlere Doğru*, 21. She is referring here to Atay's subsequent fame as a writer.

10 Ibid., 27.

these [areas inhabited by] these lawless monsters. They had no guards or protectors. Even if there had been, who could have guaranteed that they would not join forces with the assailants? The Armenian convoys were travelling down these roads, slowly melting away as they progressed.

There was no massacre, but it cannot be denied that along the way they underwent damage, suffered [and were diminished by] casualties. . . .

On the subject of the deportations the German High Command agreed with us, they were with us. So [now] why these accusations, why these calumnies? Why are we alone being targeted? Why don't the Armenians accuse Germany and the Germans? Was it not that same Germany which was our ally? This is all because we are confronted by the Christian World (*Ehli Salib*), the blind and deaf Christian world.

During the deportations on the roads that the Armenian convoys travelled down or the provinces that they stopped in, the Vali, or the *kaimakams*, or other high ranking officials, or the gendarmes were taking Armenian girls and young women. They would immediately bring them home and marry them. That is when the tragedy of the Turkish woman and the Turkish child began. The Armenian woman who had been taken into the Muslim home began to wreak her revenge and project her hatred for all that was Turkish and Muslim against the poor and innocent [Muslim] woman [of the house]. Insults, mistreatment . . . Beatings and torture for the children whose only crime was being Turkish. The Turkish husband said nothing.[11]

We had such a case in the family. My uncle had a pretty aristocratic wife and a lovely child, they were getting along famously. Yet my uncle also fell for the fashion (*moda*) of taking Armenian women. While the Armenian convoys were passing through Aleppo, he took an Armenian woman and brought her home. We knew nothing about this. One day our aunt (*yenge*) came to us in tears and told us about this. My mother and father were very upset by this and immediately sprang into action. It had to be done quickly because it was necessary to finish [the business] before the act of marriage. Otherwise after the marriage it would be too late and nobody would be able to do anything.

My mother and father used all their influence and gave the Armenian girl back to her family; but it had not been easy. My uncle insisted that he wanted to marry her. According to the laws of the time, there was nothing

---

11 Ibid., 28.

to stop this. In this event my mother and father were able to solve the problem without a family drama.

The elder son of my nurse Remzi had also fallen in love with an Armenian girl and spoke of the matter to my mother. [He told my mother,] "Please, sister, you are the only one who can help me. Please do not say no. I have decided I will marry her. I do not want to go against your wishes. If I cannot marry her, I will be in despair, I may even shoot myself."

He managed to convince my mother, the problem was not my mother but my father. When my mother brought up the issue with my father, he exploded:

"We have just finished with one Armenian girl, what now, another Armenian girl? No, this cannot happen!"

My poor mother pleaded with him,"My dear husband, this child has made his mind up, let us be magnanimous. Let us say yes, otherwise Remzi is going to go against our wishes and marry the girl. Besides, Remzi is a bachelor and at the age of marriage, it is not like the other matter, there will be no family scandal."

She finally convinced my father and my father consented. The Armenian girl Siranoush became a Muslim and took the name Nimet. They came together to kiss my father's hand. My mother even gave them a wedding feast with music and dancers.

Turkish families were taking in Armenian girls not only through marriage, but by making them foster children. They were all given the name Ikbal [meaning "good fortune"]. They had brought us two girls, slightly older than me, some ten, twelve years old. My mother wanted them, my father was hesitating. I did not want them at all.

[I declared,] "These children have lost their mothers and fathers, they have been through so much suffering, can they ever forget that? If they ever do you any harm, can I ever forgive them and love them? Can they ever be a friend to any Turkish family, any Turkish home?" I used all my influence and my father was convinced. He returned the girls to the convoy. But my mother kept insisting, "So what, we could bring them up and take good care of them. We could have converted them to Islam."[12]

Besides these individual cases of rescuing Armenian children, there was another very important case. Cemal Pasha, although he was the Commander of the Fourth Army, was originally the Minister of the Navy.

---

12 Ibid., 29.

He kept this position throughout the war. Cemal Pasha had saved some fifty or sixty Armenian boys. His idea was to make these [Armenian boys] sailors (*levend*) and take them into the navy. In the *devşirme* tradition he would convert them to Islam and take them into the navy. He put these boys in an empty monastery in the Jabal at Antoura, converted them to Islam, and gave them Turkish names. These children were better taken care of than the soldiers. For some five years they lived a comfortable life in Antoura. When the towns were suffering from the famine, they were well-fed and clothed. All this until we were defeated. Then they immediately went back to their old religion, became Armenians again, and forgot all our kindness they had seen for five years. They joined the French Army because there were already Armenian volunteer regiments. They all became pitiless Turk haters. . . .

It is a shame about the Armenians, they committed treason and got what they deserved. . . .[13]

[On Halide Edib]

. . . This little woman was not like the other women in Cemal Pasha's circle, she did not pander to him, crossed her legs in front of him, allowed the Pasha to light her cigarette, even entered into political discussions with him. This little woman had ideas of her own, she voiced them, and even imposed them.

From the very first day she had won me over, my interest in her increased daily.

Who was this woman? She was Halide Edib, a writer. It immediately became known in her circle that she was a Jewish convert. Rather, her father Edib Efendi was a Jewish convert to Islam, a *dönme*. He had been a minor official in the Yıldız palace.

But his daughter was against the palace. She was a Turkist, a Turanian. A semitic Turanian, that is to say, a racist (*Semitik bir Turancı yani ırkçı*)! To use today's terminology, she was a craniologist (*kafatascı*).

Yet she had such a Biblical beauty, a beauty straight out of the Old Testament, she looked so like the pretty girls of *beni Israel*.

---

13 Ibid., 30–31. On the issue of the Antoura orphanage, see my "'Your Religion is Outdated.' Orphans, Orphanages and Halide Edib during the Armenian Genocide. The Case of Antoura." Forthcoming in *Revue des Etudes arméniens contemporaines* (December 2018).

Halide Edib had come to Syria on a mission. She was to open schools with the aim of spreading Turkish culture, to teach Arab children Turkish, make them love Turkishness, and in this way Turkify Syria. Halide Edib Hanım was some sort of Turkish missionary and good will envoy.

In fact, there was a school near Beirut which the French had abandoned during the war. This was a big, handsome, palatial school in its own parkland. This school was given to Halide Edib. Everything was already in place in this French school, all of its equipment was still in place, from desks to beds in the dormitories. All of its bedsheets were pure cotton, in fact, French cotton. In short, it was a perfect school.[14]

The school was opened but it was a school without pupils. . . . In those days I was attending the German school, and I liked my school very much. Yet one day Cemal Pasha said to my father: "Brother, we want Arab children to go to our schools, yet even our own children go to foreign schools. Halide Hanum is most offended, most hurt. Is she not right?"

This was an order. Accordingly, we were taken from the German school and put into Hanım's school.

I used to walk to the German school by myself with my schoolbag on my back, simply, without fuss. . . . There was no way I could go to my new school on foot, nor were there trams or buses in wartime Beirut. So we started going to school in a luxurious *phaeton* in great pomp. . . . Despite all this it took me an hour longer to get to school that to my German school.

As to our schoolmistress Halide Edib Hanim, she was in her palatial quarters, resting . . . the classes were empty. Teacher ladies from Istanbul, with made-up eyes (*gözleri sürmeli*), dressed in pink hijab (*maşlah*) and pink headscarves of *crepe d'amour* cloth pulled tightly around their heads, promenaded in the corridors. Who were they to teach? There were no pupils in the school.

Maybe, Halide Edib was a good writer, but what is certain is that she was a bad organizer and administrator. I went to her school for three months, I did not even attend one day of classes. Yet in these three months an opera was composed, based entirely on Talmudic themes; its music was created by a Lebanese composer Vedia Sabra.

I knew Vedia Sabra very well, because she used to give me private piano lessons. The name of the opera was *Shepherds of Canaan* (*Kenan Çobanları*).

---

14 Münevver Ayaşlı, *Geniş Ufuklara ve Yabancı İklimlere Doğru*, 30–31. This is the Notre Dame de Nazareth referred to above.

We put this opera on the stage and acted it in the presence of Governors, Commanders, and Police Chiefs.

This opera, *Shepherds of Canaan*, had wounded me deeply and made me think bitter thoughts. Because this play was acted out thoughtlessly and arrogantly in front of those who held the fate of the country in their hands. . . .[15]

In short, the "cultural imperialism" envisioned by Cemal Pasha had not taken off, it did not work. After three months I gave my father an ultimatum, "I will not listen to you or Cemal Pasha, I will not go to that school." My father must have agreed as they put me back in the German School.[16]

This school game had barely lasted two years. As soon as Cemal Pasha left Syria, the school was closed down, Halide Edib Hanım and all her teachers went back to Istanbul. Just in time too, because if they had stayed in Beirut, they would have had a rough time.

When the Ottoman army retreated and the enemy armies came, all the Beirutis started slandering the Turks. It was said that Hanım and her teachers had removed all the precious furniture and goods from the French school and taken them to Istanbul. I did not believe this; but there were other rumours. It was said that Hanım and her teachers had bought many things from the big stores in Beirut and run off without paying their debts. This is possible in the following fashion. The Beiruti store owners and merchants, to be in the good graces of Cemal Pasha, had tried to look cute to Hanım and her teachers. These unctuous (*yalpak*) Lebanese had offered all the ladies credit. They probably almost forced their goods on them saying, "Buy, buy, buy as much as you like, you can pay when you want to!" The teacher ladies, believing the unctuous Lebanese, did buy, but when the war front suddenly collapsed and they had to leave in a hurry, they probably did leave behind some debts; but this could not have been much. What would the poor teachers buy? One or two *mashlahs* and headscarves . . . I know very well how the unctuous Lebanese can flatter when it suits their interests. . . .[17]

---

15 Münevver Ayaşlı, İşittiklerim Gördüklerim Bildiklerim (Istanbul: Boğaziçi Yayınları, 1990), 64–65.

16 Münevver Ayaşlı, *Genis Ufuklara ve Yabancı Iklimlere Doğru*, 32.

17 Ibid., 34–36.

Life in Sofar

. . . The summers are very hot in Beirut. Everyone, that is to say, of course, those who have the means, do not stay in Beirut but go up to the Jabal. We also went up to the Jabal. . . .

Our house in Sofar was very nice. The Cemal Pasha family had also rented a house in Sofar, but it was more like a palace. They were numerous and lived close to us. Cemal Pasha would also come to Sofar from time to time. I became very good friends with Cemal Pasha's children. We were almost like siblings. Cemal Pasha had five children, four sons and one daughter. His two oldest sons, Ahmet and Mehmet, were studying in Germany. The twins Kamuran and Necdet were my age. The youngest was called Behcet. We used to call him Bubi.

My brother had come home for the summer holidays, my mother was very happy. Apart from our two pretty carriage horses, my father had bought a beautiful purebred Arab for my brother. This horse was unique. We had named him Mahbub. My brother was very happy.

Who cared about the war?[18]

Our house in Sofar was very pretty. It was on the main street. In Beirut we used to frequent the good families; but in Sofar we became very good friends, because Sofar is a small place, people ran into each other several times a day. Sofar was also the summer residence of the good Lebanese families like the Tabets and the Sursocks. The Tabets and the Sursoks were the richest. We had become close friends in Sofar. Madame Tabet came to have morning coffee with my mother nearly every day. Madame Tabet had four sons. Two remained in Egypt because of the war, the other two were with her. Her eldest son George was unwell, he never went out and sat in the garden resting in an armchair with a blanket on his knees. He would salute us respectfully in a very well-brought-up manner and ask how we were. Her younger son Eduard was a very handsome boy. They became good friends with my brother.

But the real Queen of Lebanon was Linda Sursock. It was rumoured that she was Cemal Pasha's mistress. In fact, the famous French novelist Pierre Benoit wrote a novel about her, *La Chatelaine du Liban*, it was about her affair with Cemal Pasha. Linda's husband was a very handsome young man who was very rich. They had two children, Ibrahim and Marie, I became good friends with them. . . . Linda had a two wheeled buggy called

---

18 Münevver Ayaşlı, *Geniş Ufuklara ve Yabancı Iklimlere Doğru*, 37.

a Tono (*toneau*). She used to drive it herself, always accompanied by her best friend and confidante, Mademoiselle Ksep. They would go by our house and we would exchange greetings. She would also sometimes come for a coffee.[19]

The new house

[*Münevver's mother wanted to move into a house in Beirut with a view of the sea. After some searching, a very handsome house was found. It belonged to the Bassoul family but it had been rented to a French dentist who had to leave. The Bassoul family was ready to rent the house but stated that they would not take responsibility for the furniture. As the neutral Dutch Consulate was taking care of French interests, the house had to be rented through them.*]

. . . The Consul actually did not want to get involved, but in a few days two *kavas* [footmen] from the Dutch Embassy and an official came and took some of the furniture. However, they did not want the bigger pieces and left them in the house. [20]

My mother liked Beirut so much that if Beirut had remained ours I am sure we would have settled there after my father retired from the Regie. . . .

[The private train]

. . . Cemal Pasha's family were visiting with us again. [Cemal Pasha's older sister] Hala Hanım Efendi and her entourage, after staying with us for a month, invited us to Damascus and we gladly accepted. Both my mother and I wanted to see Damascus. So here we are, me, my mother and our guests, on the way to Damascus. We are crossing the Lebanon mountains.

---

19 Ibid., 38–39. Leila Fawaz notes that the Syrian politician Faris al-Khuri mentioned in his private papers that "[t]he Sursocks described themselves as Ottomans, and in his papers, Khuri noted the friendship that Jamal Pasha had with Michel Sursock, a friendship which some family members believed extended to Sursock's wife and cousin, Linda Sursock." See Fawaz, *A Land of Aching Hearts*, 122. Ayaşlı is entirely wrong about the book by Pierre Benoit *La Chatelaine de Liban*. The book has nothing to do with Cemal Pasha or Linda Sursock being a French equivalent of a "penny dreadful."

20 Münevver Ayaşlı, *Geniş Ufuklara ve Yabancı Iklimlere Doğru*, 47. After the end of the war the house and its furniture would become the ruin of the Tayyar Bey family. They had a continuous stream of house guests, including Cemal Pasha's family.

It is spring, Mount Lebanon is like paradise on earth. The aroma of lemon and orange groves, wild tulips, wild lilacs in the fields. Cemal Pasha's sister, the lady, sends word to the driver, "Stop the train," she orders. The train stops and we get off to gather wild tulips and wild lilies. Then the lady sends word to the driver, "Get the train moving." The train moves.

It is wartime. There is no coal. Trains run on the lovely pines and cedars of Lebanon. The train moves by burning those beautiful pines and cedars. It moves so slowly that a young and agile person could get on and off easily.[21]

[Münevver dislikes Cemal Pasha]

. . . I loved the sultans and the men of religion. I loved my religion and my country. I did not at all like the men in power. I hated them; because, despite my tender age, I understood that for my country these men were not good, but bad men. It was because of this, because he was among these men that I did not like Cemal Pasha. My mother, father, and brother liked the Pasha.

I should also make it clear that in his private life, Cemal Pasha was not a bad man, he was always polite, kind, and considerate. We never saw him in pyjamas or wearing slippers. He was always in uniform and his hair was well-groomed.

One day during the evening meal the Pasha appeared very thoughtful and absent-minded. He did not eat much and left the table early. We also got up and retired to our rooms.

I asked my mother, "What is wrong with the Pasha?"

"They are fighting in Gaza. The Pasha is worried about the war. He has not had any news."

Sometime past midnight there was a pounding on our door. We could hear the Pasha, he was shouting, "Sister! Sister!" My mother got dressed and went down. When she came back, I asked her what the commotion was about. [She replied,] "The battle has been won in Gaza.[22] The Pasha is overjoyed, he has woken everybody up, he is drinking champagne and offering us all champagne." I answered, "Rather than drinking champagne he should offer prayers of thanks."

---

21 Ibid.
22 This would be the first battle of Gaza on March 27, 1917 when the British suffered heavy casualties and had to retreat. Rogan, *The Fall of the Ottomans*, 326–327.

Some 50–60 years after this event, at the College de France in Paris, Monsieur Massignon would [tell a story].[23] The scene: the coronation ceremony of Faisal, the young King of Iraq, to which Monsieur Massignon is invited. He would remember the occasion, laughing until tears ran down his eyes. [He said,] "We celebrated the coronation of the Hashemite King of Iraq, Faisal, the king and his entourage decked out in old Prussian uniforms, with food cooked by a French chef and listening to waltzes played by an orchestra brought in from Vienna."

So we celebrated the victory at Gaza with French champagne. . . .[24]

[Cemal Pasha's snobbery]

Cemal Pasha's greatest wish was to attract good Turkish families to Syria and Lebanon. He wanted to see well-brought-up (*kibar*) Turkish families around him. He particularly liked the aristocratic and *alafranga* families of Istanbul [*alafranga* meant "westernized" as opposed to *alaturca*—SD]. Somebody who was just the type that Cemal liked was Ismet Bey [also known as *le beau Ismet* (*handsome Ismet*)]. Ismet Bey spoke French like a Frenchman, English like an Englishman, and his manners were those of a perfect European. Cemal Pasha liked to learn poise and conduct (*adab ve erkan*) from people such as these. Ismet Bey astonished Lebanese socialites who were in love with all things French. They also spoke French, but not like Ismet Bey. They also pretended to be Parisian, but it was as if Ismet Bey had come from Paris yesterday. The admiration of the Lebanese socialites for Ismet Bey raised his value in the eyes of Cemal Pasha. In any event, Ismet Bey was from a very *alafranga* family. It was the Edhem Pasha family. This family had produced many notable people[, such as] the great painter Osman Hamdi Bey and the architect Sedat Edhem Bey.[25]

---

23 Louis Massignon was a famous French orientalist. Münevver Ayaşlı would later go on to study at the College de France and claims in her writing to have "become great friends" with Massignon. Yıldız, *Münevver Ayaşlı*, 79.

24 Münevver Ayaşlı, *Geniş Ufuklara ve Yabancı Iklimlere Doğru*, 50.

25 Münevver Ayaşlı, *Geniş Ufuklara ve Yabancı Iklimlere Doğru*, 52. The Edhem Pasha family is the family of Ibrahim Edhem Pasha, onetime Grand Vizier of the Ottoman Empire, his son Osman Hamdi Bey, famous for his work in the sphere of archeology and orientalist painting, and Sedat Eldem, a famous modernist architect influenced by Frank Lloyd Wright. Ismet was known in the Eldem family as "*le beau Ismet*." Personal communication from Edhem Eldem. In French in the original. On Ibrahim Edhem Pasha see Edhem Eldem, "The Story of the Little Greek Boy Who Became a Powerful

[Loss of the hope of victory. The Ottoman defeat. The Turks leave]

... As the years advanced, we gradually lost our hope of victory. Now most of us were ready to accept a fifty-percent victory. Every day it was beginning to look like the enemy had more than a fifty-percent chance [of winning]. Our hopes fell to forty, thirty, twenty, and ten percent. It was as if we were getting used to the idea of defeat. Every day we expected bad news, news of catastrophe....

... Another piece of unexpected news ... Cemal Pasha has abandoned the Fourth Army to the Germans and has returned to Istanbul. .... His family have also left for Istanbul. All the Turks in Syria and Lebanon are gradually returning to Istanbul. ....

The other piece of terrible news was the entry of British troops into Jerusalem in 1918.[26] This was terrible news not just for us as the Turks, but for the whole of the Islamic world.[27] This was the victory of the Christian world (*Ehl-i Salib*).[28] [Even] our ally Catholic Austria was celebrating, the church bells were ringing for joy in Vienna.

As the Turks were leaving, my father wanted to send us ahead, saying he would join us later. I was the only one who agreed with him. I said "Dear father, I am afraid we should go. You can come later, you can come more easily alone." My mother and brother wanted to stay. My mother did not want to leave the Beirut she loved so very much. My brother did not want to leave his horse Mahbub whom he loved like his life. The family was divided, my father and I in favour of leaving, my mother and brother wanting to stay. When they came around to the idea of leaving, it was too late, the roads were cut, and we were feeling the breath of the enemy. My mother and brother were hopeful, saying, "The British and French are civilized,

---

Pasha: the Myth and Reality in the Life of Ibrahim Edhem Pasha, ca. 1818–1893." Unpublished paper cited with the permission of the author.

26 Ayaşlı is wrong about the date. The British entered Jerusalem on 11 December 1917. Eugene Rogan, *The Fall of the Ottomans*, 350: "By sunrise on 9 December, 401 years of Ottoman rule in Jerusalem had come to an end." Çiçek, *War and State Formation in Syria*, 263: "On 13 December Cemal Pasha left Damascus for Istanbul."

27 Ayaşlı was not wrong in her reference to the "Christian world." Howard Bliss, the president of the Syria Protestant College, would refer to the event as "the redemption of Jerusalem," or the "deliverance of Jerusalem from the Turks." AUB Archives. Howard Bliss Collection 1902–1920. Box 19, File 5.

28 Münevver Ayaşlı, *Geniş Ufuklara ve Yabancı Iklimlere Doğru*, 55. It is interesting that she uses the term *ehl-i salib*, which actually means "crusaders."

in any case we are not officials or military we are the officials of a French firm. . . ."[29]

. . . Six days of vacuum . . . No army, no government, no enemy . . . You may well ask, "How can that happen?," but happen it did. In these six days, who is in charge? Hüseyin Kazım Bey and Monsieur Alfred Sursock.

This is what came to pass. The Vali who replaced Azmi Bey in Beirut (I believe his name was Ismail Hakkı Bey) was very much under the influence of Hüseyin Kazım Bey, doing everything he demanded. Under the influence of Hüseyin Kazım and Alfred Sursock, the Turkish Vali left Beirut before the enemy arrived, leaving the city completely abandoned. The people of Beirut were stupefied. They remained quiet asking, "How can this happen?" They remained quiet, waiting for the enemy. All we saw in the streets was the magnificent carriage of Monsieur Sursock drawn by his splendid white horses. In it [one always saw] Hüseyin Kazım on the right and Alfred Sursock on the left. The Arab press of Beirut was running banner headlines praising Hüseyin Kazım, declaring, "The great friend of the Arabs Hüseyin Kazım Bey!" On the other side, that is to say, the enemy side, there was indecision. They could not believe that Beirut was to fall into their laps like ripe fruit, and they hesitated, fearing a trap.

We are waiting, waiting for the enemy. Which enemy are we waiting for? The British? The French? The victorious British general who had won on this front was General Allenby.

After six days of indecision a very sad and tragic event occurred. The Turkish flag came down over the Serail. In its place up went a flag we did not recognize. It was not the British or the French flag. Everyone stared in amazement. We discovered that this flag was the flag of the newly created state of Syria. We were to expect the King of Syria, Faisal. This was none other than Faisal, the son of Sharif Husayn, the same Faisal who had deserted to Lawrence from the Turkish headquarters at Jerusalem.

King Faisal was met by Hüseyin Kazım Bey and Alfred Sursock who gave him possession of the city.

Suddenly, another fantastic story: King Faisal is going to marry Rikkat Hanim, Hüseyin Kazım Bey's daughter. Many people who had put distance between themselves and us began to get close again. This was because the commander of the Syrian army which had entered the city with King Faisal

---

29 The Tobacco Regie was a French company.

was my father's school friend, Shukri Pasha. He sent word to my father: "Does Tayyar Bey wish for anything?"

The Beirutis were throwing their fezzes in the air, shouting, "Ya Tayyar Bey!"

My father thanked him, asked him for nothing and did not pay a courtesy call on Shukri Pasha.[30]

Just as the marriage of Rikkat Hanim and King Faisal did not happen, King Faisal's rule in Beirut did not last long. The Syrian army pulled out and was replaced by the French army followed by the Armenian brigades (*Ermeni alayları*). The situation was very bad for us. We all started to wait for the British army, whom we saw as saviors.

The Armenian soldiers were raiding all the Turkish homes at night, searching for Armenian girls and children. One night they raided the home of our Remzi Efendi, who had a little Armenian girl called Marie, and took her. They tried to take his wife Nimet, who was an Armenian convert, but when they found they were legally married and had a child, they gave up on Nimet. This was a horrible situation. After things got sorted out our Remzi Efendi played the hero: "If they had taken Nimet, I would have shot them and then myself."

Remzi had a son. He had named him Vahideddin, after the new sultan. . . .[31]

. . . The Armenians did not come, but the French dentist, in whose house we were living, came back to Beirut with the first available conveyance, like a wounded monster. The first thing he did was throw us out of the house. . . . Moreover, the creature started a legal suit against my father who was tried in the French military court. Consider our situation. Our father, defeated and a prisoner, at the hands of the French military court [was bad enough, but] what was worse, the creature was not wrong. . . . We were fleeced, fleeced, all the money we had saved from the salary paid in gold coin, our horse, carriage, our three beautiful Arab horses, particularly my

---

30 Münevver Ayaşlı, *Geniş Ufuklara ve Yabancı İklimlere Doğru*, 56. Ayaşlı is somewhat confused about the events here, which is to be expected as she was writing nearly fifty years later. Faisal never came to Beirut. The Arab general in question is Shukri Pasha al-Ayyoubi who had also been military governor of Damascus after the Turkish withdrawal. Gelvin, *Divided Loyalties*, 26: "[The] leader of the departing Ottoman army had also designated al-Ayyubi to secure the city."

31 Münevver Ayaşlı, *Geniş Ufuklara ve Yabancı İklimlere Doğru*, 57. Thus a boy with an Armenian mother is named after the last sultan of the Ottoman Empire.

brother's splendid Mahbub, all our precious carpets, antiques, all of it was sold in order to pay compensation to the French doctor.

I cannot describe how low the morale of my mother and brother had sunk. Every time my father went to the military court, we would shudder with fear: was he going to come back in handcuffs? Are they going to imprison our father? We had lost our horses and goods, let us hope not to lose our lives!". . .[32]

. . . After the French, the British army also entered Beirut. With the English a time of plenty started in the city. Butter, cheese, jams, chocolate, cocoa . . . The English were feeding their troops on these, and the troops were selling these [provisions] cheaply to the local population. We had not seen chocolate for five years. . . .

As usual I was watching the world from my window. My observations: the British officers are very handsome, elegant. As to the enlisted men, frighteningly ugly, small, spindly, tiny bright blue eyes, long and sparse yellow hairs. These [hairs] were in plain view because the arms and legs of the English soldiers were bare. This was the first time that we saw soldiers wearing shorts. The English soldiers did not molest us in any way. Only, and that from a distance, showing their garden-hoe-like teeth, they would say, "I love you, I love you" to any young girl or woman they saw.[33]

. . . We had given up on Beirut. We now experienced very difficult days in this Beirut where we had such good times. We waited impatiently for the day we would return to Istanbul. We missed Istanbul severely. But when [were we to go back?]

One day we heard car horns, sirens, marches, we asked, "What is happening? What now?" Then we learned that an armistice had been declared, not peace, just armistice. For us, this was a glimmer of hope, however weak. Yes, it was decided to return the civilian prisoners. Oh my God, thanks be to You! Now are waiting for a ship big enough to accommodate all of us.

Again, it was Hüseyin Kazım Bey and Monsieur Alfred Sursock who were taking care of the civilian Turkish families, working to ensure that they be rescued as soon as possible from the life of prisoners.

Finally a huge ship arrived, a British-built transatlantic liner; but what a wreck! Throughout the war years it had served as a troop carrier between India and Egypt, but its engines were healthy and strong. The ship docked,

---

32 Ibid. It is likely that the house they were living in had been confiscated by the Turks, although Münevver does claim that they paid rent.
33 Ibid., 59.

the Turkish families began to embark. Everybody in the hold, because there were no cabins. Again, through the good offices of Hüseyin Kazım Bey he managed to procure a cabin for us and his own family.

The Turks are scrambling up the gangway as if they were escaping from prison. . . . As if they were running from a madhouse. The Turks are running up the gangway, as if they expect any minute that somebody would pull them back.

The ship slowly moved away from the dock and headed for the open sea. On the quay, the few friends the Turks had left and the more curious onlookers had come to see how the Turks were leaving. Some Arabs, who had hated the Turks, were casting angry gazes as if to say, "Serves you right! See how you are leaving!"

Farewell, beautiful Beirut, farewell, beautiful Lebanon! We cast our eyes back at the places we had loved, sad and bitter, until we could see them no more.

I had been an eight-year-old girl when we left Istanbul. Now I was returning to Istanbul at 13, almost a young lady. How happy we were when we came here with great hopes, how much we had loved Aleppo, Beirut, Lebanon. Now we are returning to Istanbul, broken, crushed, desolate, and accepting our fate. . . . My God, what is this pain of ours? We lost our homeland Rumeli for ever and returned to Istanbul. Now we abandon these lands that we have loved like our own country and go back to Istanbul. What is this, my God? The price we must pay for our glorious past?[34]

---

34 Ibid., 60–61. Münevver's family were from Salonica. Her account largely matches that of Hüseyin Kazım seen above, except for the scene of the glorious send-off described by Kazım.

Chapter 5

Naci Kaşif Kıcıman

Naci Kaşif Kıcıman

[*Naci Kıcıman was the chief intelligence officer of Fahreddin Pasha, the defender of Medina during the long siege of the city by the forces of Sharif Husayn in the Arab Revolt of 1916–1918. He was a close confidant of the Pasha and kept detailed notes on each stage of the siege. After the war he wrote to Fahreddin Pasha asking him for permission to publish the memoir. The text of the memoir is very interesting as it combines Naci Kıcıman's observations with official documents and orders issued by Fahri Pasha. Hence the text varies between very dry reporting on military matters and extremely emotional outbreaks where the author rails against "the treason of the Arabs" etc. He was taken prisoner after the fall of Medina and spent three years as a prisoner of war in Egypt. The memoir was published for the first time in 1922 in installments in the "Tercüman-ı Hakikat" newspaper, with the title, "How we lost the Hijaz." Kıcıman went on to hold several important posts in Republican Turkey, becoming an expert on municipal government and serving as a governor in Sinop, Bolu, Trabzon, Sivas, İsparta, and Siirt. Fahreddin Pasha was to serve later as the ambassador of the Republic of Turkey in Kabul.*

After the outbreak of the Arab Revolt on June 5, 1916, an Ottoman army, the Hijaz Expeditionary Force [Hicaz Kuvve-i Seferiyesi] under the command of Fahreddin Pasha, was to hold Medina until January 10, 1919, more than two months after the Mondros Armistice of October 30, 1918. The force, some 14,000 troops well supplied with artillery and ammunition, was too powerful for a frontal attack by the Bedouin forces of the Arab Revolt. Indeed there was some disagreement among the Allied forces and the Arabs as to whether Medina needed to be conquered at all. Some, such as T. E. Lawrence, felt that holding down the Ottoman forces in Medina was more useful than a costly frontal attack. Lawrence favored continuous pressure on the Hijaz Railway, the lifeline of Medina. Others, such as Emir Faisal, felt that the conquest of

Medina was essential for the establishment of a viable Arab state. In fact, Medina was not entirely cut off until April 8, 1918 while the last reinforcements arrived in March. As non-Muslims may not set foot on the sacred land of the Hijaz, it was also deemed not possible to bring in Christian regular British and French troops as the British feared that this would provoke an intense reaction from Muslim Indian subjects who would see it as deliberately defiling the holy lands.[1]

In March 1918 the German Commmander in Chief of Ottoman forces, General Liman von Sanders had advised in favor of an evacuation of Medina, enabling the much-needed troops to defend Palestine. Yet he had been overriden by Enver Pasha because of the symbolic value of Medina for the Muslim world.[2]

After the surender of Medina, Fahreddin (Türkkan) Pasha was taken to the Kasr al Nil prisoner of war camp in Egypt, where he was kept for six months. He was then transferred to Malta as a "war criminal" and kept in the Fort Salvatore barracks for two years. He was allowed to return to Turkey in 1919. In 1920 he joined the Kemalist forces and fought against the Greeks.][3]

Letter from Fahreddin Pasha to the author

I received your writings on the Hijaz. I was very pleased and touched, I thank you very much. I prayed for you for having rescued from oblivion "the defense of the Hijaz" while the sweat has not dried and the blood spilled is still warm. May you be blessed! . . . I am searching for the documents you asked for. Because I did not keep a diary, only one or two of my notebooks survided the war. I will send you what I have, and I will later send you what I find. You say that you are not qualified to write the story of the "defence of the Hijaz." Your sincerity is enough. Be tranquil.[4]

---

1 Naci Kaşif Kıcıman, *Medine Müdafaası: Hicaz Bizden Nasıl Ayrıldı* [*The Defense of Medina: How we lost the Hijaz*] (Istanbul: Sebil Press, 1994). On the siege of Medina see also Martin Strohmeier, "Fakhri (Fahreddin) Paşa and the end of Ottoman rule in Medina (1916–1919)," *Turkish Historical Review* 4 (2013): 192–223; Elie Kedourie, "Surrender of Medina. January 1919," *Middle Eastern Studies* 13 (1977): 124–143; Rogan, *The Fall of the Ottomans*, 302–303; Faulkner, *Lawrence of Arabia's War*.

2 Sanders, *Five Years in Turkey*, 207: "Nothing but political and religious interests caused Enver to call attention again and again to the great importance of Medina. . . . It was unnatural and impracticable to continue indefinitely the defense as far as Medina."

3 Naci Kaşif Kıcıman, *Medine Müdafaası*, 16.

4 Ibid.

[The end of the road]

[*Kıcıman noted the historic irony that Medina was being defended by the Muslim army of the Ottoman Sultan against Arabs who claimed descent from the Prophet Mohammad. Kıcıman is scathing in his treatment of the Bedouin fighters:*][5]

. . . Although the Bedouin had known for four hundred years that the Ottoman forces they were fighting were Muslims, because of extensive propaganda and because we were allied with the Germans they were fooled into believing the we were infidels (*kafir*).

From the front lines they would shout "*Nasrani* (Christian)!" In retaliation we would have our imam chant the *ezan* (the call to prayer). This they answered by shouts of "*kezzab* (liar)!" and rained bullets on the imam. One day Sergeant Osman, a hero who had set out on a reconnaissance sortie, was captured by the rebels. His ears, nose, and reproductive organ were cut off, then the rebels disembowelled him.[6]

[*In retaliation after a particularly savage encounter with the Bedouin:*] Fahreddin Pasha ordered that the heads of three dead Bedouin be cut off and exhibited publicly in Medina.[7]

[Propaganda and counter-propaganda]

[*Both sides published propaganda tracts referring to Islam to justify their position. The main thrust of the declaration published in the "El Qibla" newspaper in Mecca was that the Turks had committed heresy by translating the Qur'an into Turkish. Also there were passages recounting how Cemal Pasha had given parties where Muslim women served alcoholic drinks.*][8]

. . . Fahreddin Pasha was constantly exposed to this [propaganda] while he patrolled with his forces all along the front. He had established a newspaper called the *El Hijaz* in Medina to counter the propaganda of Mecca and prevent the confusion in the thoughts of those Arabs who had remained loyal. However, because of problems in distribution the paper did not produce the expected results. The newspaper did not circulate in

---

5   Ibid., 39.

6   Ibid., 55.

7   Ibid., 287.

8   Ibid., 61. See also Talha Çiçek, "Visions of Islamic Unity: A Comparison of Djemal Pasha's *al Sharq* and Sharif Husayn's *al Qibla* periodicals," *Die Welt Des Islams* 54 (2014): 460–482.

the lands of Ibn Rushd or Ibn Saud. Although there were many Arabs in the *Haremeyn* who were loyal to the government, it was not possible to use them even for propaganda and espionage. In time they all joined the Sharifian side. . . .[9]

[How to bribe a Sheikh. Bedouin relations with the Ottomans]

. . . When I had been appointed to Medina, the Protector and Commander of Medina was Basri Pasha who had been at this post for seven years. He knew all the Sheikhs of the area personally. They would pay the Pasha periodic visits each year, declare their loyalty, and receive their gifts.

. . . When these gifts were distributed, Basri Pasha would keep me by his side. He knew how many men each sheikh had at his command and his standing in the tribe, and he would gauge each gift accordingly. This Ottoman pasha sat behind a crystal table under which he had two sacks, each containing one thousand gold liras. The pasha would deliberately put each of his feet on one of these bags and would make sure to make a noise every time he shifted his feet. The Sheikhs sitting opposite him would take in this scene. After the conversation with a Sheikh was over, the pasha would put one of these sacks on his lap, he would [then dip his hand] in the sack and extract a full handful, half-handful, or a quarter-handful, according to his estimate of the Sheikh's importance. The men would take their gold, kiss his hand, and I would show them out, but the pasha would not move.

After the Sheikhs had left he would tell me,

"Now, Naci, write!"

"What am I to write, Your Excellency?"

The pasha would think [and answer],

"So-and-so was a Sheikh of Sheikhs so I gave him a full handful. This makes eighty liras. So-and-so was [only] a Sheikh so I gave him half a handful. That makes fifty liras."

. . . If the gold coins overflowed between his fingers he would count that as one [full] handful and have me write eighty. According to these measures the gift that he could hold with three fingers was twenty-five liras. According to these calculations he would throw the chits I had written into the sacks and the accounting session would be over. . . .

9   Naci Kaşif Kıcıman, *Medine Müdafaası*, 61–62.

. . . The new Emir of Mecca, who had been appointed by the government in Istanbul, did not know how to deal with the Arab tribes. He did not know how gold was to be used in the Hijaz. Therefore he had no influence on the military campaign and did not consult those with experience. In a short while, he returned to the cool waters and the green mountains of Lebanon.

However, the only reason why the revolt spread was gold and provisions. Whichever side would give the most gold until the first blow was struck would have the Bedouin support. Later we would distribute wheat, oats, and other provisions to the tribes along the railway but this only delayed their revolt. We were already too late in distributing provisions to the tribes of the *Haremeyn*. Because of this, because of hunger, and for the purposes of looting, they joined the rebels. . . .[10]

. . . In fact, the tribes around Medina hesitated for a long time. Not believing that Sharif Husayn could actually oppose the state, they remained loyal to the government. They continued to receive their subsidies and the provisions to be distributed to their tribes. The question of whether the Bedouin would join Sharif Husayn or stay loyal to the Ottoman state was closely linked to the economic and social circumstances in these dificult times.

The Bedouin, according to an old custom, would call anything related to the state *Haqq al Dawla* [The right of the state—SD], be it officials [or] officers. Everything was part of the great personage of the state, to the extent that they even called the trains in the Hijaz *cahş-üd devle* ([in Arabic,] *Jahsh al Dawla*), meaning "the beast of the state." Therefore, the concept of the state for the Bedouin comprises such a complex of meanings that they could not understand how Sharif Husayn could raise the flag of revolt against such powerful and magnificent entity. This was why they remained along the railway lines and continued to receive the wheat that the state continued to provide.

---

10 Ibid., 65–67. The Young Turk government appointed Sharif Ali Haidar, the head of a competing branch of the Hashemites, to replace Sharif Husayn. Fahri Pasha was planning to install him in Mecca. Indeed. Kıcıman is right to point out that the initial enthusiasm of the Bedouin was due in no small part to the the promise of booty. Rogan, *The Fall of the Ottomans*, 301: "Once the first battles had been won and the towns taken, the tribesmen took their booty and went home." See also Çiçek, *War and State Formation in Syria,* 227 nt 46: "The tribes located along the Hijaz railroad in northwestern Arabia— Huweitat, Beni Atije, and Fukara were paid 10,000 ltq in gold by August 1916 in return for their loyalty. . . . Nuri Shalaan was paid 3,000 ltq in gold yearly."

. . . There are some parts of the desert where they do not know how to bake bread. They roast the wheat grains like coffee and chew it with teeth that always remain strong and white like pearls. Happy is the traveler or the warrior who is able to take with him a few grains in a little goatskin pouch together with a few dates.[11]

Thus, it is very dangerous to try to raise in revolt this long-suffering population of the Hijaz. However, because they are highly intelligent men, if they do not immediately see that the government reacts rapidly and summarily punishes the rebels, they will be quick to see that the government is weak, and that is just what came to pass. Despite this, right until the end Sharif Husayn was not able to gather a serious force around him.

. . . The Fourth Army, to counter the sugar and rice distributed by Sharif Husayn and our enemies, allocated the wheat from the Hawran to the tribes who remained loyal to the government. Wagonloads of wheat would be delivered to every loyal tribe and they would present themselves weekly to the railway station that were designated as their distribution center where they would receive their wheat from the distribution official.[12]

[The arrival of the last *Sürre-i Hümayun*][13]

These days (August 1916) we saw the arrival of the last *Sürre-i Hümayun*. The *Sürre* is the ceremonial cover of the Ka'ba that is sent every year by the Sultan who is also the Caliph of Islam. Together with this it was the custom to distribute precious gifts and money to the people of Mecca and Medina. We were ordered to open the road to Mecca so that the Commander of the *Sürre* (*Sürre Emini*) could deliver [the precious gifts] to Mecca.

---

11 Naci Kaşif Kıcıman, *Medine Müdafaası*, 110–111.

12 Ibid., 111–113. Cemal's preference to use this wheat to buy the loyalty of the tribes was one of the reasons for the famine in Lebanon. Çiçek, *War and State Formation in Syria*, 236: "Cemal Pasha had to dispatch large amounts of food to tribes in the region to secure their loyalties."

13 The *Sürre-i Humayun* was a yearly ceremony of symbolic gift-giving, whereby the Sultan who was also the Caliph (*Halife*) of Islam would send symbolic gifts of money and precious objects to the holy cities of Mecca and Medina. As one of the titles of the Ottoman Sultan was "Servant of the Holy Sanctuaries" (*Hadem ul Haramayn-Sharifayn*), this ceremony had high symbolic significance particularly during the siege of Medina when Fahreddin Pasha was trying to secure the loyalty of the Arab tribes. Heavily caparisoned camels would lead the procession. In Kıcıman's memoir, in a photograph on page 58, Fahreddin Pasha is shown holding the bridle of the leading camel. On this see my *The Well-Protected Domains*, 16–44.

The Commander of the Fourth Army Cemal Pasha was determined to get the *Sürre* to Mecca. He feared that if the precious gifts were turned back halfway, this would have very bad effect on Turkish Muslims. It was feared that they would come to have a bad opinion of the government. Because of this and many other reasons, the Commander of the *Sürre* stayed for a long time in Medina. He was waiting for the opening of the route to Mecca. However, it was not clear when and if the road would ever be opened, and even if it was, whether it would be secure. Later, the officials of the *Sürre-i Humayun* went back [to Istanbul] unofficially one by one. . . .

. . . Although the *Sürre* was a historic practice, the people benefiting from the *Sürre* were so worthless and shallow that it is defies belief. The distribution of the contents was also so bizarre. But I will refrain from criticism out of respect for its memory.[14]

. . . A Sheikh had come to Medina as a special envoy of Sultan Mehmed Reşad Khan. It was heard that he had a letter of introduction requesting that he be admitted into the tomb of the Holy Prophet. It was also heard that the Sheikh, who was a sheikh of the Nakshibendi order, had had an audience with the Sultan just before he left. The Sultan, who was very sad and melancholy, said to him as he gave him the letter of introduction, "What can I do, nobody listens to me! . . ."[15]

A few days after the *Sürre-i Humayun* arrived in Medina, Emir Ibn Rushd came to visit on the occasion of the Eid al Fitr. He was welcomed with full military honors. Field pieces were fired and there was a fireworks display. The Emir had arrived with some sixty armed slaves [as bodyguards] and a few sheikhs serving as secretaries.

At the Headquarters of the Expeditionary Force, the Emir and his entourage were offered a feast that they could not have imagined in their dreams. September 27 [1916], Thursday was the day of the Eid. The Eid prayer was ceremoniously concluded as usual in the Haram Sharif. Here I find it appropriate to make mention of a small thing that can cast light on the minds of the Bedouin. The guard brought by the Emir would go around armed even in the *masjid* of the Holy Prophet. However, the Bedouin only rarely visit places like towns where there are mosques and *masjids*, and, although they are the beloved of Allah, they are very ignorant about prayers or even about the Qur'an. During the Eid prayer they would look right and

---

14 Naci Kaşif Kıcıman, *Medine Müdafaasıı*, 57.
15 Ibid. Sultan Mehmet Reşad was renowned for his piety.

left and try to copy what others were doing. But their faith was very strong. They would seize the metal bars of the Prophet's resting place (*Babı Tövbe*) and after shouting "Ya Mohammad!" (Peace be onto His Name) they would commence to carry on a conversation with the Prophet as if he were an old friend, tell him their woes, and ask for his help. Then, as if they were sure that their wishes had been granted, they would leave in peace. If it were only possible for others to see the way in which these ignorant but innocent Bedouin approached those railings, stroked and kissed them with intense piety which could never be faked, I am sure many more people would seek the road of salvation.[16]

On the second day of Eid, the Holy Gifts of the *Sürre* (*Mahmal Sharif*) were loaded onto caparisoned camels. They then proceeded, led by a band, and behind them came the *Aghas* of the *Haram Sharif*, military and civilian personel on right and left, the camel cavalry, and the official guard. The lead camel's very long silver bridle was held by Fahreddin Pasha, Emir Ibn Rusd, and the Commander of the *Sürre*, Memduh Bey. In this fashion the procession repaired to the *Haram Sharif* and the *Mahmal Sharif* was put in its appointed place.

On the next day, the defense lines half an hour to the south of Medina were inspected. In honor of Emir Ibn Rusd there were machine gun and grenade drills. The Emir was then taken to the Uyun Gardens, after which he witnessed the shooting practice of the camel corps. One day he was taken to the aerodrome where he boarded an airplane on the ground. He firmly refused to fly. His guards made sure the airplane did not take off by sitting on the wings.[17]

The beginning of the catastrophe in Medina

While all this ceremony was going on, the situation of the troops was deteriorating. Medina was ridden by intense malaria and along the rail lines many cases of scurvy were seen. All of this was taking a heavy toll on officers and soldiers alike. Provisions were cut to 165 grams of wheat and 5 grams

---

16 Ibid., 100.
17 Ibid., 101. This was obviously a display to make sure Ibn Rushd stayed loyal and to spread the word about the force of the Ottomans among the Bedouin. The defenders of Medina were right to mistrust Ibn Rushd. Cicek, *War and State Formation in Syria*, 221: "[A]fter a while the Ottoman government began to suspect an alliance between Ibn Rashid and Great Britain."

of cooking oil [a day]. . . . In September each officer was given monthly two kilos of oil, two kilos of sugar, two kilos of of rice, two kilos of cracked wheat (*bulghur*), and one kilo of broad beans. . . .

Of the seventy-thousand-strong population of the city, only some two or three thousand were left. . . . The officers attacked the greenstuffs and vegetables on the market in order to prevent scurvy.

One would have expected that while the defenders were so preoccupied with internal woes, the rebels would mount up the pressure. Nothing of the sort happened. There was no offensive. There were not even a few small raids. What they were doing was putting their best efforts into sabotaging the railway, and, as is usual in siege situations, trying to conquer the fort through starvation. Nor were they wrong.

This is the tally of the military force in Medina. The total strength of the Forty-Second and the Fifty-Fifth regiments was six batallions, each consisting of 3,000 soldiers, the Camel Regiment (*Hecinsüvar Alayı*), consisting of four companies, each numbering one hundred, the mule cavalry numbering one hundred and fifty, 18 machine guns, two field guns, one mortar, one mountain artillery battery, one battery of heavy mountain artillery, heavy artillery batteries made up of eight guns including one Shneider gun and two Mantelli guns, one signals regiment, one regiment of sappers, one Nordenfelt team. It was thus quite clear that Sharif Husayn was not about to defeat this force with his bedouin. He had either to call for British help, or to ask for the entry into Medina of the Muslim soldiers from their Muslim colonies. However he was afraid that once [the Muslim soldiers] arrived here, they would never leave. Thus, he chose to wait for developments, restricting himself to sabotage and harassment activities along the railway. . . .[18]

. . . Because the defenders of Medina did not fear a frontal assault, they did not worry about insignificant skirmishes and set about construction activities in the city. Construction and repairs were proceeding apace. A broad avenue was being constructed in front of the *Bab us Salaam*. The land

---

18 Naci Kaşif Kıcıman, *Medine Müdafaası*, 103. The inaction of the Arab tribes in these days is probably to be attributed to the general indecision in the Allied camp and the Arab forces as to what should be done about Medina. One argument, put forward by Lawrence and others, was that as long as Fahri Pasha was cooped up in Medina his forces could not be used to reinforce the Palestine front. "Altogether these troops numbered around 14,000 men, a formidable force which required a strong Arab military presence in order to prevent the Ottoman troops from sorties." See Strohmeier, "Fahri Pasa and the End of the Ottoman Rule in Medina," 200.

around the *Haram Sharif* was to be cleared to a perimeter of forty meters and decorated with flower beds.

When the heat reached unbearable degrees, the Commander of the Fourth Army asked Fahreddin Pasha if wanted an ice machine. [The Pasha replied,] "My Pasha, I alone drink fifteen beakers of water a day, you can imagine the needs of my soldiers. How can ice last in such heat?" A short time afterward, an ice factory was set up and started distribution in Medina. It must be said that ice brought new life to Medina. In Istanbul, when people put ice into water they were always told "Watch out! You will get indigestion, boil it first!" Here, nobody cared. Besides, there was not enough ice to waste by boiling. The ice water was downed quickly because we feared that the ice would melt and the water become warm.

Sometimes we would pool our shares of ice as a great sacrifice to make ice cream. This was like some fantastic dream, so we gulped down the ice cream, fearing we would never see it again, to the point where we became ill.[19] Another use for ice was to pick fresh new dates and put them into the ice machine to transform them into fresh date ice cream. Anyone who has not tasted this in heat reaching forty-eight degrees in the shade can never appreciate the taste.[20]

Cemal Pasha bids farewell

. . . These days Cemal Pasha, the Commander of the Fourth Army and the General Commander of Syria and Western Arabia, is ending his term of service. He sent a farewell message to all of the armed forces. The following words were dedicated specifically to the Expeditionary Force in the Hijaz:

> My heart is particularly full of gratitude and wonder regarding my comrades at the furthermost reaches of my command who have heroically defended the Holy Seat of the Prophet (*Merkad-ı Mukaddesi Nebevi*) with great deprivations and difficulties (*en büyük metaib ve mevani içinde*). Despite the paucity of their numbers they have defended [the Holy Site] against the vastly superiour numbers of the rebels who have been acting with the British and the French. I am sure that the Power of the Almighty will always be beside those sons of the fatherland who labor for his Holy Prophet.

---

19 Naci Kaşif Kıcıman, *Medine Müdafaası*, 105.
20 Ibid., 105–106.

Was Cemal Pasha trying with these words of praise to cover up the mistakes he made in the Hijaz or was he seeking forgiveness of the mothers, fathers, sisters, and fiançeés of those Turkish lads who had been martyred by the cowardly bullets of the rebels, this was not clear. . .[21]

The defenders of Medina eat locusts instead of meat

[*On June 7, 1918 Fahreddin Pasha issued the following order:*]
    . . . What difference is there between a sparrow and a locust? It is simple: the latter does not have feathers. . . Like the sparrow, it has wings and it flies. It eats plants. Like the sparrow, it is nervous, like the sparrow, it is peevish. . . It is choosy about what it eats and it eats clean things. It is also accustomed to good living. It takes great pleasure in lemon and tobacco. The main sustanence of the Arabs of Hijaz, Asir, Yemen, and Africa is the locust. The Bedouin owe their health and strong constitutions to the locusts they eat. Camels and mules also eat locusts with great pleasure. It also has healing properties; it is well known as a cure for those with weak knees, consumption, and hemmaroids. It is like an elixir for rheumatism. Particularly its eggs are extremely beneficial. Unfortunately, we waste them by burying them in the ground and pouring lime on them.

I have had the locust examined and inspected by our doctors. After their deliberations, the doctors all speak of it with great admiration and endlessly describe its nourishing and medicinal qualities.

It is true that it damages crops, but do not some birds also do the same? Why have we become the enemy of the locust despite all of its qualities? The locust is both nourishment and cure. We should benefit from it, just like the flesh of game. It has been proven by experience that it is more beneficial than many of the vegetables we eat. . . . There is no difference between it and the shrimp and the lobsters that are such a delicacy on the coast.

The locust can be eaten in all climes. Its eating is considered a *sunna*. The Prophet (Blessed be His name) has said it is *halal*. Although the Imam-ı Malik orders that its eating is permitted providing the head is removed and that it is cooked on an open fire, the *ulama* of the Hanafi school condone its eating raw as has been recorded in the *Tenvir ül Essar* and other books quoting it.

---

21 Ibid., 119. Cemal left Syria on December 13, 1917.

The locust of the Hijaz is fatter and tastier than those of other regions. . . . Locusts can be eaten as described in the following four recipes.

(1) The harvested locusts are dried in the sun like *çiroz* [a recipe for drying fish in the sun—SD] for two or three days. Their head and legs are removed. The remaining body is fried in oil and eaten like a fried dish (*kavurma*).

(2) It is boiled in water, head and legs removed. Then it is mixed in with rice or *bulghur pilav*.

(3) Boiled locusts are put on a plate and lightly seasoned with olive oil and lemon.

(4) The fried parts of the locust are pounded into powder and conserved in containers like meat conserves and stored in packs and boxes. This is the favourite manner of eating it among the Bedouin. This is their only food during military campaigns. In some of our battles against them we had taken sacks of this locust powder. At the time we did not know its value and we threw it away and wasted it. It is a sin to disdain eating the locust, which is ordained by the *sunna*.

Yesterday there was "fried locust" on the menu at headquarters. My comrades and I ate it with great pleasure and found that it tasted even better than preserved tongue. A locust salad with olive oil and lemon is particularly delicious.

[*Kıcıman then describes how fried locust was served to the officers:*]

The Pasha was served first. We were all looking at each other, giving one another significant looks asking, "What shall we do? How are we to eat it?" The Pasha wanted to set the example. But I saw from his face that despite the smile and beneficent expression, he had great difficulty swallowing the fried locusts. [22]

---

22 Ibid., 180–183. Liman von Sanders dismissed the starvation of the Ottoman troops in Medina: "He [Fahreddin Pasha] repeatedly telegraphed to the Army Group that he and his men were condemned to starvation, but that was only the customary Turkish exaggeration." Sanders, *Five Years in Turkey*, 231.

[The last train. Medina is cut off. Desertion begins]

. . . On April 8, 1918 a train arrived from the north. This train, which brought our letters, our newspapers, our food, and other things—I say this with great regret—was the last train. After this the "defenders of Medina" would be in a bewildered state between civilization and nomadism. Although we were in Medina, it was no longer possible to live as civilized beings. Naturally, nor could we be expected to live like Bedouins.

On April 10 we sent our last train from our Medina to the civilized world. This [train,] which was taking our last greetings, our last letters, was shrieking piercingly and pitifully as if it knew it was never coming back. But none of the comrades in the Expeditionary Force were paying any attention to the metallic shrieking of this mass of steel and iron. They were only thinking of their holy duty of defense. In this they were right. Because they were the heroes determined to defend the "Green Dome" just as the [Ottoman] armies had done for centuries. These heroes were beyond simple and commonplace human sentiments. . . .[23]

. . . Medina was under siege, but the beseiged did not know it. Everything was kept secret, and, as in the past, attempts were being made to reestablish contact. Fahreddin Pasha communicated with all the officers in Ma'an and Der'a; in Damascus and Istanbul there were no officials who had not heard the cries of the pious defender of Medina. The telegrams written by our Honored Commander were so heart-wrenching that if any possibility at all existed of extending a helping hand, it would have been impossible not to do so. I am very sorry that I am not able to reproduce the originals of these cries for help for all to see. What was the response from Istanbul or Damascus? Istanbul merely ordered Damascus to examine the situation locally.

Here I have to openly declare that if the command of Palestine and Syria had remained in the hands of Cemal Pasha, that is to say, if he had not bid farewell to his army and retired into oblivion, he would have repaired the Hijaz Railway and cleared the road to Medina. The Lightning Army Group (*Yıldırım Orduları Grubu*) was commanded by cold-blooded German officers who saw the Hijaz front as a useless burden. . . .[24]

---

23   Naci Kaşif Kıcıman, *Medine Müdafaası*, 152–153: "*Medine müdafiileri Medeniyet alemi ile bedevilik arasında ne yapacağını şaşırmıştı.*"
24   Ibid., 157. Kıcıman was right about the German attitude towards the Hijaz Expeditionary Force. See Liman von Sanders's views above.

. . . The stage that had been awaited by both the defenders and the attackers for a long time was finally reached. Medina, which had never in its history been so well equipped with weaponry and military force, was beseiged by local Muslims, Arabs who had been tricked by the enemy. Was this to be the end of the service that had begun in the time of Sultan Selim I, the "Protector of the Holy Presincts," the service that had been provided at the cost of thousands of martyrs. . .?

The fact that it would be necessary to withstand all the burdens of the siege while the roads were blocked led to disputes and rumors, particularly among the Arab troops. Desertion was increasing daily. The pasha had been obliged to issue the following order on April 20, 1918:

(1)   All deserters will be shot on my orders.
(2)   Anyone catching a deserter will be rewarded with fifteen gold pieces. Anyone who can provide information and proof of intended desertion will be given five gold pieces. Anyone uncovering plots to desert will be given ten gold pieces.
(3)   This order will be communicated to all units.[25]

There was an ailment that was gnawing away at the strength of the Hijaz Expeditionary Force: desertion. . .

Why did desertion, which had begun with the Arab soldiers, slowly spread to the Turkish troops? To some extent this was understandable for the Arabs. But for Turks, this was a shameful thing. We were hearing that, on the other fronts, there was desertion because of mistreatment of soldiers and the oppression of officers. Yet, those who deserted from the Expeditionary Force knew that they would never see their homes again. The deserters from Medina, who were thousands of kilometers from Damascus, even if they were armed, could never make it to the Adana border. This meant that there had to be another reason for these desertions. This important reason was sought for and finally found. It was discovered that in Medina there was a secret organization to encourage desertion among the Arab, Turkish, Circassian, and Kurdish troops. The members of this organization were tried before a court martial and found guilty. Hasan Mühellel and Ahmed Mısri from Medina,

---

25 Ibid., 162–163. On desertion from the Ottoman forces see Beşikçi, *The Ottoman Mobilization of Manpower in the First World War.*

and Abdul Hamid from Homs were condemned to death. On Tuesday, April 30 [1918] they were destroyed by the volley of an unflinching firing squad. . . .

. . . While the Defenders of the Hijaz were preoccupied with their own worries, what was going on in the other, greater theaters of war? While we were hoping for relief from them, Ma'an had fallen and the Palestinian army had started to retreat. The telegraph station at Der'a was crying out in mourning, "Farewell! Farewell!" The fall of Damascus and the joining of the enemy armies of Iraq and Palestine meant that all our hopes were dashed. All ties with the motherland were cut forever. . . .[26]

[Kıcıman's views on Arab fighters]

On the night of August 7, 1918 the rebels began an artillery barrage from Culeycile. So the rumors were true, Sharif Ali was to start his offensive after all. The fighting was fierce. The artillery battle lasted three days. Thanks to the force and competence of our gunners and the incompetence of the rebels, we destroyed three of their guns. Naturally, the attackers remained stationary. After an artillery barrage of three to four days, they should have attacked with infantry and bayonets. But no son of the desert was yet born to do such a thing. Nor were the mercenaries willing to risk their lives. So what was Sharif Ali doing here? Why had he come all the way from Bir-i Darwish?

We were hearing some rumors. The paymasters of the self-styled "King of the Hijaz," who supplied him with weapons and ammunition, were taking him to task saying, "What are you waiting for? While we are spilling our blood daily you are sitting comfortably in your corner. Empty talk does not make an ally! Draw your swords and charge. Otherwise we will cut off your money!"

According to these rumors, those who dared to come against our guns at Culeycile, from the highest to the lowest, were all bought with money. Was it not useless to expect additional sacrifices from men such as these? Without learning what it meant to honor a flag or feel partiotic stirrings, was it not the height of arrogance and ignorance to fire even one shot at an army which had covered itself in glory for centuries?

---

26 Ibid., 169. The British forces entered Damascus on 1 October 1918.

The rebels who understood this decided to withdraw on the night of August 11, 1918 and immediately acted on their decision. The camel corps who had born the brunt of the fighting combed the area [the next day]. The Bedouin had all fled. So maybe their paymasters were satisfied. Why not, what more could be expected? Artillery fire had lit up the desert sky and even caused the radio antenna in Yanbo and Port Said to quiver. Was this not enough?[27]

[News of the Armistice]

. . . The darkest day of Ottoman history was upon us. On October 31, 1918, the telegram announcing the Armistice arrived. It was read only by the Commander, and because he could not bear the bitter news alone, he had invited a few close aides to share his pain caused by the disaster. These officers were the Intelligence Officer Naci Kaşif and the Signals Officer İdris Behiç Bey. When the Pasha closed his doors and instructed his orderly, Mercan, to not let anyone in, it was near midnight. . . . He said, "You are not to tell anyone what you will now hear or talk about the documents you will see. You will swear on your honor!"

The two young officers, who were shaken by the unbearable weight of a historic tragedy, swore accordingly. He began in a soft voice that even the ants could not hear, like water overflowing from a brimming pool: "The Palestine front has been breached. Liman Pasha has fled in his pyjamas. Damascus has fallen. Armistice has been signed." He then proceeded to read the telegrams relating to these events. . . .[28]

. . . On November 6, 1918 we received the following telegram. It was the "death knoll" that would strike at the heart of the defenders:

To the Commander of Medina Fahreddin Pasha.

To the Commander of Asir Muhiddin Pasha.

Despite the unbelievable sacrifices you have made in the last four years in the defence of our religion and honor, the collapse of our allies have obliged the Ottoman State to sign an armistice with the Allies. One of the articles in the armistice agreement states that all Ottoman military units in

---

27 Ibid., 245. Kıcıman was not wrong about British payments. See Rogan, *The Fall of the Ottomans*, 309: "By the end of 1916, the British government had provided nearly 1 million pounds in gold to the sharifian cause"

28 Naci Kaşif Kıcıman, *Medine Müdafaası*, 328.

the Hijaz, Asir and Yemen are to surrender forthwith to the nearest Allied commander.

You who have carried out your honorable duty for years will, of course, understand that your compliance with this order is only to prevent the total destruction of the Motherland. I am sure you will be able to shoulder this heavy burden just as you bore those sacrifices that have earned the admiration even of our enemies. I want you to rest assured of the friendly feelings of the English state and I wish you a swift and safe return to our sacred homeland.

Grand Vizier and Minister of War.

Ahmet İzzet.[29]

This announcement was like a lightning bolt for the Commanding Pasha and anyone who heard it. Although he had tried to keep the [telegram] secret for the good of the defenders and the safety of the fort, unfortunately, he was not able to prevent the spread of this dark news. The fact that this order was sent by an enemy telegraph station and was repeated for days aroused the suspicion of the Commander of the Fort.

During this period, the telegraph station of Yanbu al Bahr and Port Said would contact the Medina telegraph and ask for an answer. They wanted to learn whether or not the defenders of Medina had received the message in order to inform their superiors. The Pasha responded to this with absolute silence. It was as if this order had never reached Medina, as if the electronic waves filling the skies above Medina had not touched our antenna, as if by some unfortunate miracle of science our microphones did not receive these repeated appeals. . . .[30]

[*Fahreddin Pasha was suspicious of the wording of the telegram.*] What did they mean by "swift return to the homeland"? Was this not some strange wording? If this fort for which we have given so many martyrs to defend for all these years is not our homeland, where is our homeland? Do we not see it as a sacred part of our homeland. . .?[31]

[*Nonetheless, contrary to Fahreddin Pasha's orders, some of the officers acknowledged the receipt of the telegram.*]

---

29   Ibid., 331.
30   Ibid., 332.
31   Ibid., 333.

Correspondence with Emir Ibn Sa'ud[32]

We wrote a letter in Arabic to Ibn Sa'ud. At the time of the Ottomans, the title of the Emir was "the Governor (*Vali*) and Commander of the Najd." Letterheaded stationery printed in Istanbul had been sent to him for his use. The Emir used this stationery for his correspondence. This is what Fahri Pasha told Emir Ibn Sa'ud in his letter: "Come to Medina with your soldiers. Let us go to Mecca together and capture Emir Husayn who had rebelled against his Sultan. Let us take Mecca back from him and put down the rebellion."

In his answer Emir Ibn Sa'ud used words to the following effect: "If the German and Austrian Emperors accept the frontiers of my Emirate, then I will come."

Fahreddin Pasha answered these inappropriate words thus: "The ancestors of the Ottomans aided the Selçuk army against their enemies, thus enabling them to defeat them. As a reward, the Selçuk Emperor gave them the lands of Söğüt and Domaniç. Before you put forward such a demand, perform a similar service so I can recommend to the Sultan that he give you such a reward." Emir Ibn Sa'ud did not answer this second letter.

The said letters were dictated to me by Fahri Pasha in Arabic. I sent them by a special messenger *(najjab)*. A *najjab* is a Bedouin who delivers messages in the desert and is paid five gold pieces each time. This correspondence is being mentioned here for the first time in history. Nobody except Fahri Pasha and myself knew until today whether such correspondence ever took place between Fahri Pasha and Emir Ibn Sa'ud.

After we evacuated Medina and we were taken [as prisoners] to the Red Sea coast, the British put pressure on the adjutant of the Pasha and his batman asking them, "What did the Pasha write to Ibn Sa'ud?" They answered, "We do not know!" When they joined us later, I asked the adjutant what they had asked them. He told me and stated that they had answered that they did not know. I smiled inwardly.[33]

---

32 One of the reasons Emir Abdallah was hesitant about a frontal attack on Medina was because he was using British subsidies meant for fighting Ibn Sa'ud. Thus, Fahreddin Pasha was operating on the basis of "the enemy of my enemy is my friend." See Kedourie, "The Surrender of Medina. January 1919."

33 Naci Kaşif Kıcıman, *Medine Müdafaası*, 334–335. The reference here to Söğüt and Domaniç is part of the foundation myth of the Ottoman state. According to legend, when the eponymous founder of the Ottoman state, Osman Ghazi, came upon a battle

[A comparison between the defenders of Medina and the Armenian resistance in Urfa.]

One of the issues that has to be recorded here is a written order circulated by Fahri Pasha that was to be destroyed after reading. In this circular the Pasha referred to the desperate resistance shown by the Armenian fighters in 1915 in Urfa, during the suppression of the Armenians (*Ermeni tenkili*) that he had been a witness to. By making this comparison he wanted to exhort and encourage the defenders of Medina to further sacrifices.

As is well known, the Armenians, who for centuries led a peaceful and prosperous life eating the Turkish nation's bread, falling victim to the perfidy of the foreigners, had stabbed us in the back when we were weakest. They created armed gangs and massacred thousands of innocent Muslim Turks. Verily, it was inappropriate to compare [their acts to] the sacrifices made by the defenders of Medina, who were part of the Turkish nation that had punished the treason [of the Armenians] and caused their unjust and unsupported aims to collapse. The defenders of Medina could not be compared to this gang of brigands who had been bought by our enemies. The defenders of Medina were fighting for the holy lands that had been ruled for four centuries by their ancestors, and specifically the "Holy Shrine of the Prophet" and their religion of one thousand years. And against whom? Against a personage who, claiming descent from the Holy Prophet all along, went against the wishes of the majority of the Arabs, was bought with English gold, took the title of "Sharif," and led a bunch of looters (*çapulcu*).

For this reason it was obviously inappropriate to compare the defenders of Medina with the Armenian brigands. Yet, Fahreddin Pasha had made this allusion in his circular not to compare the two cases but simply to give the defenders courage. He simply wanted to say: "These Armenian brigands desperately defended a hopeless and wrong cause in worsening conditions. Why do you not show more effort? Take them as an example."

Despite this, from the general gist of the circular it could be mistakenly understood as if—only from a military perspective—Fahreddin Pasha

---

between the Byzantine and Selçuk armies, he joined in the fray and ensured the victory of the Selçuks. As a reward he was awarded the region of Söğüt in western Anatolia, which later became the symbolic location of the birth of the empire.

approved and admired the treasonous efforts of the Armenians. That was why he ordered it to be burned. [34]

The last days. The arrival of the "poisonous microbe"

. . . Since the beginning of the defense of Medina various negative influences were seen. The external enemy began an intensive poisoning of the minds just at the right time, and he found among the beseiged some elements who were willing to spread his propaganda and false news. The Arab officers and enlisted men in the fort, in their discussions during nighttime meetings made plans to spread such spurious rumors, but they did not dare. When they saw that among the Turks there also were those who were prepared to believe the rumors from the outside, only then did they set their chins wagging. It was at this time that, according to the program set up by the enemy, a new rumor started to spread. According to this, a special envoy had been sent from Istanbul to Medina. He had already gone through Port Said, disembarked at Yanbu Al Bahr and was to depart Bir-i Darvish the next day.

In my memoirs I had said that this "fake Mahdi" was a "poisonous microbe" that had penetrated the fort. It was after this that the real disaster started. On the night of December 18–19, 1918 a captain, who had arrived on an English torpedo boat, appeared before the lines of our defenders at Culeycile and shouted, "Good tidings, friends! I am going to take you back to the motherland!"[35]

However, those children of the motherland, no matter how happy and content they may be in their mother's lap, would never feel the same sort of elation as they felt in this [our] spiritual motherland. In fact, the bearer of catastrophe was not going to bring them freedom. On the contrary,

---

34 Ibid., 335–336. Fahreddin Pasha had in fact been the commander of a 6,000-strong Ottoman force, backed by artillery, ordered to put down the Armenian self defence rising in Urfa. The Armenian resistance began on September 29, 1915 and lasted for 25 days. Fahri Pasha "put his cannons in place and then sent a message to Yotneghperian (the Armenian leader), in which he expressed his admiration for the insurgents' exploits but added that they should now surrender." They did not and perished nearly to a man. Kevorkian, *The Armenian Genocide*, 618–619.

35 Naci Kaşif Kıcıman, *Medine Müdafaası*, 349–350. The "poisonous microbe" was in fact Captain Ziya Bey who had been sent with a written order from the Minister of War ordering Fahri Pasha to surrender. Strohmeier, "Fahri Pasa and the end of Ottoman Rule in Medina," 211.

he was going to make them abandon the holy city that they had defended with such great sacrifices. In order to prove that the document he brought was genuine, and to show that it was different from the leaflets thrown out of airplanes or left secretly, he had brought letters to many of the officers and men, even money. As soon as the Commander Pasha read the document, he immediately issued the following order:

> By the grace of God (*Avn-i inayet i Rabbaniye*) and the delivering spirit of the Prophet (*imdad-ı ruhaniyet-i Peygamberiye*), I order you to remain alert at your posts, and if you are approached by anyone individually or in groups, who act in any way contrary to the orders we have issued, I request that you immediately carry out your military and religious duty.
>
> Friday, 20 Kanunuevvel 334
> Commander of the Expeditionary Force
> Fahreddin.

This was strong advice, but more of a warning. . . Before, when someone arrived from the outside, they were forbidden to communicate [with the defenders]. But each time this led to grumbling such as, "Why? Why is he not let free?" It was in order to avoid such negative interpretations that the captain, who was, after all, an officer in the same army, was allowed to circulate freely within the fort. Yet he, far from being a good soldier, was more of a charlatan. The Commanding Pasha, who had [even] previously censored newspapers checked again before he allowed their distribution, by letting this officer go free allowed the defenders to be poisoned, the resolve of the fort to be shaken, and, as a result, [leading] to the division of the beseiged into two camps.

Given that nothing was finished yet, he should have remained fast to his previous position of caution. Unfortunately, his generosity was to cost the defenders dearly. [36]

Gossip had seriously shaken the determination and faith of the defenders of the fort. Yet, the Commanding Pasha, not paying any attention to this, wrote his answers. He was particularly angered by the objections of his chief of staff Emin Bey. Emin Bey declared that one hundred and fifty people died each day, which meant that the order of the Ministry of War should be obeyed and the fort surrendered. Colonel Necip Bey, who was present at the deliberations, knew that the final responsibility rested with

---

36 Naci Kaşif Kıcıman, *Medine Müdafaası*, 352.

the Pasha and declared, "You know best (*siz bilirsiniz*)!" Yet Ibrahim Bey, the second in command of the chief of staff, stated, "I will commit suicide before I surrender to barelegged Bedouin (*baldırı çıplaklar*)."

The answers to be written to Istanbul were carefully deliberated over for four days. The Pasha declared in his answer that until he received a direct imperial order (*irade*) from the sultan, he would continue to defend Medina. He told the Ministry of War that the "Fort of Medina" was not like any other besieged fort. Because it was the seat of the Shrine of the Prophet (*Merkad-ı Nebevi*), it constituted the basis of the Caliphate which had been defended for centuries by the caliphs and the sultans, and thus could only be surrendered by a direct order from the sultan. The Pasha would accept no other order.

Captain . . . Efendi, carrying these replies and the money sent to the defenders' families, crossed our lines at Culeycile on December 24, 1918. . . .[37]

The Declaration of those in favour of surrender[38]

To all brother officers and enlisted men of the Hijaz Expeditionary Force!

It is time to wake up!

The whole world except the Hijaz Expeditionary Force has been at peace for two months. The peace treaty with our country was signed on the thirty-first of October. Yes, we use the word "peace," but it is really an "armistice." For us this is a peace treaty. Yes, we use the word "peace" because according to [the conditions of] the Armistice, all troops of all our armies have been demobilized. Only a small force has been left.

Iraq, Syria, Hijaz, Asir, and Yemen have been completely separated from us.

Article 16 of the Armistice: Arabia has become completely independent. Apart from the forces of the Hijaz Expeditionary Force, all other forces have been completely evacuated from Arabia. An Arab Government in Damascus has long since been functioning. It has started organizing and applying its policies. The only force that has not obeyed these orders, and has refused to obey the orders that have been sent by telegraph and delivered in person by Captain Ziya Bey, is the Commander of the Hijaz Expeditionary Force and

---

37 Ibid., 353. Kıcıman refuses to use his name.
38 Ibid., 357.

his lackeys. Apart from those brainless few, we are thoroughly convinced that to stay and die here after everything is over is useless and [tantamount to] murder.[39]

According to the conditions of the Armistice, our fleet has been temporarily surrendered to the Allies. The Allied fleet lies before the Dolmabahçe Palace. The Allied forces have occupied the Straits and Istanbul. Until all the conditions of the Armistice have been met, the Allied fleet will not leave Istanbul. It will not send provisions to the motherland. It will not give money to our government. If we do not surrender Medina to the closest Allied commander, we will be considered to be in a state of mutiny against our government and the Allied forces. We will be deprived of all our civil rights!

The result is pointless. We will die here from hunger! Why and for which aim? What power and strength do we rely on? We are obliged according to the Armistice conditions to evacuate all our positions, surrender to the nearest representative of the Arab Government, surrender in whatever location to be determined by the Allied Commander in Egypt!

. . . Our Commander is now telling us, "The Government tells us to surrender the keys of Medina to the British! The British officers and the soldiers of the Sharif will rob you. Rather than surrender on these terms, with our weapons, it is better to die." The Commander and his lackeys are lying. They say, "If we receive an imperial order, we will fulfil the requirements of the Armistice." However, in a constitutional government the Sultan does not bear final responsibility. Everything is carried out according to the wishes of the people and its government. The Armistice had been accepted by Parliament. This is all the justification we need![40]

To ask for an imperial order means killing one hundred and fifty men each day. Our Commander knows very well that no imperial order or any other order will ever come. Even if it does, he will continue stubbornly [to refuse]. In fact, the British envoy, who has understood that our Commander had gone temporarily insane, declared that he was ending the negotiations. . . .

The result: The whole world has bowed down to the bayonets of the Allies. There remains only one choice for the Hijaz Expeditionary Force, those who are between life and death and are dying [at the rate of] one hundred and fifty a day. To save twelve thousand Muslim lives, we must immediately

---

39 Ibid., 358. The Mondros Armistice was signed on October 30, 1918.
40 Ibid., 358–359. The formulators of the declaration seem to be unaware that Article 16 of the Mondros Armistice made no such declaration of "Arab Independence."

accept the parts of the Armistice that concern us and immediately begin negotiations with the Allied commander right in front of us. . . .

Arab and Turk; two governments will live as brothers from now on. Were we not always brothers? Were we not connected to each other by religion and history? Can the Sacred Race of the Arabs (*kawmi nejib*) become our enemy by becoming independent? Even they themselves will answer, "No! No!" We will work together. His Highness the Sharif, appreciating the manner in which the Hijaz Expeditonary Force has heroically carried out its duties for four years, provided camels for our safe passage to Yanbu Al Bahr. They have sent medicines for our sick and arranged for our comfortable transfer to the coast. Can there be a greater manifestation of humanity? Can there be a greater manifestation of brotherhood? If they had not done so, or told us to go walking, what were we to say, "No, never, we are victorious, we will kill and hang, we demand motorcars, we demand everything and only then we will come out?" Which brave warrior is prepared to accept on his conscience the weight of the hundreds that are pointlessly dying every day because of a madman?

Today is the day of decision. There is not a moment to be lost, innocent soldiers are dying. Let us immediately decide. This declaration is for those who have not yet understood the situation. The majority have understood. We must stop these murders and give the command of the Hijaz Expeditionary Force to the highest-ranking officer. Those who are prepared to join us should make themselves and their followers known to the "Central Committee."[41]

[The last days of Fahreddin Pasha]

[*In the final days before the surrender, Fahreddin Pasha esconced himself in the shrine of the Prophet, the Haram-i Sharif.*]

Everyone was in a state of great anxiety because the Pasha had made a solemn promise. He had said the following: if one day we were to lose all hope of defense, all his comrades in arms were to perform their ablutions and unite around him in the garden of the *Haram-i Sharif*. There he would have

---

41 Ibid., 361. In fact, the declaration may have had a point about Arab good will. Baghdadi officers in the Sharifian forces who had defected from the Ottoman army actually referred to Ottoman dead as *shahid* (martyrs) and rebuked the French Algerian Muslims for fighting against their "Muslim brethren." Kedourie, "The Siege of Medina," 130.

the *ezan* chanted from all the minarets, he would ask Allah and his Prophet to bear witness and at the end of this religious ceremony, the military band would strike up the "Ottoman March."

The Pasha would then draw his revolver and fire at the ammunition piled up in the garden of the *Haram-i Sharif*. Thus the whole Expeditionary Force, rather than surrender their swords to the enemy, would ascend to the skies in the explosion of Mauser bullets, artillery shells, and bombs, wrapped in our red flag. Rather than see that banner, which never bows down, insulted in the hands of enemies, it would serve as a gift to the angels and *khouris* in heaven so that they could cover their heads with it in times of prayer. . . .[42]

. . . Everyone outside [the *Haram-i Sharif*] were in great fear. All expected a great explosion at any moment. However, the Pasha would never try such a thing unless he had gone mad. Five, six hours ago they [those in favour of surrender] had prepared a medical report attesting to the insanity of the Commander, hoping by this move to seize and do away with him. They had sent to him a delegation made up of eight or ten of the highest-ranking medical officers. Everyone feared the Pasha. [This delegation] had respectfully asked his permission to enter his presence. The Pasha understood what was going on. With great calm and attention he received the medical delegation. The Major who was the head of the delegation spoke slowly:

"Your Excellency, we have heard that you are unwell and that is why we came to visit you. If you permit, we would like to examine you." If the doctors had been able to lay hands on the Pasha, they would have immediately prepared a report stating, "the Commander Pasha is insane!" But the Pasha was too clever for them.

"Thanks be to God, I am well. My health is fine. I do not need to be examined. I simply did not sleep well last night. That is why I have sought sanctuary here. Please give my regards to those who sent you so that you could report that the Commanding Pasha had gone insane. He is very much in command of his faculties."

---

42 Naci Kaşif Kıcıman, *Medine Müdafaası*, 398–399. Kedourie does not set great store by this threat, quoting Ziya Bey, the Ottoman officer sent to deliver the order of surrender. Kedourie, "The Defence of Medina," 133: "Fakhri was intensely religious, but he had at the same time a vein of practical shrewdness in him. To commit suicide in the Haram purely from religious sentiment, his insistence on his duty of protecting the Prophet's tomb, was due chiefly to the fact that religion was his chief instrument of discipline."

The doctors left without accomplishing anything. . . .

. . . The night was wearing on. Sharif Abdallah could not remain in Bir-i Darwish and had come up on the defences at Culeycile. He called Necip Bey on the telephone and threatened him severely. Supposedly, the Arabs were in an uproar, they were preparing to attack Medina. A massacre was imminent. He would not be able to hold them much longer. He had castigated Necip Bey, declaring, "You belong to an army that has deposed Abdulhamid. Why don't you just grab Fahreddin Pasha and throw him out?"

What a sad irony for the Ottoman Army! Regretably, the first statement was a fact of history. The second was about to take place. . . .[43]

. . . The night was wearing on. The Commander of the fort was in the *Haram* with his revolvers. It was absolutely necessary to disarm him. His orderly Mercan made as if to drop the lamp by accident. The Pasha's cipher man Kadri Bey managed under cover of darkness to take out two of his revolvers, but he was not able to get to the Pasha's small Browning that he always kept under his cushion, nor to get to his sword. . . .

. . . Meanwhile, the historic event was to take place in the Pasha's bedchamber. The delegation that was given the task of arresting the Pasha was coming up the stairs. The Pasha was still in bed. . . . Those entering the chamber pretended to kiss his hands and beg his forgiveness, yet they firmly seized his wrists. The Pasha understood that he had been tricked and, furious at this base behavior, had roared like a chained old lion: "May God damn you! So you will finally deliver your Commander to the enemy? May God heap his curses upon you!" But these people were not of the kind to heed such words. They were not even aware that they had taken him outside without his trousers or his jacket. He screamed, "Have you no shame? Look at the state of me!" They brought his clothes, dressed him and took him down the stairs. . . .

After the Commander of the fort was arrested on January 10, 1919 the following declaration was issued: "This morning around six-thirty, His Excellency the Commanding Pasha, of his own free will left his chambers in the Haram-i Sharif and was driven to Culeycile by way of Bir-i Ali. There is no doubt that his security will be provided for on the roads and he will be treated with respect."

---

43 Naci Kaşif Kıcıman, *Medine Müdafaası*, 400.

[*This did in fact happen. Emir Abdallah received Fahri Pasha with full military honors and treated him with respect. The Arab troops that entered Medina on January 13 were undisciplined and widespread looting occurred, to the point where, according to one Arab officer, "[t]he people of Medina lost more in the days following the Sharifian occupation than they had during the two years of Fakhri's rule."*][44]

---

44 Kedourie, "The Surrender of Medina. January 1919," 136. Strohmeier records that the great majority of the population of Medina had fled by 1918. Strohmeier, "Fakhri Pasa and the End of Ottoman rule in Medina," 216. Emir Abdallah recalled that Fakhri Pasha was "depressed and angry" and was "looking round like a caged lion and finding no escape." Rogan, *The Fall of the Ottomans*, 396.

Conclusion

The *Atrak* and the Arabs

This book has been an attempt to describe the last years of the Ottoman presence in the Arab lands as seen by the Ottomans themselves.

The native people of the Arab lands called them "Turks" (*atrak*), as did their enemies. Yet how they defined themselves was always more nuanced and complicated. Falih Rıfkı, writing in the 1930s, definitely saw himself as a Turk and had become a committed Turkish nationalist. Hüseyin Kazım, even when writing learned works in the Biblioteque Orientale in Beirut on the Turkish language, saw himself as an Ottoman, and severely critiqued the state for alienating its Arab subjects. Yet, even he was scathing about the Syrians' character, whom he accused of toadying up to Ottoman officials.

For Ali Fuad, the distinction was also clear between the Arab nationalists who had betrayed the Ottoman state and the "Turkish nation." They had committed treason and were therefore punished by the Turkish nation. For Naci Kıcıman, who was to find himself trapped in that irony of ironies, defending the tomb of the Prophet Mohammad against Arabs who claimed descent from that same prophet, the Turks were the true Muslims who were defending Medina. Enver Pasha had been advised by his German staff, including the commander in chief Liman von Sanders, and some Turkish generals like Mustafa Kemal, to evacuate Medina and use the forces thus made available to defend Palestine. Yet he refused, declaring that the symbolic value of Medina for the Muslim world made it imperative that it be held. Falih Rıfkı is highly critical of this decision, yet even he declares that "a Turkey without Medina would be the suicide of imperialism," thus conflating Turkey and the Ottoman Empire. It is also important to note that when Enver and Cemal visited Medina in 1916 they were making history as the highest-ranking Ottomans to ever visit the city. Both Rıfkı and

Ali Fuad have a very jaundiced view of Enver Pasha's ostentatious piety as he made a show of being overcome with emotion and cried constantly because he was treading on hallowed ground. Ali Fuad's observation is particularly ironic when he states that Prince Faisal wore "an inscrutable expression." Naturally, here we have to bear in mind that Erden is writing with the benefit of hindsight and citing T. E. Lawrence who wrote that Faisal actually stayed the hands of his followers who wanted to kill Enver and Cemal, stating that they were his guests. One wonders how the war would have turned out if he had been less of a stickler for desert protocol.

As the Young Turk regime had not given up on the idea of using Islamic solidarity to preserve the loyalty of the Arabs, Cemal held weekly audiences after Friday prayers with the *ulama* and other notables of Damascus. Yet, Cemal's bumbling attempt to garner the empathy of the Syrians by quoting from the Qur'an became a travesty because he actually misquoted the holy text.

Cemal actively cultivated the fear that his reputation evoked. Ali Fuad cited Es'ad Shuqair, the Syrian sheikh who had become something of a court jester in Cemal's court, who remarked on how the buildings of Damascus or Beirut would be festooned with Turkish flags when Cemal visited. Someone told him, "I would much rather hang out a flag than hang myself."

Falih Rıfkı's disparaging references to the Arabs of Medina, who had made a vocation out of exploiting pilgrims, and his conviction that Istanbul was the true Muslim city is a clear manifestation of the Turks' own sense of superiority. Rıfkı is scathing in his ironic depiction of what he calls "Ottoman Imperialism," as a hopeless project. In *Ateş ve Güneş* the concept does not come up at all. This is hardly surprising: when the book was written in 1918, the war had just ended and the fate of the Ottoman Empire was yet to be decided by the victorious allies. Rıfkı stated that their only hope was that President Wilson would dampen the British and French thirst for revenge and that the Turks would also be able to shelter under the fragile umbrella of the "Fourteen Points" and be granted some form of "self-determination." He hoped against hope that the victors would say, "the Turks fought heroically, Turkey is a power in the Orient."[1]

In *Zeytindağı* the Ottoman Empire has become a much derided *ancien regime*. The robust young republic is depicted as having come into existence

---

1   Falih Rıfkı, *Ateş ve Güneş*, 7.

despite the failed "Ottoman Imperialism." "Our Imperialism, Ottoman Imperialism, was a fantasy built on the following premise: The Turkish nation is incapable of creating a state by itself!"[2] The obvious subtext is "Yes we did, and how!"

In subsequent editions of *Zeytindağı* Rıfkı's attitude would become even more severe, "Ottoman history has been a world of lies. Lying is not shameful in the Orient."[3] Turkey was now looking West and the "Orient" was a thing of the past. Unlike when he wrote *Ateş ve Güneş*, when he did not know the end of the story, by the time he published *Zeytindağı* the Turkish Republic was about to celebrate its tenth anniversary. Mustafa Kemal had gone from being nothing more than a general with a brilliant war record to being "Father of the Turks."

There are indications that in the immediate aftermath of the war the links between the Arabs and the Turks had not been severed. Jafar Al Askari, who was the military governor of Aleppo in 1919, stated in his memoirs that one of his major worries was that they "had to . . . contend with Turkish propaganda among the Muslims." He had to work against the "pro-Turkish propagandists" whose "pernicious influence on the Arab cause" might have seriously undermined the authority of the Arab government. Some Iraqis were fleeing British rule in Iraq and wanted to go to Turkey where they would "find safe haven." Al Askari attempted to persuade them not to go, but "That was tantamount to jumping from the frying pan into the fire." Yet with some who had "set their faces towards Turkey," he was ultimately unsuccessful.[4]

Al Askari was right to worry about Turkish propaganda. Talha Çiçek has shown that in the years 1919–1921 when the Kemalist nationalists were fighting against the French in Turkey, they actively co-operated with Arab fighters in Syria. Turkish propaganda leaflets circulated throughout Syria and word of Kemalist victories against the Greek invaders were publicly celebrated in Arab cities.[5] Yet even as they were tactically collaborating with the Arabs in Syria, a report prepared by a Kemalist *cadre* stated, "It is a

---

2   Falih Rıfkı, *Zeytindağı*, 27.

3   Online edition of *Zeytindağı*, 7–8, accessed March 11, 2017, www.kitapsevenler.com.

4   Jafar Al Askari, *A Soldier's Story. From Ottoman Rule to Independent Iraq: The Memoirs of Jafar Al Askari* (London: Arabian Publishing, 2003), 172–173.

5   Talha Çiçek, "Osmanlıcılık ideolojisi ve Osmanlı Hakimiyeti Sonrası Türk Arap ilişkilerinde Değişim ve Süreklilik" [The Ideology of Ottomanism and Continuity and Change in Turkish Arab Relations] *Divan* 33 (2012): 173–192.

simple truth that the natural racial constitution of the Arabs renders them incapable of governing themselves."[6]

The Great War as a Turkish war

Within all the memoirs cited in this book, with the possible exception of Hüseyin Kazım, the war is described as a *Turkish* war. Thus, it is no accident that the modern day official account of the war by the Turkish military should be titled "The Turkish War in World War One." Falih Rıfkı makes no mention of the Arab troops that made up the bulk of the army marching on Egypt. Ali Fuad mentions them only as a potential source of trouble and sedition in the case of an Entente landing in Lebanon. For Naci Kıcıman, the "defenders of the fortress of Medina" were all Turkish lads from Anatolia, whereas we know that the garrison included a considerable number of Arab troops; the Arab army is nothing more than a band of "barelegged looters." For little Münevver, the only Arabs that appear at all are the family coachman, her father's *majordomo*, the self-seeking Lebanese petty traders, and the Arabs who give them dirty looks as they are leaving Beirut. With the possible exception of Hüseyin Kazım (let us recall the touching send-off of the Turks by the Arabs in Beirut in his account), the mindset of the other four authors is entirely conditioned by the political, social, and intellectual *millieu* of the first half-century of the Turkish Republic in which they lived, wrote, and published. Thus, the memoirs all have the benefit of hindsight.

No doubt, the feeling of estrangement and increasing prejudice against the Turkish "other" was felt also by the Arabs who inhabited the Ottoman Twilight. As put by the *doyen* of Lebanese history, Kamal Salibi,

> Until the early years of the twentieth century Arab Moslems . . . remained supremely conscious of their religious and political unity with Turkish Moslems, and their loyalty to the Ottoman Sultan seldom wavered. Arab dislike for the Turks was, nevertheless common, and there was no lack of mutual prejudice and tensions between the two races which the early Arab nationalists could exploit.[7]

On the Turkish side, the "mutual prejudice" played out into what I have called the "stab in the back syndrome" and the "good riddance syndrome"

---

6   Ibid., 187.
7   Kamal Salibi, *The Modern History of Lebanon* (Delmar: Caravan Books, 2004), 156.

that would pick up steam in the 1930s. These two "syndromes" became the clearest expression of the essentialist nationalism of the Kemalist era, a phenomenon that has been described as "one of the safest and comforting intellectual harbors of the human mind."[8]

Another aspect of World War I as a "Turkish war" is the fact that their German allies are treated as if they were insignificant and portrayed in a negative light in the memoirs. Falih Rıfkı mentions Von Falkenhayn as being almost instrumental in Cemal Pasha's fall. In the same vein, he states that "the Germans wanted to colonize the Ottoman Empire after the war." In Ali Fuad's account of the desert war, there is no mention of Kress von Kressenstein, the man who was second in command after Cemal, and who, indeed, planned the campaign. Nor is there any mention of the orientalist Curt Prüfer, the liaison man attached to Kress, who was responsible for everything from translating Kress's orders to "smoothing over ruffled feathers at high command." Sean McMeekin has shown that Turkish-German relations had been stretched to the breaking point in the last years of the war.[9]

Cemal's chief of staff stated that the Suez Campaign was a hopeless task, essentially desired by the Germans to tie down British forces in Egypt. Ali Fuad takes pains to refute the French propaganda that "the Germans had whipped the indolent Turks into action." He was to claim that all the infrastructural "miracles" (water works, roads, military towns, etc.) were the work of the Turks and were designed by Turks. Even little Münevver giggles, "Liman Pasha fled in his pyjamas," referring to the fact that he had nearly been taken prisoner. This is all in keeping with the official tendency in the Kemalist narrative to play down the German angle, and, when reference was made to it, to stress that the "CUP allowed themselves to the dragged into the war by the Germans," a view that has now been totally discredited, as we have seen above.[10]

This official sidelining of the German ally is all the more surprising, given that, as I have argued above, even in the last year of the war, the Ottomans, certainly Enver, were still hoping for a German tactical victory

---

8   Murat Belge and Jale Parla, Preface to *Balkan Literatures in the Era of Nationalism* (Istanbul: Bilgi University Press, 2009).

9   McMeekin, *The Berlin-Baghdad Express*, 168

10 The same tendency to play down German involvement was seen the official treatment of the Gallipoli Campaign where the victory is essentially a Turkish victory. See Ayhan Aktar, "Rewriting the history of Gallipoli: a Turkish perspective," *Honest History*, July 25, 2017.

on the Western Front which would entitle them to have a seat at the table for a negotiated peace on favorable terms, enabling them (hopefully) to keep some of their Arab provinces. Presumably, the Sykes–Picot Agreement would then become null and void.[11]

Aspects of the macabre in the memoirs

In nearly all of the memoirs cited in this book there are macabre scenes. The Ottoman forces besieged in Medina were under strict rationing, yet their German allies had given them a generator and an ice machine. They were, therefore, able to make ice cream. Kıcıman extols the exquisite taste of the date ice cream that they made. Yet, the same garrison was forced to eat locusts. Fahreddin Pasha, their commander, actually provided several choice recipes for locust dishes. The trope of locusts works in two opposite ways in Medina and Syria. In Syria and Palestine, the locust plague is a symbol of the deprivation and misery of the "days of the Turks," as witnessed in Salim Tamari's work.[12] In besieged Medina the locust became a means of sustenance.

When Emir Ibn Rushd visited the Medina garrison as the ally of the Ottoman forces, he was treated to a display of military might as the besieged troops carried out maneuvers in his presence, presumably to convince him to stay loyal. One part of the display consisted of the Emir being placed in an aircraft whose engine was started. Because the Emir was terrified of the thing actually taking off, he made his bodyguards perch on the wings. .

Münevver Ayaşlı's account of her privileged existence as a spoiled young girl in an upper-class Ottoman family also has its macabre episodes. One such scene is the train journey to Aleppo when the women are terrified that they would be struck by the "Aleppo boil," which, according to legend, emerged on a person's body when they first sight the fortress of Aleppo. Believing this superstition, the credulous ladies take off their shoes and stick their feet out of the window, reasoning that if they are to be struck by the boil it will at least be on the part of their body which will not be visible.

Another episode in Ayaşlı's account also takes place on a train. When Cemal Pasha's sister is returning to Damascus from a visit to Beirut, she

---

11 See the relevant section in the Introduction, "The last days in the overall context of the Great War."

12 Tamari, *The Year of the Locust: A Soldier's Diary and the Erasure of the Ottoman Past* (Berkeley: University of California Press, 2011).

is given the Pasha's private train. Münevver joyfully recounts how, as they were crossing the ante-Lebanon mountains in the spring, the great lady would order the train to stop so that little Münevver could descend to pick flowers.

In Ali Fuad's memoirs, again, the motif was flowers. We read how on the day of Cemal Pasha's wedding anniversary, his staff in Damascus decided to offer their congratulations by presenting him with a room full of newly budding apricot blossoms which filled the place with their fragrance. This touching ceremony takes place the day after May 6, 1916 when seven Arabist patriots were hung and, in fact, were still suspended from the gallows in the Government Square in the city barely a few hundred meters away from the "apricot room." Ali Fuad at least felt a pang of conscience about this ghoulish scene as he remarked that he "shuddered" at the spectacle.

In a more light-hearted vein, Ali Fuad recounts an anecdote where some of the young officers who were billeted at the Mount of Olives hospice are chastised by the Mother Superior of the convent for cleaning their razors with bed sheets, very like naughty schoolboys at a boarding school.

The same Ali Fuad likened himself to Saint-Just and included long (and incongruous and therefore untranslated) passages in his memoirs lauding the French Revolutionary leader.

The Augusta Victoria Hospice seems to have made quite an impression on all the officers who spent time there. Falih Rıfkı waxed lyrical upon first setting eyes on the building and exclaimed, "A big, crushing, spotlessly clean German building!" Ali Fuad stated, "The Hospice of Augusta Victoria was a temple of peace and industry," referring to it as "a magnificent structure." The photograph of Cemal and his staff taken in front of the entry arch to the building is another example of the macabre and the ironic; Cemal and his entourage seem impervious to the fact that they are posing in front of *bas reliefs* of angels in the arch behind them.[13]

Falih Rıfkı with his tongue-in-cheek references to "Ottoman Imperialism"; Ali Fuad with his measured irony regarding Cemal's lawlessness; Hüseyin Kazım with his open condemnation of the "bad faces and bad words" of the Turks; Naci Kıcıman with his frequent jibes at "barelegged plundering Bedouin"; and, finally, little Münevver's snub, "those unctuous Lebanese": these are all part of the Ottoman twilight in the Arab lands.

---

13 See Plate 1.

The same twilight has left behind other, more tangible traces. Parts of the Jordanian desert are strewn with Ottoman uniform buttons, British ration containers, spent shells, and pieces of uniforms. Hundreds of these items have been found by the surface surveys carried out by the Great Arab Revolt Project. When I asked Dr. John Winterburn, who is the Landscape Archaeologist for the project, what they did when, on the few occasions, they came across bones, he told me that they were left undisturbed and *in situ* out of respect.[14]

---

14 *The Great Arab Revolt Archeological Project* is carried out jointly by the University of Bristol and the al-Hussein Bin Talal University in Jordan. It is a major project working on the archeological remains of the Great Arab Revolt in Jordan. The project's website lists four reasons as to why the work is so important; one of these reasons is that the remains in Jordan "represent the collapse of the Ottoman Empire and therefore the background to the emergence of the modern Turkish nation-state and national identity." I would like to thank Dr. John Winterburn and the directors of the project for their generous permission to use the photographs of artefacts that were found in various site locations. The poignant example of the uniform buttons recalls Simon Schama's dictum about the Polish forest, "It is haunted land where greatcoat buttons from six generations of fallen soldiers can be discovered lying amidst the woodland ferns." See Simon Schama, *Landscape and Memory* (New York: Vintage Books, 1995), 24.

Bibliography

Archival Sources

Başbakanlık Osmanlı Arşivi (BOA, Ottoman Archives), Istanbul.
American University of Beirut (AUB) Archives. Howard Bliss Collection. Box 16, AA 2-23-2
  and Box 18, AA 2-3-2.

Published Official Documents

*Birinci Dünya Harbinde Türk Harbi, IV. Cilt., 1.Kısım.: Sina Filistin Cephesi, Askeri Tarih
  ve Stratejik Etüt Başkanlığı* [The Turkish War in the First World War, vol. IV, part 1: The
  Sinai and Palestine Fronts, Directorate of Military History and Strategic Studies]. Ankara:
  Genelkurmay Başkanlığı Harp Tarihi Dairesi, 1979.
Birinci Dünya Harbinde Türk Harbi: Avrupa Cepheleri [The Turkish War in World War I: The
  European Fronts]. Ankara: Genelkurmay Başkanlığı Harp Tarihi Dairesi, 1979.
La Verité sur la Question Syrienne: Commandement de la IV ème Armée [The Truth on the
  Syrian Question. Command of the Fourth Army]. Stamboul: Imprimerie Tanine, 1916.

Newspapers

Le Temps, June 27, 1916, www.gallica.bnf.fr/ark:/12148/bpt6k2425894. Accessed February 7,
  2017.
L'Orient Arabe, October 20, 1917, www.gallica.bnf.fr/ark:/12148/bpt6k2425894. Accessed
  February 7, 2017.

Secondary Sources

Adak, Hülya. "National Myths and Self Narrations: Mustafa Kemal's *Nutuk* and Halide Edib's
  Memories and the *Turkish Ordeal*." *South Atlantic Monthly* 102, nos. 2/3 (2003): 509–528.
Adıvar, Halide Edib. *Memoirs of Halide Edib*. London: John Murray, 1926.

Ahmad, Feroz. *The Young Turks: The Committee of Union and Progress in Turkish Politics 1908–1914*. Oxford: Oxford University Press, 1969.

Ajay, Nicolas Z. "Political Intrigue and Suppression in Lebanon during World War I." *IJMES* 5 (1974): 140–160.

Akarlı, Engin. *The Long Peace: Ottoman Lebanon 1860–1920*. Los Angeles: University of California Press, 1993.

Aksakal, Mustafa. "The Ottoman Empire," in *The Cambridge History of the First World War*, ed. Jay Winter, vol. 1, 459–479. Cambridge: Cambridge University Press, 2014.

———. *The Ottoman Road to War in 1914: The Ottoman Empire and the First World War*. Cambridge: Cambridge University Press, 2008.

Aktar, Ayhan. "A Propaganda Tour Organized by Djemal Pasha. The Arab Literati's Visit to the Gallipoli Front, 18–23 October 1915." In *Syria in World War I: Politics, Economy, and Society*, ed. Talha Çiçek, 61–86. New York: Routledge, 2016.

———. "Rewriting the History of Gallipoli: A Turkish Perspective." *Honest History*, July 25, 2017.

Al Askari, Jafar. *A Soldier's Story: From Ottoman Rule to Independent Iraq: The Memoirs of Jafar Al Askari*. London: Arabian Publishing, 2003.

Antonius, George. *The Arab Awakening: The Story of the National Arab Movement*. London and New York: Kegan Paul, 2000. First published in 1938.

Atay, Falih Rıfkı. *Ateş ve Güneş* [Fire and Sun]. Istanbul: Pozitif Press, 2009.

———. *Babanız Atatürk* [Your Father Atatürk]. Istanbul: Pozitif Press, 2017.

———. *Çankaya. Atatürk Devri Hatıraları* [Çankaya. Memoirs of the Ataturk Era]. Istanbul: Pozitif Press, 2009.

———. *Zeytindağı* [Mount of Olives]. Istanbul: Pozitif Press, 1932, 1956, 2014, 2017.

Ayaşlı, Münevver. *Geniş Ufuklara ve Yabancı Iklimlere Doğru* [Towards Broad Horizons and Foreign Climes]. Istanbul: Timaş, 2003.

———. *İşittiklerim Gördüklerim Bildiklerim* [Things I Saw, Heard, and Know]. Istanbul: Boğaziçi Yayınları, 1990.

Belge, Murat, and Parla Jale. Preface to *Balkan Literatures in the Era of Nationalism*. Istanbul: Bilgi University Press, 2009.

Bernsten, Dorthe, and David Rubin, eds. *Understanding Autobiographical Memory: Theories and Approaches*. Cambridge: Cambridge University Press, 2012.

Beşikçi, Mehmet. *The Ottoman Mobilization of Manpower in the First World War: Between Voluntarism and Resistance*. Leiden: Brill, 2012.

Bogosian, Eric. *Operation Nemesis: The Assassination Plot that Avenged the Armenian Genocide*. New York: Little Brown & Co., 2015.

Boustani, Antoine L. *Histoire de la Grande Famine au Mont-Liban (1914–1918): Un Génocide Passé sous Silence*. Beirut: Presse Chemaly & Chemaly, 2014.

Boyar Ebru. *Ottomans, Turks and the Balkans. Empire Lost, Relations Altered*. New York: Tauris Academic Studies, 2007.

Çelik, Zeynep. *Empire, Architecture and the City: French Ottoman Encounters 1830–1914*. Washington: University of Washington Press, 2008.

Cemal Paşa, *Hatıralar* [Memoirs]. Istanbul: Iş BankasıYayınları, 2008.

———. *Hatıralarım* [My Memoirs]. Istanbul: İş Bankası, 2006.

Çiçek, Talha. "Erken Cumhuriyet Dönemi Ders Kitapları Çerçevesinde Türk Ulus Kimliği İnşası ve 'Arap Ihaneti'" [The Construction of Turkish National Identity in the Light of Early Republican School Textbooks and "Arab Treason"] *Divan* 17 (2012): 169–188.

———. "Myth of the Unionist Triumvirate: The Formation of the CUP Factions and their Impact in Syria during the Great War," in *Syria in World War I: Politics, Economy, and Society*, ed.Talha Çiçek, 9–36. London: Routledge, 2016.

———. *War and State Formation in Syria: Cemal Pasha's Governorate during World War I 1914–1917*. London: Routledge, 2014.

Cleveland, William L. *Islam Against the West: Shakib Arslan and the Campaign for Islamic Nationalism*. Austin: University of Texas Press, 1985.

Connerton, Paul. "Seven Types of Forgetting." *Memory Studies* 1, no. 1 (2008): 59–71.

Dabbous, Abdallah. *Muzakkerat Abdallah Dabbous* [The Memoirs of Abdallah Dabbous]. Beirut: n.p., 1993.

Deringil, Selim. *The Well-Protected Domains: Ideology and Legitimation of Power in the Ottoman Empire 1876–1909*. London: I. B. Tauris, 2011.

Dwyer, Philip. "Making Sense of the Muddle; War Memoirs and the Culture of Remembering." In *War Stories. The War Memoir in History and Literature*, ed. Philip Dwyer, 1–27 New York: Bergahn Press, 2017.

Eddé, Carla. *Beyrouth: La Naissance d'une Capitale*. Paris: Sinbad Alles, 2009.

———. "Le Savoir Encyclopedique ou la Continuation de la Guerre par d'Autres Moyens." Paper presented at the symposium *La Premiere Guerre Mondiale au Proche Orient: Experiences, Saviors, Memoire*. Held at St. Joseph University, November 3–4, 2014.

Edib, Halide. *The Memoirs of Halide Edib*. London: John Murray, 1926.

El Safa, Mohammad Jaber. *Tarikh Jabal Amel* [History of Jabal Amel]. Beirut: Dar el Nahar, 1918.

Eldem, Edhem. *Pride and Privilege: A History of Ottoman Orders, Medals and Decorations*. Istanbul: Ottoman Bank Archive and Research Center, 2004.

———. "The Story of the Little Greek Boy Who Became a Powerful Pasha: The Myth and Reality in the Life of Ibrahim Edhem Pasha, ca. 1818–1893." Unpublished manuscript in the author's possession.

Erden, Ali Fuad. *Birinci Dünya Savaşında Suriye Hatıraları* [Memoirs of Syria during the First World War]. Istanbul: Iş BankasıYayınları, 2006.

Erikson, Edward J. *Ordered to Die: A History of the Ottoman Army in the First World War*. Westwood: Greenwood Press, 2001.

Faulkner, Neil. *Lawrence of Arabia's War: The Arabs, The British, and the Remaking of the Middle East in WWI*. New Haven: Yale University Press, 2016.

Fawaz, Leila. *The Land of Aching Hearts: The Middle East in the Great War*. Cambridge, MA: Harvard University Press, 2014.

Firro, Kais M. *Inventing Lebanon*. New York: I. B. Tauris, 2003.

Fortna, Benjamin C. *The Circassian. A Life of Eşref Bey, Late Ottoman Insurgent and Special Agent*. London: Hurst, 2016.

Galvin, James J. *Divided Loyalties: Nationalism and Mass Politics in Syria at the Close of the Empire*. Los Angeles: University of California Press, 1998.

Ginio, Eyal. "Presenting the Desert to the Ottomans during WWI: The Perspective of the *Harb Mecmuası*." *New Perspectives on Turkey* 33 (2005): 43–63.

Gingeras, Ryan. *Fall of the Sultanate. The Great War and the End of the Ottoman Empire, 1908–1922*. Oxford: Oxford University Press, 2016.

Gőçek, Müge. *Denial of Violence: Ottoman Past, Turkish Present, and Collective Violence Against the Armenians 1789–2009*. Oxford: Oxford University Press, 2015.

Halbwachs, Maurice. "The Collective Memory." In *The Collective Memory Reader*, ed. Jeffrey K. Olick et al., 139–155. Oxford: Oxford University Press, 2011.

Halid, Çerkeşşeyhi Zade Halil. *Türk ve Arap* [The Turk and the Arab]. Cairo: n.p., 1912. Reprinted edition, Istanbul: Melissa Press, 2016.

Hanioğlu, Şükrü. *Ataturk: An Intellectual Biography*. Princeton: Princeton University Press, 2011.

———. *Preparation for a Revolution: The Young Turks. 1902–1908*. New York: Oxford University Press, 2001.

———. *The Young Turks in Opposition*. New York: Oxford University Press, 1995.

Hobsbawm, Eric. *Interesting Times: A Twentieth-Century Life*. London: Allen and Unwin, 2002.

Hoyek, Elias (Patriarche). "Les Revendications du Liban. Mémoire de la Delegation Libanaise a la Conference de la Paix." *La Revue Phenicienne* (Noel 1919): 24–288.

Jalabert, Henri S. J. *Jesuites au Proche-Orient. Notices biographiques*. Beirut: Université de Saint Joseph, Faculté des Lettres et Sciences Humaines, 1987.

Jamal Pasha. *Memoirs of a Turkish Statesman*. London: Hutchinson, 1922.

Kadri, Hüseyin Kazım. *Meşrutiyet'den Cumhuriyete Hatıralarım* [My Memoirs from the Constitutional Period to The Republic], ed. Ismail Kara. Istanbul: Dergah, 2000.

Kaiser, Hilmar. "Regional Resistance to Central Government Policies: Ahmed Djemal Pasha, the Governors of Aleppo, and the Armenian Deportees in the Spring and Summer of 1915." *Journal of Genocide Research* 12, nos. 3–4 (2010): 173–218.

Kayalı, Hasan. *Arabs and Young Turks: Ottomanism, Arabism and Islamism in the Ottoman Empire 1908–1918*. Los Angeles: University of California Press, 1997.

Kedourie, Elie. "The Surrender of Medina. January 1919." *Middle Eastern Studies* 13 (1977): 124–143.

Kevorkian, Raimond. *The Armenian Genocide: A Complete History*. London: I. B. Tauris, 2011.

Khalidi, Anbara Salaam. *Memoirs of an Early Arab Feminist: The Life and Activism of Anbara Salaam Khalidi*. Trans. Tarif Khalidi. London: Pluto Press, 2013.

Khalidi, Tarif. "The Arab World." In *The Great World War, 1914–1945*, vol. 2: *The Peoples' Experience*. ed., J. Bourne, P. Liddle and I. Whitehead et al, London: Harper Collins, 2001.

Khater, Lahad, *Ahd al Mutasarrıfin fi Lubnan* [The Period of the *Mutasarrıfs* in Lebanon]. Beirut: Editions Lahad Khater, 1982.

Kouyoumdjian, Ohannes Pacha. *Le Liban: A la Veille et au Début de la Guerre: Mémoires d'un Gouverneur 1913–1915*. Paris, 2003.

Lejeune, Philippe. *Le Pacte Autobiographique*. Accessed January 12, 2017. www.edisciplinas.usp.br/pluginfile.php/1896026/mod_resource/content/1/lejeune_pacte autobiographique-pacte_1.pdf.

Lewis, Geoffrey. "An Ottoman Officer in Palestine." In *Palestine in the Late Ottoman Period*, ed. David Kushner, 402–415. Leiden: Brill, 1986.

Mandelstam, André. *Le Sort de l'Empire Ottoman*. Lausanne and Paris: Librarie Payot, 1917.

Manzano, Eduardo, and Roberto Mazza, eds. *Jerusalem in World War I: The Palestine Diary of a European Diplomat, Conde de Ballobar*. London: I. B. Tauris, 2011.

McMeekin, Sean. *The Berlin-Baghdad Express: The Ottoman Empire and Germany's Bid for World Power*. Cambridge, MA: Harvard University Press, 2010.

Mick, Christoph. "1918: Endgame." In *The Cambridge History of the First World War*, ed. Jay Winter, vol. 1, 133–171. Cambridge: Cambridge University Press, 2014.

Middleton, David, and Derek Edwards, eds. *Collective Remembering: Inquiries in Social Construction*. London: Sage Publications, 1990.

Morgenthau, Henry. *Ambassador Morgenthau's Story*. Ann Arbor: Gomidas Institute, 2000.

Mouawad, Youssef. "1915–1918: La Grande Famine du Mont Liban." *Historia : Une Histoire du Liban des Phéniciens a Nos Jours* (December 2016–January 2017): 116–124.

Mouwad, Youssef. "Jamal Pacha, en une version libanaise. L'usage positif d'une légende noire." In, *The First World War as Remembered in the Countries of the Eastern Mediterranean*, ed. Olaf Farschid, Manfed Kropp, Stephan Dahne, 425–447. Beirut: Orient Institut, 2006.

Nedim, Mahmud Bey. *Arabistan'da bir* Ömür: Son Yemen Valisinin *Hatıraları* [A Lifetime in Arabia: The Memoirs of the Last Vali of Yemen]. Istanbul: ISIS Press, 2001.

Neiberg, Michael S. "1917: Global War." In *The Cambridge History of the First World War*, ed. Jay Winter, vol. 1, 110–132. Cambridge: Cambridge University Press, 2014.

Ostle, Robin de Moor, and Stefan Wild, eds. *Writing the Self: Autobiographical Writing in Modern Arabic Literature*. London: Saqi Books, 1998.

Pamuk, Şevket. *A Monetary History of the Ottoman Empire*. New York: Cambridge University Press, 2000.

Pennebaker, James W., Dario Paez, and Bernard Rime, eds. *Collective Memory of Political Events*. New Jersey: Mahwah, 1997.

Presland, John. *Deedes Bey: A Study of Sir Wyndham Deedes 1883–1923*. London: Macmillan, 1942.

The Qur'an: A New Translation. Trans. Tarif Khalidi. London: Penguin Classics, 2009.

Rogan, Eugene. *The Arabs: A History*. New York: Basic Books. 2009.

———. *The Fall of the Ottomans*. New York: Basic Books, 2015.

Salibi, Kamal. *The Modern History of Lebanon*. Delmar: Caravan Books, 2004.

Sanders, Otto Liman von. *Five Years in Turkey*. Annapolis: United States Naval Institute, 1927.

Schama, Simon. *Landscape and Memory*. New York: Vintage Books, 1995.

Schilcher, Linda. "The Famine of 1915–1918 in Greater Syria." In *Problems of the Modern Middle East in Historical Perspective*, ed. John Spagnolo, 239–258. Reading: Ithaca Press, 1992.

Schuman, Christoph. "Individual and Collective Memories of the First World War." In *The First World War as Remembered in the Countries of the Eastern Mediterranean*, ed. Olaf Farschid, Manfed Kropp, and Stephan Dahne, 247–265. Beirut: Orient Institute, 2006.

Strohmeier, Martin, "Fakhri (Fahreddin) Pasha and the End of Ottoman rule in Medina (1916–1919)." *Turkish Historical Review* 4 (2013): 192–223.

Suny, Ronald Grigor. *"They Can Live in the Desert but Nowhere Else": A History of the Armenian Genocide*. Princeton: Princeton University Press, 2015.

Tamari, Salim. "Arabs, Turks, and Monkeys: Ottoman Ethnographic Mapping of Palestine and Syria." In Salim Tamari, *The Great War and the Remaking of Palestine*, 25–43. Los Angeles: University of California Press, 2017.

———. "Muhammad Kurd Ali and the Syrian-Palestinian Intelligentsia in the Ottoman Campaign against Arab Separatism." In *Syria in the World War I. Politics, Economy and Society*, ed. Talha Çiçek, 37–60. London: Routledge 2016.

———. *The Year of the Locust: A Soldier's Diary and the Erasure of the Ottoman Past*. Los Angeles: University of California Press, 2011.

Tauber, Eliezer. *The Arab Movements in World War I*. London: Frank Cass, 1993.

Tautel, Christian, and Pierre Wittouck, S. J., eds. *Le Peuple Libanais dans La Tourmente de la Grande Guerre 1914–1918 d'apres les Archives des Peres Jésuites au Liban*. Beirut: Presses Universitaire St. Joseph, 2015.

Toprak, Zafer. *Türkiye'de Milli Iktisat 1908–1918* [The National Economy in Turkey 1908–1918]. Istanbul: Yurt Yayınları, 1982.

Toros, Taha, ed. *Ali Münif Bey'in Hatıraları* [The Memoirs of Ali Münif Bey]. Istanbul: ISIS Press, 1996.

Vecihi, Muhittin. *Erkan-I Harb Binbaşısı Vecihi Bey'in Anıları: Filistin Ricatı* [The Memoirs of Staff Officer Lieutenant Vecihi Bey: The Retreat from Palestine]. Istanbul: ArbaYayınları, 1993.

Walker Dennis. "Clericist Catholic Authors and the Crystallization of Historical Memory of WWI." In *The First World War as Remembered in the Countries of the Eastern Mediterranean*, ed. Olaf Farschid, Manfed Kropp, and Stephan Dahne, 91–129. Beirut: Orient Institut, 2006.

Watenpaugh, Keith David. *Being Modern in the Middle East: Revolution, Nationalism, Colonialism and the Arab Middle Class.* Princeton: Princeton University Press, 2006.

Winter, Jay. "War Memoirs, Witnessing and Silence," in *The War Memoir in History and Literature*, ed. Philip Dwyer, 27–47. New York: Bergahn Press, 2017.

Wirtz, Philipp. *Depicting the Ottoman Empire in Turkish Autobiographies. Images of Past World.* New York: Routledge, 2017.

Zein, Zeine N. *The Emergence of Arab Nationalism.* New York: Caravan Books, 1973.

Zürcher, Erik Jan. "Young Turk Memoirs as a Historical Source: Kazim Karabekir's 'Istiklal Harbimiz'" *Middle Eastern Studies* 22, no. 4 (1986): 562–570.

Index